M000095249

DAN K. EBERHART

THE

AMERICA'S GLOBAL ENERGY RENAISSANCE

SWITCH

GREENLEAF
BOOK GROUP PRESS

This publication is designed to provide accurate and authoritative information in regard to the subject matter covered. It is sold with the understanding that the publisher and author are not engaged in rendering professional services. If expert assistance is required, the services of a competent professional should be sought.

Published by Greenleaf Book Group Press
Austin, Texas
www.gbgpress.com

Copyright ©2015 Dan K. Eberhart

All rights reserved.

No part of this book may be reproduced, stored in a retrieval system, or transmitted by any means, electronic, mechanical, photocopying, recording, or otherwise, without written permission from the copyright holder.

Distributed by Greenleaf Book Group

For ordering information or special discounts for bulk purchases, please contact Greenleaf Book Group at PO Box 91869, Austin, TX 78709, 512.891.6100.

Design, cover design, and composition by Greenleaf Book Group
Interior tables, graphs, and illustrations design by HMX™
Interior photograph "Man Camp" (page 139) licensed by ©Ken Cedeno/Corbis
Lyrics from "In Heaven There Is No Beer" (page 103), words and music by Ralph Maria Siegel and Ernst Neubach. Copyright © 1956 by Beechwood Music Corp. Copyright Renewed. All rights administered by Sony/ATV Music Publishing LLC, 424 Church Street, Suite 1200, Nashville, TN 37219. International Copyright Secured. All Rights Reserved. Reproduced by permission of Hal Leonard Corporation.
Figures 12.2, 12.3a, and 12.3b (pages 146 and 147) : Courtesy of the Federal Reserve Bank of Minneapolis.

Cataloging-in-Publication data is available.

Print ISBN: 978-1-62634-258-3

eBook ISBN: 978-1-62634-259-0

Part of the Tree Neutral® program, which offsets the number of trees consumed in the production and printing of this book by taking proactive steps, such as planting trees in direct proportion to the number of trees used: www.treeneutral.com

TreeNeutral®

Printed in the United States of America on acid-free paper

15 16 17 18 19 20   10 9 8 7 6 5 4 3 2 1

First Edition

To Kylee

CONTENTS

Foreword by Tom Ridge 1

PART I: Why Energy Matters

CHAPTER 1: New Oil: Godsend or Devil's Spawn? 6

CHAPTER 2: So What Is Fracking Anyway? 14

CHAPTER 3: Energy (In)Security: What Do You Do When the Lights Go Out? 22

CHAPTER 4: The Fear Factor 32

CHAPTER 5: Energy Security: What Lies Beneath Changes the Flow Up Top 39

CHAPTER 6: Will We Run Out? Hubbert's Pimple & Peak Oil Theory 50

PART II: Can't We Just All Get Along?

CHAPTER 7: Vilification. Let's Talk 60

CHAPTER 8: The Energy Mix: No Free Lunch 66

CHAPTER 9: Why People Are Fighting Shale: Of Frackivists,
Methane Emissions, and Moral Panic 85

CHAPTER 10: Regulations: Can't Live with 'Em, Can't Live Without 'Em 97

PART III: Boom or Bust. Distinctly America.

CHAPTER 11: The Wizards of Marcellus 110

CHAPTER 12: Boom! Working Girl Trickonomics and Other Shady Spots 127

CHAPTER 13: How OPEC Plays Dice with the Universe 149

CHAPTER 14: Should We Be Worried? 158

PART IV: Practice What We Preach

CHAPTER 15: Let's Talk Crude   168

CHAPTER 16: LNG: What Is It—and Why Can't It Go to Japan or Ukraine?   190

CHAPTER 17: Yet Another Veto   198

PART V: What's Next?

CHAPTER 18: Captain America—the American Ideal Returns   212

CHAPTER 19: 2035   229

Acknowledgments   245

Endnotes   247

About the Author   265

FOREWORD BY TOM RIDGE

This is a book about "The Switch"—a tidal wave of oil and gas flowing, quite unexpectedly, out of the West. A switch in polarities and politics, changing the entire direction of world energy imports and exports. A switch that has thrown traditional energy monopolies like Russia and OPEC off-axis, prompting new—and dangerous—energy games.

In the last five years, America, its allies, and adversaries have experienced the globe's biggest paradigm shift in energy security ever. Oil and gas extraction has been revolutionized thanks to the development of hydraulic fracturing and horizontal drilling, techniques grown and perfected in the United States. Whereas petroleum and gas shortages, embargoes, and high-priced imports were the reality of the 1970s and the decades following, America faces a startling reversal of fortune. We now have unprecedented energy abundance thanks to the plumbing of hydrocarbons locked in shale formations across a dozen U.S. states.

Just when we thought that gasoline prices would always remain sky high, that North American energy independence was a pipe dream, or that oil, money, and power were the natural inheritance of Saudi sheiks and Russian energy czars, U.S. shale discovery arrived in full force in 2010 to transform our domestic energy picture—and possibly the calculus of geopolitical power.

New technologies and new education about renewables have given us the tools to change our energy future. Yet, our legislators dither over national energy policy. We are still arguing about the goal of "American energy independence," when in fact the globe is so interconnected that we should, realistically, create a new goal of *energy interdependence* and fair pricing for all. We've got brainpower, intellectual capital, and the resources to come up with a comprehensive "smart energy policy" rather than be fixated from time to time on one or two sources. "Smart policy" means an "all-in" energy policy that includes shale and conventional oil and gas, nuclear, solar, wind, biomass, geothermal, you name it. It includes measures to capture carbon dioxide emissions and preserve our national treasures. The U.S. also has the resources to share our technologies abroad and create new avenues for *energy diplomacy*. But we are still far from achieving these goals; the American people need to know more about energy in order to participate much more actively in policy choices for the future. That is what Dan Eberhart's highly readable and beautifully researched book, *The Switch*, is all about: making choices, and intelligent ones based on facts.

The Energy Cocktail

Today, our decisions about energy are shifting moment by moment. National security, energy alliances, terrorism, ideology, hydrocarbons and environmental concerns are mixing in an explosive cocktail made even more volatile by new revenue streams from oil, coal, and gas.

For example, the recent Iran nuclear deal will signify a switch, if not a reduction, in that country's uranium enrichment program that many Western analysts believe is aimed at building a nuclear bomb. Iran, the world's most active state sponsor of terrorist groups, may have to curtail its nuclear program for awhile, but it gets to ramp up oil production in exchange. Once sanctions are lifted, the Iranian regime has vowed to double petroleum output for export, raising disturbing questions about energy wealth and its ability to fuel hostile regimes, splinter groups, and their war chests.

Iran isn't alone, either. In this remarkably thorough book, Dan Eberhart, an international energy consultant and president of Canary, LLC, the nation's largest private wellhead oilfield services company, discusses the origins of energy conflict and confrontation among Saudi Arabia and other OPEC members, Russia and Ukraine, China, Europe, and the United States.

Eberhart presents "big picture" energy as you've never thought about it before. His take on America's energy panics and "blackout" mentalities, its working girl "trickonomics" in modern "frac" towns, and his "you are there" description of big-muscled hydraulic fracturing projects and the recycling facilities instrumental in their clean up offers a fascinating view of a renewed American industry and its wake-up call to the American dream.

On shale technologies, geopolitics, and the long-range impacts of hydrocarbons and other energy options on communities and the environment, Eberhart writes candidly and with surprising balance, describing risks and benefits of each energy type. But perhaps most important, Eberhart gives readers unfamiliar with the energy story a powerful fundamentals handbook. Eberhart truly understands how wars over oil and gas start and end; whether states and the Feds ultimately duke it out to forge reasonable environmental protections during energy exploration; and whether we encourage—or limit—controversial oil and gas extraction techniques and a national energy policy to ensure an energy-abundant future.

I can't think of a more important and easy-to-absorb blueprint for understanding that future than this book. Soon, Americans will be electing leaders who will make critical choices about the economy, energy, national security, and environment. A coherent national energy policy—approved by American voters and carried out with strength and focus—could mean the difference between an eternal Game of Thrones, a desecrated planet, and the stability and prosperity all world citizens crave as their birthright.

PART I

WHY ENERGY MATTERS

CHAPTER 1

NEW OIL: GODSEND OR DEVIL'S SPAWN?

Remember the Great Recession of 2008?

You might have lost your job or defaulted on your mortgage. Perhaps you were spared but watched neighbors or friends searching fruitlessly for work online or in newspapers that no longer carried classified job ads.

In 2008, like most Americans, you probably saw the depressing spiral of economic turbulence as a sign that times were bad and that worse times were coming. What you may not have seen was that in the dust of real-world recession, in the worst economic downturn since the Great Depression of 1929, a game-changing technology was being developed miles beneath our feet—something you'd probably never heard of, called fracking.

In 2008, "hydraulic fracturing" was a term that, at best, only a rig operator or a Harvard geologist would know. Today, it's the subject of thousands of news articles, scores of conferences, dozens of demonstrations, and intense legal and political debate.

This technology—given the nickname "fracking" in the ensuing years—promises to deliver virtually infinite supplies of energy available cheaply, at our doorsteps. It promises a rebirth of American jobs, abundance, and higher living standards in many rust-belt towns and farm communities that had turned into ghostly Pleasantvilles. It promises to deliver *millions of barrels of oil and billions of cubic feet of natural gas each day*. It promises economic rebirth in many states, boom times in Western Pennsylvania, Texas, North Dakota, Colorado, and Oklahoma.

In 2008, the U.S. was set to spend $100 billion a year to import liquefied natural gas (LNG) from West Africa, the Middle East, even Australia and Russia. But now, American natural gas production has reached records of 72 billion cubic feet per day; the U.S. created as much as 27 million cubic feet in 2014 alone.[1] Fracking, in other words, has kick-started a new era of American energy security, which we haven't seen since the Pennsylvania and Texas oil rush days of the mid-nineteenth and early twentieth centuries. In less than five years, fracking has saved the U.S. $40 *billion* in energy imports, fueled the growth of cleaner natural gas power plants, and created an estimated 240,000 new jobs in the energy and allied sectors. By 2020, shale gas production alone is set to create 600,000 jobs; and by 2040, U.S. jobs tied to unconventional oil and gas will have reached 3.5 million, according to an IHS Global Insight report.[2]

Fracking. To many a godsend . . . to others the devil's spawn.

There are vehemently strong anti-fracking sentiments worldwide. To many, despite its unarguable economic benefits, fracking is considered an environmental hazard that must be banned at all costs. As I write this book, Colorado, California, England, France, Bulgaria, and South Africa are becoming epicenters of legal and citizen activity, even panic, aimed at banning or severely restricting the practice. As of December 2014, New York State has prohibited fracking altogether. Many fear that hydraulic fracturing is an outright threat to the moral, social, and environmental fabric of their neighborhoods.

What's more, with the fracking floodgates open and the Organization of Petroleum Exporting Countries (OPEC) refusing to curtail production, the worldwide supply of oil has skyrocketed. Gasoline prices have plummeted. That's good and bad, as we'll soon see.

With the recent media attention placed on fracking, the term has attained household status for many.

Still, you shouldn't be embarrassed if you aren't clear on the term.

If you can't define it, you're not alone.

Despite news coverage, I've discovered that many people still don't recognize the word "fracking" or the term "shale play"—the rock formation most frequently fracked for oil and gas. Case in point: Consider these statements made by shoppers at the local H-E-B food mart in Houston, Texas. Even in this well-known mecca for the oil and gas industry, the general populace is confused.

"Fracking? That's something to do with baking, right?"

"I have no clue what fracking is."

"Isn't a shale play something that has to do with the tar sands in Canada?"

"Shale makes me think of Geology 101 from college."

One shopper, Marjorie DuBois, counts herself among those in the dark. My team asked her, "Do you know what fracking is?"

"I have no idea," she replied.

"How about a shale play?" we asked. "Ever heard of that?"

Again, DuBois was stumped. "No idea," she said.

College English professor Blanche Johnson was equally mystified. When we asked her to define fracking, she was at a loss. "Without Googling, sadly, I have no idea," she said. "Not even a clue."

A man named Tyler laughed at his lack of fracking knowledge and lamented that his wife, a former controller for an oil and gas company, wasn't with him. "She would know, but all I know is it has something to do with oil and gas," he said.

Lori Martindale, who works in advertising, had heard of fracking and had a basic understanding of the technique: "It has something to do with pumping fluid into cracks into the ground to extract minerals," Martindale said. "But beyond that I don't know."

It's this confusion that this book seeks to address. Why? Because fracking—or more specifically the energy derived from it—*will* alter our global alliances, cause wars, stop wars, fuel economic growth, affect manufacturing and associated industries, and help accelerate the production of goods and services in American and even global communities.

In fact, the changes have already started. American energy is already redefining our relationship with the Middle East, has already inspired the

Ukrainian president to visit Washington to ask *us* for energy assistance, and has sent nations like Nigeria scrambling to find new buyers in a suddenly very crowded market.

Yet that's just the tip of the iceberg.

- In early 2015, OPEC has been forced to establish policies that have lowered the price of crude oil to under $50 a barrel—the lowest levels in four years. This is a particularly astonishing development, given the cartel's historic ability to keep prices high, generally above the $100/barrel mark, for many years.

- Russia's ruble is in free fall; its oil-and-gas-dependent economy is in recession. In mid-December 2014, the Russian Central Bank made an almost unprecedented move of increasing a key interest rate from 10.5 percent to 17 percent. The following morning's brief rebound was quickly wiped out by midday, when the ruble hit a new record low (about 72 to the dollar). Some Russian banks even reacted with self-imposed blocks on currency exchanges.

- Countries such as Libya, Iran, and Venezuela—which all require oil prices over $110/barrel to balance their budgets[3]—are in a world of hurt. Continuing low oil prices could wreak havoc on their economies, causing extreme poverty, riots, or even revolution.

In short, the U.S. has produced a global energy supply shock. Traditional energy suppliers are stunned that U.S. shale resources could have changed the balance of accessible energy supplies so rapidly worldwide.

A U.S. energy renaissance is far from secured, however. Already, 90 percent of the new oil and gas wells in the U.S. employ costly hydraulic fracturing methods to increase oil and gas yields. So-called "unconventional" drilling is becoming the norm.

But rigs are shutting down as prices drop, and shale energy remains costlier to produce and faces many battles ahead. Can our newly reborn energy industry survive if the price of oil stays under $50/barrel? Will the U.S. public decide that the environmental risks aren't worth the gains? Will politicians step up to help with a comprehensive energy policy—one that promotes energy independence, while maintaining environmental stewardship—or will they continue to bicker rather than produce quality legislation?

Right now our Congress is in the crux of deciding how our goal of "energy independence" should play out. There are tough choices ahead, and the political party divides on many issues are widening.

It's up to us to decide what we want for America.

Surprise—This Book Isn't About Fracking

I believe history books will look back and shed a positive light on fracking as a technology that changed the face of the world as we know it today, but in the end, fracking is a tool. Much in the same way as Bell's telephone or Gutenberg's printing press ushered in paradigm shifts in their eras, fracking will revolutionize ours.

It's not the inventions themselves but what these inventions *have done* that give them this distinction. It's the spread of knowledge enabled by the press. It's the instant communication afforded by the telephone. In fracking's case, it's the *shift in power* that will change your life and your children's lives in ways that you may not have imagined.

It's no exaggeration to claim that fracking is the most radically disruptive oil and gas invention to come along thus far—even if you've never heard of it before. It is incredible that something so few people know about or understand is dramatically changing the world.

But this book isn't about fracking. It's about the Switch.

Consider this simple fact: In 2014, the *United States overtook Russia and Saudi Arabia as the world's top oil producer.*

We stand on the precipice of a monumental switch as a tidal wave of oil and gas flows, quite unexpectedly, out of the West. A switch in polarities and politics, changing the entire direction of world energy imports and exports. A switch that has disrupted traditional energy monopolies.

A switch that deserves serious consideration. Not just because of environmental concerns. But because of the entire kaleidoscope of conversations that is being fundamentally changed by a new U.S. energy source.

Should we lift our forty-year ban on exporting oil and gas abroad to bolster economic growth and help reduce or wipe out the federal deficit? Should we build the Keystone XL pipeline, and at what cost to local environments? Do we leverage our energy as a geopolitical weapon, or as a force of advocacy for open markets and free trade? Should we combat Russian aggression in Eastern Europe by shipping LNG to Ukraine? Can we counter the violence and sadism of terrorist groups like ISIS by helping allies cut off the groups' energy supplies—and their military revenue?

The answers to these questions—asked of the American people in the next two to three years—will change the world for decades.

IS FRACKING REALLY SUCH A BIG DEAL?[5]

FRACKING HAS CREATED AN ABUNDANCE OF DOMESTIC ENERGY

Percentages used below are the increase from 2008 to 2014.

↑74%
Increase in oil production

↑29%
Increase in natural gas production

U.S. FIELD PRODUCTION OF CRUDE OIL
(Thousand Barrels per Day)

9,000,000	
8,000,000	
7,000,000	
6,000,000	
5,000,000	
4,000,000	

'04 '05 '06 '07 '08 '09 '10 '11 '12 '13 '14

U.S. NATURAL GAS MARKETED PRODUCTION
(Million Cubic Feet)

28,000,000	
26,000,000	
24,000,000	
22,000,000	
20,000,000	
18,000,000	

'04 '05 '06 '07 '08 '09 '10 '11 '12 '13 '14

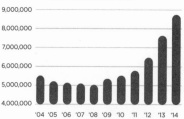

25%
of U.S. energy production comes from fracking

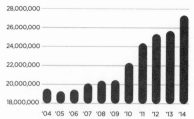

89%
of U.S. domestic energy needs are now being met

54%

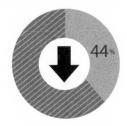

44%

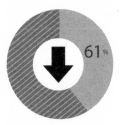

61%

decrease in oil and petroleum imports

less OPEC member crude oil imports*

decrease in total natural gas imports**

Fracking has made the U.S. the world's top oil producer.

The country is poised for energy self-sufficiency, thanks to fracking . . . and that is A VERY BIG deal.

CHAPTER 2

SO WHAT IS FRACKING ANYWAY?

Fans of the famous TV series *Battlestar Galactica* (1978) first heard the term "frack" as an expletive, a euphemism for the similar four-letter word. Amusing, but not exactly accurate for our purposes. Closer to home: One Urban Dictionary contributor described planetary fracking as "shoving a lubricated probe into an earth hole to extract gas."

Geology.com provides a more technical definition: "Hydraulic fracturing is a procedure that can increase the flow of oil or gas from a well. It is done by pumping liquids down a well into subsurface rock units under pressures that are high enough to fracture the roc. . . ." The methods are now being used to develop organic-rich shales in many parts of the world.[1]

But what does that mean? Why is fracking so hotly debated? And what on God's green earth is shale?

Fracking involves blasting as much as two million gallons of water, sand, and a unique brew of chemicals—anything from coffee grounds to ceramic beads, acids, household cleaners, and gels—into a single well bore to break apart oil- and gas-bearing rock formations. Gas and liquids can then escape freely from multiple tiny fractures (some of them less than 1 mm wide) within the fractured shards of rock.

Shale is a fine-grained, clastic sedimentary rock—clastic meaning it's composed of broken pieces of older rock—that lends itself especially well to the fracking process.

Because shale oils and gases aren't pooled in large single-dip reservoirs like conventional petroleum and gas reserves are, extracting oil and gas from shale requires complex steps. In many cases, it's not enough to puncture and frack a single shale target: horizontal drilling is needed. This comparatively recent technology allows operators first to drill thousands of feet vertically below the earth's surface. The drill then turns horizontally, boring with high-power machinery through a shale formation that may be miles long. Steel casings and gaskets of hardened cement paste are inserted into the well bore to seal the well to prevent hydrocarbons from escaping into surrounding rocks or water supplies. Once the drilling is completed, hydraulic fracturing fluid is pumped at very high pressure, along with a mixture of chemicals and sand, to produce tiny fractures in the shale. The sand, known as a proppant, keeps the tiny fractures open, enabling trapped or "tight" oil and gas to flow back out of the earth through the well bore.

The result? Much higher production of oil and gas.

But why is fracking so controversial? You may have heard some of the media coverage regarding environmental issues.

Perhaps, like Joseph Aldolino, a networking specialist interviewed at our local H-E-B, you have heard that fracking can harm the environment.

"I know what fracking is," Aldolino said. "It's when we drill and you're pouring all these dangerous chemicals farther down into the ground. I know they do it to try to get natural gas."

Lorna Smythe, who works in customer service, agreed: "As I understand it, fracking is getting oil and gas from the rocks or the earth—and it's dangerous to the environment."

Robin Weber, a fitness professional, went further. "Fracking is causing possible earthquakes and contaminating the water supply totally," she explained. Weber also mentioned people suffering from nosebleeds and even the prevalence of cancer clusters in fracking areas.

Not everyone agreed. "Fracking is breaking up rock to get at precious energy resources that we have, as opposed to tapping into large pools of oil," said Mike Hughes, an orthodontist. "I would vote 'yes' to fracking. I'm all for it. I say we get all fracked up."

As these comments demonstrate, public perceptions of fracking are mixed.

HOW FRACKING WORKS

First off, a well must be built. Wells may be greater than 8,000 feet deep and have a width of up to 20 inches. The well is located on a "pad" site, and there can be more than one.

Maintaining small diameter wells on the pad site keeps the surface presence to a minimum, which results in a smaller environmental ◀◀◀ footprint due to fewer access roads and pipelines needed.

Next up is the placement of steel pipes, or casings, set in place with a cement paste inside the well.

Cementing the pipes is imperative, as they act as a ◀◀◀ protective shield so gas and oil do not reach surrounding rocks or water sources, causing contamination.

The pipes are there to protect groundwater contamination and vary in depth, depending on how far down groundwater exists at the pad site.

When the right depth is reached by the well it takes a dramatic turn, literally. No longer solely vertical, the well shifts to the right or left at the "kick-off" point and goes horizontal between 1,000 and 6,000 feet.

"Kick-off" point
▶▶▶

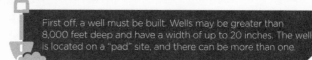

6,000–10,000 feet

With the well all set-up . . . let the fracking begin!

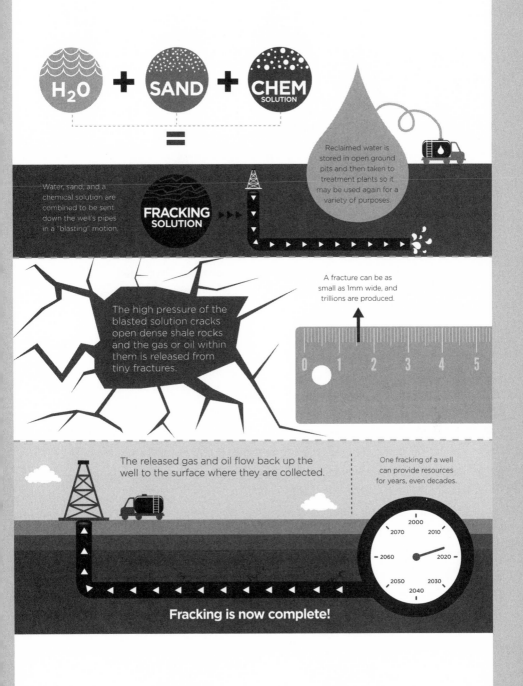

H₂O + SAND + CHEM SOLUTION = FRACKING SOLUTION

Water, sand, and a chemical solution are combined to be sent down the well's pipes in a "blasting" motion.

Reclaimed water is stored in open ground pits and then taken to treatment plants so it may be used again for a variety of purposes.

The high pressure of the blasted solution cracks open dense shale rocks and the gas or oil within them is released from tiny fractures.

A fracture can be as small as 1mm wide, and trillions are produced.

0 1 2 3 4 5

The released gas and oil flow back up the well to the surface where they are collected.

One fracking of a well can provide resources for years, even decades.

Fracking is now complete!

2000 2010 2020 2030 2040 2050 2060 2070

Opponents of fracking have fiercely attacked the practice as dangerous to the planet and to local neighborhoods disrupted by noise, methane pollution, and drilling machinery. Fracking also requires huge volumes of water per well—a strain on resources in dry areas like Texas, parts of Colorado, and California.

Environmentalists cite the potential dangers of disposing of and recycling fracked water, much of it contaminated with toxic chemicals and runoff. And although many states are now requiring "green completions," including cleaning, filtering, and recycling fracked water, some improperly sealed wells can and have leaked methane, the primary component of natural gas. Anti-fracking activists (or "fractivists") have cited instances and documented reports showing that shale fracturing and methane contamination may compromise the safety of private and community well water. For example, in July 2014, the Pennsylvania Department of Environmental Protection reported 209 local water supplies had been negatively impacted by oil and gas activities (although the department did not report the nature of each impact).

At the same time, defenders of shale oil and gas give abundant examples of economic and even environmental benefits—from U.S. job creation to lower natural gas prices and reduction of energy imports to increased investment in the petrochemical and pharmaceutical industries. In addition, methane from natural gas—the same methane that worries environmentalists—actually has many clean-air benefits. For instance, it burns cleaner than coal or oil and has supplanted many U.S. coal-fired plants to generate electricity.

In a May 2014 phone interview, Mark Brownstein, associate vice president of the Environmental Defense Fund (EDF) and its chief counsel on U.S. climate and energy, pointed out that natural gas is significantly preferable to coal, which is still the top fuel for electricity generation in the United States. Natural gas produces approximately 50 *percent less* carbon dioxide than the coal alternative. It's worth noting that the increase in shale gas supplies has resulted in dramatic U.S. price decreases that are essentially forcing many coal-fired power plants into retirement, Brownstein said.

So what's the answer? Does shale energy produce pristine natural gas—a pure alternative to dirty coal? Or is fracking leaving our virgin lands in ruin?

Personally, I think the answer lies somewhere in between. Oil and gas, like any industrial process, is certainly not 100 percent "green." Neither are all its leaders out to destroy the environment, sweep dirty secrets under the rug, and pursue a dollar at the cost of healthy water, clean air, or worse—ruined lives.

Yes, we can pinpoint areas of corruption and stories of terrible accidents. But for the most part, members of the oil and gas industry work hard to keep their footprint minimal. Would they work as hard if the environmental groups didn't breathe down their necks every step of the way? Maybe not. It's a good thing we have checks and balances.

When mistakes happen, the incidents get more than adequate news coverage, the public is rightly outraged, and processes are improved.

The environmental story gets told a lot—and it's certainly a vital one. We *must* come to reasonable solutions to address environmental concerns. In fact, I have a whole chapter devoted to environmental discussion. If you want to skip right to it, go to Chapter 9.

But, to be honest with you, I'm here mostly to tell another fracking story. The—in my opinion—more interesting, arguably more important, story. The story that gets missed in the cacophony.

That story is about power.

WHAT IS SHALE?

Shale formations occur over millions of years through a process of heating and compression, or compacting, during mountain building.

◄◄◄ Shale

55%

Shale is a type of sedimentary rock. Nearly 55% of all sedimentary rock is shale, and it usually forms in sheets.

Shale is formed from the carbon-rich carcasses of primitive animals and plants—**fossils!**

When a fossil settles into a playa, river, basin, or ocean, over time it becomes part of shale rock.

Roughly **70%** of the Earth's surface is covered by shale.

SHALE + =

Shale is the most commonly fracked rock, because it contains abundant oil and gas.

The Bakken Shale Play—located in Western North Dakota and Eastern Montana, plus parts of the Williston Basin—has shale dating back to the Late Devonian, Early Mississippian age—over **359 million years ago!**

MILLIONS OF YEARS BEFORE PRESENT

| 200 | 300 | BAKKEN | 400 |

JURASSIC

PERMIAN

MISSISSIPPIAN

SILURIAN

TRIASSIC

PENNSYLVANIAN

DEVONIAN

The United States has a lot of shale.

CHAPTER 3

ENERGY (IN)SECURITY: WHAT DO YOU DO WHEN THE LIGHTS GO OUT?

The darkness descended ahead of the dusk before its prescribed time. It came just after 5 p.m. EST, on November 9, 1965, as tens of thousands of commuters along the East Coast were making their way home. Some were headed to restaurants for dinner or to the nearest bar to drink away the evening. Others rushed to join their families. And just as children were trudging home in the twilight through piles of leaves or practicing piano and violin in their living rooms, the lights dimmed, flickered on, then off. Province by province, state by state, electricity surged through the interconnected power stations of Ontario, Quebec, New York, New Jersey, Connecticut, Massachusetts, New Hampshire, Rhode Island, and Vermont. Then each station failed. What followed was fifteen hours of darkness for more than thirty million people living and working in the most energy-hungry corner of North America.[1]

News Flash: New York, "The City That Never Sleeps" is forced to slumber by candlelight.

"Theaters closed for the night. Times Square, usually a glimmering crossroads of light, was dark. Thousands of travelers stranded in New York were forced to sleep in hotel lobbies. The New York Times report that 'the city's hotels looked like bivouac areas.' Nearly ten thousand commuters were stuck on subway cars, unable to escape the darkened subway tunnels. About midnight, the Transit Authority began sending food and coffee to those trapped underground."[2]

What had happened? How could it happen? A new kind of public anxiety, even desperation, was born across 80,000 square miles of pitch black.

"The first thing that went through my mind was that there was an enemy attack," said Gerry Heydt, then a Purdue University graduate student in Indiana.[3] Heydt was on his way with fellow students to an "all-you-can-eat" chicken special at a local restaurant when he heard radio news of the blackout. Heydt was immediately concerned about his parents' safety because they lived in New York, but he couldn't reach them by phone. Another New Yorker, Mae Rosenzweig, one of the commuters trapped on a train underground, remembered that "some people were getting panicky and coming up with ridiculous explanations [that] the city was bombed. . . . They thought the Russians were bombing [the city]. . . . Fortunately, there were other people who pooh-poohed [the idea]."[4]

As it turned out, Heydt and Rosenzweig's more fearful compatriots were all wrong. The cause of the disaster was, in fact, an engineering glitch. Human error.

It began in Ontario, Canada, where a power surge set off a chain of failures across the northeastern United States. A single faulty relay triggered a rapidly cascading collapse of interconnected utilities. At dusk, the Lewiston, New York, power station registered the combination of rush-hour and dinnertime demand as an overload, tripping the circuit. All power instantly diverted to the other lines, which in turn overloaded. Within five minutes, the entire northeastern power grid was in shambles as the effects of overloads and loss of generating capacity caused a domino effect: One station after another automatically shut down in response.

With nothing more than the light of the full moon to guide them, people walked home or grabbed taxis and buses where they could. They lit candles, found flashlights, and tried their transistor radios. Many of the radio stations without reserve generators went offline. One family in Ithaca, New

York, expecting the onset of the wife's labor pains at any moment, took out camping equipment, cooked dinner on a Coleman stove, and waited.

In the Belly of the Beast

As Americans, we have dealt with intermittent lights out before— especially during the air raid drills of World War II when East Coast and West Coast cities prepared for the possibility of enemy attack.

But in November 1965, the trip to darkness took more than a personal toll. For the first time, both producers and consumers of electricity—and the American public at large—felt vulnerable.

Suddenly we were faced with a daunting reality—our minute-to-minute reliance on the power grid. As a postwar civilization, we had displayed extreme confidence in our superior technologies and exuberant social responses to them. We had begun our race to the moon, made advances in heart surgery, medicines, and electrical engineering and computers, and built nuclear power plants. We'd brought live TV coverage to the Civil Rights movement, constructed vast interstate highways, airports, supersonic aircraft, communication satellites, and giant dams. Suddenly, Americans were forced to acknowledge how much of our lives and daily tasks were dependent on consistent, reliable energy.

Given our absolute dependence on energy, how could there ever be enough?

The President Gets Serious

Fears that there could be a repeat of 1965's Great Northeast Blackout reached all the way to the White House. Faced with public and energy industry anxieties, President Lyndon B. Johnson took immediate steps. In a message to the chairman of the Federal Power Commission, Johnson ordered a "thorough cause of the study of this failure" and put at the chairman's disposal the "full resources of the federal government . . . directing the Federal Bureau of Investigation, the Department of Defense and other agencies to support you in any way possible." He also urged the chairman to call on the country's top experts for additional engineering support.[5]

It took six full days to figure out what went wrong, but the Great Northeast Blackout demonstrated all too effectively the consequences of losing power and our vulnerability to the technological failures that can stop its flow. Like all developed nations, we depend on electricity and, as such, are crippled without it. This is common knowledge. But there's nothing like a massive power failure (aka "slap in the face") to wake people up.

Fortunately, the Great Northeast Blackout spurred people to action. Not only did citizens stock up on flashlights, batteries, Coleman stoves, and transistor radios, our engineers also took a much deeper critical look at the North American power grid. Planning for the unexpected, regional coordinating councils such as the Northeast Reliability Council (NERC) and the New York Power Pool (NYPP) were formed to develop industry standards for equipment testing and reserve generation capacity. These groups also developed preventative measures governing interconnection and reliability, so that similar blackouts would not happen again.

Yet, they did happen again.

Just after 9:30 p.m. on July 13, 1977, a twenty-five-hour blackout spawned "Hell Night" in New York City. Unlike the 1965 event, which "instantly became an emblem of civic spunk and resilience," according to *The New York Times,* the 1977 event was marked by arson, looting in the poorer neighborhoods, and 3,800 city arrests. A series of lightning strikes that sultry night caused a massive power failure at New York's Indian Point No. 3 plant, followed by a cascade of plant failures. The result was "civic disarray and uncertainty at a time of overwhelming municipal budget woes, economic deterioration, and fear caused by a serial killer known as Son of Sam."[6]

Afraid of the Dark

Around the same time, the U.S. was learning another hard lesson. Just a few years after the Great Northeast Blackout, the country was consuming *a third* of the world's oil. Imports had reached 8.4 million barrels per day, and the bulk of those barrels came from the Middle East. Because of our insatiable energy appetite, anyone could see America was on the verge of an oil crisis.

During the 1973 Arab-Israeli War (also called the Yom Kippur War), the Arab members of OPEC imposed a complete embargo against the United States, retaliating because the U.S. chose to arm and resupply the Israeli military. Arab OPEC members banned exports to other countries supporting Israel, including the Netherlands, Portugal, and South Africa.

For six months, OPEC refused to sell oil to the U.S.

Not only did the embargo throw us into recession, but oil prices went through the roof, roughly quadrupling within just three months. The price of a barrel hit $11.65 in December 1973, 130 percent higher than in October 1973 and 387 percent higher than one year before. The share value of companies listed on the New York Stock Exchange plummeted by $97 billion. Oil shortages took a toll on the everyday lives of ordinary American citizens, creating backups and lines for gasoline that extended for miles each day.

Eventually OPEC let up, ending the embargo in March 1974. But the damage had already been done. The U.S. entered a period of wage and price controls, the Watergate scandal, and "stagflation," a period of economic stagnancy combined with inflation.

In August 1974, President Ford took to the television waves to address the American public on the subject of oil prices and the need for "energy independence." Here is President Ford's original typewritten draft, along with his handwritten manuscript changes, the typescript of the president's policy on conservation, and an address a year later on ending price controls to return to the free market.

oh
pat

August 29, 1974

DRAFT PRESIDENTIAL STATEMENT

Dedicated efforts to conserve energy continue to be essential if this Nation is to achieve its goals for improving energy self sufficiency, conserving resources and improving the quality of our environment.

Today, I have established an energy savings goal for the Federal Government for the current fiscal year. I have directed that agencies hold energy consumption to a level of 15% below the amount consumed in fiscal year 1973. In addition, I have instructed the administrators of the Federal Energy Administration and General Services Administration to recommend a multi-year program to assure that energy efficiency is considered in all decisions pertaining to Federal buildings, operations and purchasing.

During the twelve month period ending June 30, 1974, Federal Government agencies achieved energy savings of more than triple the original 7% goal, and avoided costs of some $800 million. Our accomplishments last year and our new goal for the coming year should serve as an example of the potential for serious energy conservation efforts.

I call upon all Americans to join in these efforts to conserve energy.

# # #

(Pullen)PT   September 9, 1975

DRAFT OF TV STATEMENT ON OIL, TUESDAY, SEPTEMBER 9, 1975

I have today vetoed S. 1849, which would have extended for six

months price controls on domestic oil. So there is no question in the

minds of the American people and the Congress, let me state the reasons

why I have taken this action:

       -- First, to save American jobs.

       -- Second, to protect the American consumer from the continuous

rise in ~~gasoline~~ _fuel_ prices.

       It's just that simple.

       Since the 1973 embargo, America's bill for imported oil has

continued to rise -- from just over $3 billion to more than $25 billion

today -- an increase of 700 percent. I am talking about American dollars

~~which we are using~~ _young dollar_ to pay for foreign oil and for foreign jobs. Altogether,

a potential of
more than one million American jobs have been lost in this way.

If ~~I signed S. 1849~~ continuing government controls, America's start on

the road to energy independence would be delayed indefinitely. [Having

served in the Congress ~~for more than a quarter century,~~] I am well

aware of the reluctance of the ~~national legislature~~ members of Congress to face up to such a

difficult ~~sticky~~ problem just as an election campaign is getting underway.

For more than eight months, I have tried to get the members of the Congress

moving on a solution to this vital problem of energy independence. My

latest effort at a compromise with has resulted ~~only~~ in a proposed six-month extension

of an existing law -- which is no answer at all to ~~the problem.~~ // a program energy independence for the U.S.

If my veto of ~~S. 1849~~ is sustained, I ~~still~~ would will accept a 45-day

extension of price controls -- if there is assurance an acceptable plan

can be enacted during this period.

If all efforts at compromise fail, I will act to ensure an orderly

transition from government controls to the free market.

A decision on oil price controls is a vital step on the road to

energy independence. We must attack our energy problem before it

becomes a National emergency. Our time to act instead of react grows

shorter with each day and each delay. I urge the ~~Congress~~ *members of the Senate & House* to sustain

my veto and ~~work with me~~ *get on* in meeting this problem head-on -- now!

# # #

Jack Grayson knows a little something about price controls and stagnancy. As chair of the U.S. Price Commission from 1971 to 1973 under President Nixon, Grayson instituted and oversaw price controls. "No one could move their prices at all unless I approved them," Grayson told our team in a personal interview in March 2014. "Price controls went pretty far: schools, railroading, education . . . even prices for Las Vegas prostitutes! Energy was just one of the sectors I had to deal with. I didn't treat energy any different than the others."

After two years, Grayson urged President Nixon to consider that price controls were distorting the system altogether. Instead of rescinding them, though, Nixon divided the system and kept energy under strict price control.

"I disagreed with that," Grayson said. "Natural gas had been held down when it was proven to be a very viable source of energy." And this decision, he believes (with the wisdom of 20/20 hindsight), prevented the market from working.

Average gasoline prices in the U.S. jumped from an average of 38 cents to 84 cents a gallon. The recession forced the idea of energy conservation, and gas-guzzling cars became a thing of the past—at least for a while. Sales of more fuel-efficient cars soared and threatened the U.S. auto industry, while Japanese and German cars made their first serious U.S. market inroads.

Had we learned anything? The idea of "energy independence," a stated presidential goal, became real to many people. Yet it remained elusive. Like ghosts from World War II, the concepts of rationing, conservation, turning down thermostats, standing in lines, clipping coupons, and "going without" returned to our national vocabulary.

It seemed that in just a few short years, the world had gone backward. We were suddenly more vulnerable than ever before.

CHAPTER 4

THE FEAR FACTOR

By the end of the 1970s, U.S. citizens had become keenly aware of the damage an energy disruption could cause. They understood the fear that comes from economic stagnation and too little power. Fear of skyrocketing energy bills. Fear of blackmail for energy. Gasoline shortages. Fear of losing the lights.

The fear crept into our pop culture. In the Spike Lee film *Summer of Sam* (1999), the 1977 New York City blackout played out once again as Bronx residents fearing the Son of Sam killer faced mob violence, a curfew, and confrontations with police. In *The China Syndrome* (1979), a newscaster, a cameraman, and a nuclear plant manager discover a conspiracy to cover up a radioactive hazard at the plant threatening the entire Southern California population.

The fear also crept into our political decisions. In fact, for more than forty years, "energy independence" has been a stated goal of every American president. Until very recently, we weren't even close!

For example, when the U.S. economy reeled from the effects of the Arab Oil Embargo of 1973, President Nixon established "energy independence" as a crisis-inspired policy goal. He set the time frame for complete energy independence at 1980, a goal he defined not as reaching zero imports but as never again finding the U.S. in a position where another country could manipulate our supply of oil, thereby rendering the U.S. economically or politically vulnerable.

President Gerald Ford looked to 1985 as the year to achieve that goal, while President Jimmy Carter wanted to cut our oil imports by half by

1985—a goal that *was* accomplished. George H.W. Bush proclaimed that imports could be cut by one-third by 2010, but more than fifteen years later, his son George W. Bush set his sights on reducing oil imports from the Middle East by 75 percent by the year 2025. With the task unfinished, Barack Obama vowed to slash petroleum imports by one-third by 2025. However, it's the current boom in shale oil and gas that is allowing the U.S. to reach for this goal in the present day.

"Scorched Earth" and Oil Wars

No matter the president or stated goal for energy independence, fear of not having enough energy and enough access or control of oil and gas has led to repeated conflicts, especially in the Middle East. The first U.S. Gulf War (1990–1991), for example, was successfully fought against Iraq by a coalition of twenty-eight nations, including American, Saudi Arabian, UK, and Egyptian forces.

The stated dispute was about Kuwaiti oil production. Iraq's leader, Saddam Hussein, initially declared that his armies invaded Kuwait in response to that country's "overproduction" of oil, which had cost Iraq an estimated $14 billion a year when oil prices fell. Hussein also accused Kuwait of illegally pumping oil from Iraq's Rumaila oil field located on the Kuwaiti-Iraq border. When the UN called on Iraqi forces to withdraw from Kuwait, U.S. troops moved into Saudi Arabia to protect U.S. oil fields. When coalition forces comprised of troops from the U.S. and more than a dozen other countries stormed Kuwait and southern Iraq, Hussein's troops set fire to at least 600 Kuwaiti oil wells, a scorched-earth policy that clearly showed retribution for Kuwaiti (and coalition) energy production and policy.

Access to oil was also a central unstated issue in the second Iraq war waged by President George W. Bush. The American government claimed Saddam Hussein and Iraq's weapons of mass destruction posed a threat to the U.S. and its allies. Many now affirm that the war was launched for multiple motives, including oil. Even Chuck Hagel, the former U.S.

FOR THE PAST 40 YEARS, 8 PRESIDENTS HAVE PROMISED AMERICANS ENERGY INDEPENDENCE...

PRESIDENT NIXON
JANUARY 1974

"At the end of this decade, in the year 1980, the United States will not be dependent on any other country for the energy we need to provide our jobs, to heat our homes, and to keep transportation moving."

PRESIDENT CARTER
JANUARY 1978

"Never again should we neglect a growing crisis like the shortage of energy, where further delay will only lead to more harsh and painful solutions. Every day we spend more than $120 million for foreign oil. This slows our economic growth, it lowers the value of the dollar overseas, and it aggravates unemployment and inflation here at home. Now what we must do—increase production. We must cut down on waste. And we must use more of those fuels, which are plentiful and more permanent."

PRESIDENT FORD
JANUARY 1975

"I have set the following national energy goals to assure that our future is as secure and as productive as our past: First, we must reduce oil imports by 1 million barrels per day by the end of 1977. Second, we must end vulnerability to economic disruption by foreign suppliers by 1985. Third, we must develop our energy technology and resources so that the United States has the ability to supply a significant share of the energy needs of the free world by the end of this century."

PRESIDENT REAGAN
FEBRUARY 1985

"We seek to fully deregulate natural gas to bring on new supplies and bring us closer to energy independence."

NO, WE'RE NOT THERE YET.

PRESIDENT G.H.W. BUSH
JANUARY 1991

" Just as our efforts will bring economic growth now and in the future, they also must be matched by long-term investments for the next American century. That requires a forward-looking plan of action, [including] a comprehensive national energy strategy that calls for energy conservation and efficiency, increased development, and greater use of alternative fuels. "

PRESIDENT G.W. BUSH
FEBRUARY 2001

" Our energy demands outstrip our supply. We can produce more energy at home while protecting our environment, and we must. We can produce more electricity to meet demand, and we must. We can promote alternative energy sources and conservation, and we must. Americans must become energy independent, and we will. "

PRESIDENT CLINTON
SEPTEMBER 2000

" Increased energy efficiency has significantly enhanced our energy security by reducing our demand for oil . . . but much more can be done. The President and Vice President have secured substantial increases to accelerate the research, development, and deployment of alternative and more efficient energy technologies. "

PRESIDENT OBAMA
JANUARY 2012

" Nowhere is the promise of innovation greater than in American-made energy. Over the last 3 years, we've opened millions of new acres for oil and gas exploration, and tonight I'm directing my administration to open more than 75% of our potential oil and gas resources. Right now, American oil production is the highest that it's been in 8 years. Not only that, last year we relied less on foreign oil than in any of the past 16 years. "

35

Secretary of Defense, acknowledged oil's role in the Iraq War during a 2008 speech at Catholic University. "People say we're not fighting for oil. Of course we are."[1]

George W. Bush's Treasury Secretary Paul O'Neill reported that Bush's first two National Security Council meetings in 2001 included a discussion of invading Iraq. O'Neill received a briefing document, "Plan for Post-Saddam Iraq," which envisioned peacekeeping troops, war-crimes tribunals, and a division of Iraq's oil wealth. Another Pentagon document, dated March 5, 2001, was titled "Foreign Suitors for Iraqi Oilfield Contracts," and included a map of potential areas for exploration.[2]

Clearly, energy is the centerpiece of many world conflicts. Case in point: The 2014–2015 Ukrainian crisis that unfolded as both a military and energy-pricing confrontation between Russia's Gazprom, the state-owned company, and the Ukrainian government. Gazprom has held a tight energy grip on Ukraine and Eastern Europe for decades, but it is also a major supplier of natural gas to Western Europe. At three different times since 2006, Russia has turned off the gas that transits to other European nations through Ukraine's hub of pipelines. Russia claims Ukraine doesn't pay its gas bills. Ukrainian energy analysts, on the other hand, suggest that Russian President Vladimir Putin uses gas as a geopolitical weapon and that gas embargoes are saber-rattling and a method of punishment, in which Russia threatens the entire energy security of Europe.

Then there is the Japan-China territorial dispute over a group of islands known as Senkaku in Japan and Diaoyu in China. These eight uninhabited islands—essentially piles of rock in the East China Sea between the two nations—have a total area of about seven square kilometers, and both nations are claiming them as part of their national territories. They represent more than meets the eye: Not only are these bits of land strategically close to important shipping lanes, they also—you guessed it—offer access to potential oil and gas reserves.[3]

So even if we don't think about it much, energy security is as vital to a nation's well-being as a functional health-care system. Moreover, energy security is an interconnected reality; it affects the quality of life of

TOP 10 COUNTRIES

WITH THE GREATEST TECHNICALLY RECOVERABLE SHALE OIL AND/OR GAS RESOURCES

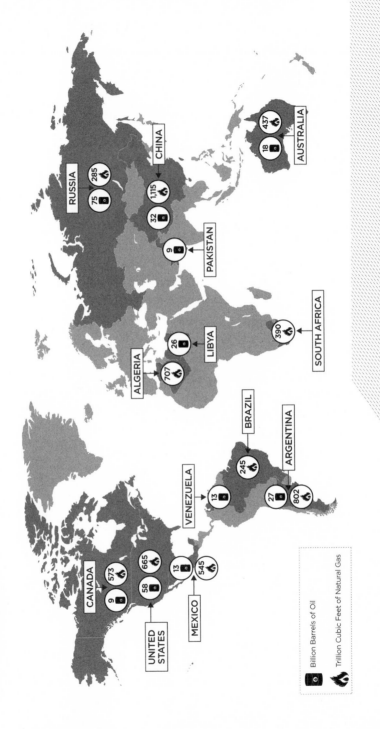

Billion Barrels of Oil

Trillion Cubic Feet of Natural Gas

every citizen anywhere on earth. It is also one of the reasons why energy self-sufficiency plays such a strong psychological role in a nation's geopolitical strategy, its willingness to share or steal assets, and even its will to power.

Clearly, we should care about who has the energy and how it's used. Having energy changes the flow of, well . . . everything.

CHAPTER 5

ENERGY SECURITY: WHAT LIES BENEATH CHANGES THE FLOW UP TOP

The Ukrainian energy business is a black box. A state secret. Only four or five analysts fully understand it. It's a tangle of corrupt officials and interconnected oil and gas pipelines, billions in Black Sea drilling contracts, and flavor-of-the-week Russian threats to cut off gas supplies or subsidies to Ukraine.

The "box" contains several wild cards. One is an ousted Ukrainian president, Viktor Yanukovych, who favors gold-footed bathroom fixtures, a $2 million private sauna, and sweetheart contracts forged with gas and coal millionaires tied to Gazprom, Russia's monopoly gas supplier. In addition, scores of armed thugs and alleged criminal organizations buttress the government officials (many of whom are Ukraine's oil and gas barons).

Even Yulia Tymoshenko, the first female Ukrainian prime minister, was convicted of oil and gas company embezzlement and abuse of power as a president of United Energy Systems of Ukraine, a natural gas trading company with strong ties to Gazprom. During Yanukovich's administration, she was sentenced to seven years in prison and ordered to pay the state $188 million—charges that international supporters claimed were politically inspired. She was later released when the new Kiev government decriminalized the activities for which she was charged.

And, finally, consider the ethnic Russian separatists recently fighting in Eastern Ukraine with sophisticated anti-aircraft weapons. In late July

2014, the collateral damage in their struggle included several Ukrainian military planes and a commercial Malaysia Airlines jetliner shot down with 298 civilians aboard, which shook the world. Much of the forensic evidence of the shootings was spirited away by separatists before investigators could arrive on the scene to determine fault.

Ukraine is a mess. Ukraine is also a microcosm of what can go wrong when countries become too dependent on outside suppliers for energy. Ukraine, in particular, exemplifies how shale development—or lack of it, in this case—can affect the security of a country and its ability to survive and prosper.

Ukraine's problem: The country is a natural gas hub standing between Russia's abundant energy fields and its customers in Central and Western Europe. It has also been engaged in a series of battles between its home gas company, Naftogaz of Ukraine, and Gazprom over natural gas supplies, prices, and debts. These disputes have escalated and now involve political leaders from several countries and threaten natural gas supplies in a number of European nations dependent on Russian suppliers that transit gas through Ukraine. Russia supplies a quarter of the EU's natural gas, and roughly 80 percent of those exports are transited through Ukrainian pipelines.

Historically, Ukraine has relied on cheap Russian gas subsidies to support its ailing economy. Beset by government and business corruption and severe economic inequality since its independence in late 1991—when the Soviet Union dissolved—Ukraine has been effectively "addicted" to subsidized energy. Thanks to Moscow's corrupt pricing policies, since Ukraine established independence, the country has struggled for economic viability, losing manufacturing market share, and accumulating massive oil and gas debt.

Europe's Dependence on Russian Gas

Since 2005, Europe has become increasingly dependent on imported Russian gas. This dependence has given Ukraine a unique position as a portal or "choke point" through which a substantial amount of all Russian natural gas transiting to Western and Central Europe flows.

"Oil and gas is what starts wars," said Chris Faulkner, the CEO of Breitling Energy Corporation, a shale-exploration firm based in Dallas, Texas, that bids on contracts in the EU and China.

In Ukraine, civil unrest started with rampant government corruption, but war started with a gas bill.

Russia cut off the gas to Ukraine and, by extension, to Eastern and Western Europe, during the bitter winters of 2006 and 2009 and again in June 2014—ostensibly over Ukraine's portion of unpaid gas bills and late fees.

It all started in March 2005, when a dispute arose over the prices of Russian natural gas supplies and the cost of Ukrainian gas transit. During this conflict, Russia claimed Ukraine was not paying its gas bill while simultaneously diverting Russian gas (which Gazprom had intended for export to the EU) through its pipelines to satisfy domestic needs.

Naftogaz eventually owned up to the deception, and Gazprom announced it would raise gas prices to Ukraine from $50 per 1,000 cubic meters to $230. Kiev refused to pay, and on January 1, 2006, Gazprom rang in the New Year by turning off the taps, almost certainly at President Vladimir Putin's behest. The Ukrainians responded by penning side deals to import gas from Turkmenistan—at reduced prices—via a Swiss-registered Gazprom subsidiary. (Such are the ways that nations save face.)

Three years later, problems erupted again. This time, Gazprom retaliated against Ukraine's continued attempts to forge EU trade deals. Russia raised prices from $250 to $400-plus, and Gazprom turned off the taps again on New Year's Day 2009, as sub-zero temperatures swept through Europe. While Western European countries had more fuel stockpiles, southeastern European countries like Bulgaria and Slovakia simply ran out of gas, closing schools and industrial plants and declaring national emergencies. The gas supplies of as many as eighteen European nations were reduced or entirely depleted thanks to the Russian embargo.

The ensuing years saw continued court battles, and a Swedish court of arbitration in 2010 ordered Naftogaz to return 12.1 billion cubic meters (430 billion cubic feet) of gas to RosUkrEnergo, a Swiss-based company in which Gazprom controls a 50 percent stake. An interim gas agreement between Russia and Ukraine was signed in 2010, specifying a 30 percent reduction in Russian gas prices in exchange for extension of a Russian lease on a Black Sea naval base at Sevastopol.

In 2014, however, arguments over Gazprom pricing and unpaid bills again resulted in a gas cutoff—this time in June, a comparatively moderate time to slap Ukraine's wrist for tardy payments. Russia once again announced it would raise Ukrainian gas prices as high as $400 per 1,000 cubic meters, as opposed to the $270-odd price Ukraine had been paying under a subsidy granted to Viktor Yanukovych's administration. This sparked angry demonstrations and protests among pro-Europe ("Euromaidan") Ukrainians, and several months later Yanukovych fled. On February 22, 2014, he was officially deposed by the Ukrainian parliament, and an interim government was set up.

As citizens and journalists exposed Yanukovych's corruption and lavish estate holdings, Moscow refused to recognize the interim Kiev government and moved uniformed (but unidentified) troops and pro-Russian separatists into Crimea. Very quickly Russia annexed Crimea and nationalized all its oil and gas companies. The move was a direct attempt to thwart Ukraine's plans to drill with Western oil majors in the Black Sea. Moscow also hiked Ukrainian gas prices by 80 percent, claiming the country owed as much as $38.4 billion for past gas fines and unpaid contracts. The new Kiev government defiantly pronounced the Gazprom bill ridiculous and refused to pay.

"Vladimir Putin uses oil and gas as a geopolitical weapon," said Ukrainian analyst Olena Tregub when our team spoke with her in May 2014. "Putin's biggest motivation is to stay in power; he claims he has to restore Great Russia as a superpower. The state of the Russian economy affects the legitimacy of his regime."

Why International Oil and Gas Trade Matters

Putin isn't the first to use oil and gas as a weapon, and he won't be the last. Remember: He who controls the energy controls the lights, the heat, the information highways, the price at the pump—all the juice that modern society runs on.

To ignore that fact is naïve.

Decisions about whether to develop accessible domestic energy sources like shale oil and gas or renewables, and decisions about pricing, infrastructure development, and import or exports, and from whom, may mean the difference between a nation's economic security and its vulnerability to intimidation or outright attack.

Ukraine, once part of the Soviet Union, is a case in point.

"[Ukrainians] were drinking their own Kool-Aid, the cheap natural gas from Russia," noted Breitling's Chris Faulkner during a phone interview in April 2014. "The country historically was paying 30 to 40 percent discounts, and Putin got them addicted, so Ukraine didn't industrialize or move their country forward. They got stuck."

Most experts agree that the key to Ukraine's long-term stability is a combination of energy self-sufficiency and massive economic and democratic reforms. Ukraine is home to Europe's third-largest shale gas reserves at 42 trillion cubic feet, according to the U.S. Energy Information Administration (EIA), but shale is barely exploited.

"It's pretty simple," Faulkner states. "You can embrace Russia and kiss the imperial ring, or you can embrace shale gas," he said. "The reality is that if you have no energy security policy in place, you're fools."

Any Country Can Become a Ukraine

Without a free and fair international trade in oil or gas, any country without developed resources or the money to buy sufficient energy outside its borders can become a Ukraine. Whether it's jacking up prices unreasonably, stopping the flow of gas or oil, destroying infrastructure, or penning unfair contracts, an energy aggressor can bring a recipient economy to its knees. As Hungarian energy ambassador-at-large Anita Orban explained in an April 2014 phone interview, "It is prices that provide the best economic and political tool for the monopoly supplier. Whoever has the monopoly calls the shots."

Is the Middle East Our Russia?

For decades the U.S. has been chiefly concerned about petroleum supplies and pricing from the politically volatile OPEC nations of the Middle East. Now, as it turns out, "Dependence on Russian natural gas has been Europe's equivalent of U.S. dependence on Middle Eastern oil," writes Pierre Noel, an energy analyst.[1]

Today, U.S. crude imports from the Middle East remain about 22 percent of total imports. And OPEC still determines cartel oil prices and supplies, which in turn have key effects on global pricing.

But Simin Curtis sees a change on the wind. As president and CEO of the Pittsburgh-based American Middle East Institute, Curtis runs an independent, nonprofit organization focused on building business, educational, and cultural ties between the United States and the countries of the Middle East. In that capacity, she meets many ministers from around that region—and all have been eyeing the shale revolution in the United States.

"I think they're very scared of it," Curtis divulged in a January 2015 phone interview with my team. "Here you have this powerhouse of America building up their manufacturing capabilities and starting to use the by-products of this gas. . . . That means that the markets that Saudi's trying to develop are going to have some stiff competition. I know that they're worried about what the implications are."

Other analysts agree that this shift in energy dominance has Saudi Arabia—and the rest of the cartel—running scared.

Jim Krane, the Wallace S. Wilson Fellow for Energy Studies at the James A. Baker III Institute for Public Policy at Rice University in

Houston, Texas, believes that concern applies to the entire Gulf Cooperation Council (GCC). In addition to Saudi Arabia, the GCC states include Bahrain, Kuwait, Oman, Qatar, and the United Arab Emirates.

"We have developed this relationship with that part of the world under the understanding that it was a mutually dependent relationship: We were depending on their exports of oil and their supply and their willingness to keep markets supplied with oil, and in return, we were offering them security," Krane told my team during an interview in June 2014. "There's more to that relationship than just oil for security, but that's certainly a big part of it."

And now that the U.S. is less dependent on foreign oil, Krane said, "There's some worry that rising oil security in the U.S. means we're going to be less concerned with that part of the world and that we may be less willing to go through quite as much trouble as we have over the past four to five decades to extend that security umbrella and keep it as robust as it has been."

As Krane pointed out, the Obama administration remains committed to the security of the region, in part because their supply helps keep the price stable—and lower—than it would otherwise be. But he recognizes signs that the U.S. is going in a different direction: "There have been other diplomatic partings of the ways that don't have much to do with shale oil. So there's all kinds of scrambling to find other ways that they can increase their strategic importance in the eyes of Washington."

"OPEC countries have resisted an increasingly open global environment of trade and investment," assert Ann Myers Jaffe and Edward Morse, Middle East energy security experts, in *Energy and Security: Strategies for a World in Transition*.[2] "They have sought to defy market forces and control the price of oil through government interference and manipulation of markets." OPEC's chief weapon is artificially regulating energy supply and investment for the benefit of Arab producing nations and their patronage networks. By controlling supply amid rising global demand, for example, OPEC reduced its spare production capacity, helping to drive up oil prices fifteenfold from *$10/barrel in 1998 to a peak of almost $150 in the summer of 2008*. In a year when we were already facing economic recession, the resulting skyrocketing cost of gas couldn't have come at a worse time.

Now OPEC is playing the game the other way around. Saudi Arabia has flooded the worldwide supply, causing the price of oil to plummet—down from $115/barrel in June 2014 to $45 in January 2015. The lower gas price may be good news for travelers, but its precipitous fall could wreak havoc on the economy. Some economists are even bandying about the term "stock market crash," saying that if energy loans start to default, a banking crisis is close behind.

Simin Curtis, however, calls the shale revolution "one of those unstoppable forces" that she expects will overcome Saudi Arabia's gamble of keeping energy down. "It might *slow* production here in the United States, but I would really be surprised if the Saudis could *eliminate* that. "What I worry about," Curtis said, "is that the countries that really just live on the edge and have not diversified enough really from oil, those countries are keeping their populations from outright mutiny because of oil."

Most people would agree: It's imperative that any country actively develop its own energy options to protect citizens' livelihoods, to ensure prosperity, and to shield the country from those who would wield oil and gas supplies as a political weapon. Those who argue that those energy resources should come from renewables are right—partially.

We *should* develop renewables. Who is going to argue against cleaner energy from solar, wind, or water? But the fact is, renewables are not a currently viable option for ubiquitous energy usage. Renewables are expensive, and nations need "energy mixes"—diverse sources of different kinds—to stabilize pricing and bring about change at a reasonable rate.

Look at Germany, for example. The country is often cited as a model for green success, as it has set a goal of 80 percent renewables by 2030. But when the Pacific Ocean tsunami of 2011 destroyed three of the Japanese Fukushima Daiichi power plants, a wave of anti-nuclear sentiment swept through Europe. Germany switched off eight of its seventeen nuclear reactors, cutting 7 percent of its electricity. Trying to reduce nuclear energy while transitioning rapidly to renewables inadvertently produced sharply higher power costs at a time of recession. In 2014, German consumers will pay €20 billion to subsidize integration of solar, wind, and biogas technologies into the German power grid, while the real market price of these renewables is an estimated €3 billion. Meanwhile, German government surcharges on electricity have soared 47 percent, and 300,000 German households have seen their electricity shut off in the past year because of unpaid bills.[3]

The Germans—and indeed the rest of their European cohorts—have since adjusted their energy programs by boosting coal purchases to offset high-cost renewables. Ironically, though, coal is among the most polluting of energy resources in the world, emitting such gases as carbon dioxide, toxic mercury, and sulfur dioxides.

At the very least, we need a gateway to an economy powered principally by clean energy sources—including natural gas from shale and other sources, which emits half the carbon dioxide of coal. An ample supply of energy from our own lands is critical to our balance of energy security—that and, as we'll learn, a reliable and updated policy on energy exports and imports. That's what energy security is all about. It's not just producing all of our domestic energy on our own, in isolation. It's coming up with solutions that include energy diversification from multiple sources, domestic and international; and tapping our own energy reserves, including shales, solar, biogas, hydroelectric, wind, offshore, and conventional resources. It means importing and exporting with nonhostile global partners who deliver reliably. And it also means integrating renewables into the mix when and where they make sense.

Our shale energy, it turns out, is a treasure. It's an unexpected bounty that can be tapped securely—and, contrary to public belief, it's a source of power not likely to run out any time soon.

Energy Security? Energy Independence?
Self-Sufficiency? What's the Difference?

By the 1970s, when Americans suddenly woke up to the realities of energy insecurity, they began to explore another idea: energy independence.

The worst consequence for our nation was to become *energy dependent*. That is, the United States could no longer produce enough oil, gas, and alternative fuels to support our burgeoning economy, despite an apparent abundance of natural resources.

Though the Arab Oil Embargo lasted only six months, its effects reverberated for decades. Even today, Americans harbor the fear of energy dependency. Baby Boomers, in particular, recall soaring oil and gasoline prices, miles-long lines at the gasoline pump, and a recession that delayed or prevented many from getting or holding onto their first real jobs.

The most important national policy concept to emerge from the Arab Oil Embargo was *energy independence*. To American presidents, "independence" meant immediate action to provide sufficient energy supplies (e.g., oil, gas, coal, renewables) on home turf to fulfill *all* of America's industrial, transport, commercial, and consumer needs, regardless of disruptive political factors or events. Independence quickly became synonymous with "energy self-sufficiency" and "energy security." However, energy experts today argue that these concepts are not really the same.

Energy independence, for example, could be interpreted as *energy self-sufficiency*, meaning the country assembles sufficient resources to function alone without fuel imports or exports for extended periods of time. This independence could, in theory, be achieved through a combination of fuel stockpiling (strategic reserves), conservation, and accelerated discovery and production of a variety of fuel sources. However, energy independence may be the more apt construct in a country like the U.S., where our economy is so interconnected with others worldwide through active global energy trade.

Energy independence could also be widened in definition to mean *energy self-sufficiency plus import-export trade with geopolitical allies only*, such as European or South American countries, Australia, or Canada. This kind of energy independence, in theory, could preclude energy imports with unfriendly or hostile nations.

Energy security, on the other hand, is the more popular recent term that analysts frequently use. Rather than suggesting complete energy independence, which in turn suggests a national energy policy of isolationism and even a complete withdrawal from global energy trade, energy security refers to a *broader concept of expanded and secured energy assets*, which includes fuel supplies and strategic reserves, new technologies, import-export trade with reliable foreign partners, and protection for the nation's entire energy infrastructure, including workers, drilling platforms, pipelines, tankers, refineries, storage facilities, environmental control and cleanup, power plants, transmission lines, distribution systems, backup and disaster recovery systems, and Internet-enabled computer networks that operate the nation's power grid.

This integrated concept, energy security, is quite different from the narrower concept of energy independence, but it is arguably much more relevant in the world of interconnected global trade and resource dependencies we have today.

Shale resources are already reducing our imports of oil and gas drastically and promising to turn America into a net energy exporter in the twenty-first century. Whether we can achieve true energy security or energy independence while remaining globally interconnected will become matters of intense national debate.

CHAPTER 6

WILL WE RUN OUT? HUBBERT'S PIMPLE & PEAK OIL THEORY

"You can only use oil once. You can only use metals once. Soon all the oil is going to be burned and all the metals mined and scattered."

—Marion King Hubbert, former geoscientist with the Shell research lab in Houston, Texas

In 1956, world-renowned geophysicist Marion King Hubbert used mathematical models to predict that U.S. oil production would reach its apex between 1965 and 1970, then decline thereafter.

He was right . . . basically. The year 1970 marked a high point of U.S. petroleum production—9.6 billion barrels—followed quickly by supply shocks, a Middle East oil embargo, and petroleum prices that quadrupled in a year, then doubled again from 1978 to 1981.

Hubbert was scoffed at, then celebrated when his predictions came true. Even the National Academy of Sciences accepted his "peak oil" theory, known today as Hubbert's peak, as correct science in 1975. The academy acknowledged its own supply projections had been overestimated, and for many years scientists followed Hubbert's lead, believing that the entire supply of planetary oil was finite and defined by a symmetrical bell-shaped curve.

This curve showed a sharp rise in oil-well production, a peak, and then a steep descent into oblivion (aka "dryness"). Hubbert, among other scientists, was extremely pessimistic about the future of fossil fuels. In

1978 he further proclaimed that global oil supplies would hit a peak in 1995 and thereafter drop off. Anyone born in 1965 or after would see the demise of petroleum supplies in their lifetimes. So perfectly symmetrical was his bell-shaped curve that fellow scientists called it Hubbert's pimple.

Jed Clampett's Elephant Oil

The reality of oil reserves is complex. Hubbert predicted "peak oil" in the 1950s, when the petroleum drilling industry was still technically immature. Most oil production derived at that time came from "elephant" oil fields—tremendously large reservoirs of easily accessible oil. One Penn State geologist, Seth Blumsack, an assistant professor of engineering policy at the school's Department of Energy and Mineral Engineering, described these elephant reservoirs as "Jed Clampett oil," the kind that *The Beverly Hillbillies* hero, Jed Clampett, discovers when he shoots a hole in the ground and oil comes spurting up in a geyser.

Hubbert may have been right about running out of the Jed Clampett–type elephant oil. However, even larger reservoirs and additions to existing ones have since been discovered in Brazil, Russia, Alaska, the North Sea, and the Gulf of Mexico. Hubbert never considered the factors of technical innovation or rising oil prices and their effects on discovering new unconventional resources, such as Canadian oil sands (most commonly found in Alberta), bitumen-rich heavy oil sources in Venezuela, undersea petroleum in Brazil, the North Sea, and the Gulf of Mexico, among other locations, or, of course, shale reserves, the "light tight" oil that has changed the supply picture so radically in recent years.[1]

Indeed, colleagues and students of Hubbert described him variously as a great teacher and intensely focused but also arrogant, insecure, and combative. He had a thin, tight mouth and also bore a striking resemblance to the avant-garde Irish playwright Samuel Beckett. Both he and Beckett had long Nordic faces and square jaws, wiry crew cuts, and steely, hawklike eyes. Like Beckett, Hubbert was a visionary. But his colleagues at Shell Oil and, later, the United States Geological Survey described him as one of the world's most difficult people to work with. Young scientists assigned to him at Shell didn't last for more than a year. Hubbert was also unaware that the nascent technology he described in a 1957 paper—hydraulic fracturing—would eventually unleash the current "fifth wave" of oil and gas.

The Fifth Wave

That's right—a *fifth* wave. Scientists have predicted the demise of petroleum reservoirs on earth *five times* in the last 125 years. And they've been wrong five times, according to preeminent energy author Daniel Yergin, whose books include *The Prize: The Epic Quest for Oil, Money, and Power* and *The Quest: Energy, Security, and the Remaking of the Modern World*.

"The world will run out of oil in 10 years."
—U.S. Bureau of Mines (1914)

"The world will run out of oil in 13 years."
—U.S. Department of the Interior (1939 and 1950)

Since Hubbert made his predictions, oil reserves have actually *increased* in size, productivity, and what is technically recoverable. Moreover, long-term data on major oil plays show that most do not follow a symmetrical bell-shaped curve, as Hubbert described. Instead of a sharp rise, a peak, and a steep decline, many petroleum fields reach long-term plateaus of near-constant production, rather than peaks and dips. New discoveries, including additional reserves found in existing fields, more than make up for productivity declines, resulting in global net increases of supply for the foreseeable future. For example, the world has produced 1 trillion barrels of oil since the beginning of the oil boom in the nineteenth century. Based on current data, geologists believe at least

5 trillion barrels of petroleum resources exist, of which 1.4 trillion is currently technically and economically accessible. Production capacity should grow from about 93 million barrels per day in 2010 to about 110 million barrels per day by 2030. This is almost a 20 percent increase. "The conclusion is that the world is clearly not running out of oil. Far from it. The estimates for the world's total stock of oil keep growing," Yergin writes.[2]

The World Running on Empty—Five Times

1. The first "running out of oil" crisis came in 1885, less than thirty years after oil was first discovered in Titusville, Pennsylvania. That year, the State Geologist of Pennsylvania declared that "the amazing exhibition of oil is only a temporary and vanishing phenomenon— one which young men will live to see come to its natural end."[3] Oil was subsequently discovered in Oklahoma, Kansas, Ohio, and Texas, with concurrent discoveries made in Russia, the Dutch East Indies, and the Austro-Hungarian Empire.

2. The second crisis came after World War I. A boom in U.S. automobile production—the number of registered cars in the U.S. increased fivefold from 1914 to 1920—prompted the director of the United States Bureau of Mines to predict that production in U.S. oil fields would peak within the next two to five years and decline rapidly from there. Discoveries in the Ottoman Empire and East Texas, aided by the use of dynamite and sonic waves, produced a glut of oil by 1931. Prices during the Great Depression dropped as low as 10 cents per barrel.

3. The third crisis came after World War II. Although 6 of the 7 billion barrels of oil provided to the Allied forces came from the United States, the U.S. itself became a net oil importer after the war— although imports were limited to only 10 percent of consumer consumption. Another oil shortage was predicted. But the opening up of vast oil fields in the Middle East once again led to abundant supplies and falling prices.

4. The fourth crisis came in 1973, during the Arab Oil Embargo. Its aftermath created an era of diminishing expectations for growth in America and concurrent worries about oil prices and supplies. "The oil and natural gas we rely on for 75 percent of our energy are running out," said President Jimmy Carter in a 1977 televised speech from the Oval Office.[4] However, massive discoveries in Alaska's North Slope and the North Sea led to a supply glut and price collapse in 1986, with oil dropping from $100/barrel to as low as $10/barrel.

5. The fifth crisis came at the beginning of the twenty-first century. Rising prices and accelerating oil consumption in China and emerging economies worldwide once again raised the specter of shortages. But shale oil and gas discoveries and the advancement of hydraulic fracturing and horizontal drilling in the United States quickly produced an oil surplus. Similar (and very large) shale oil and gas fields have been discovered in Russia, South America, Australia, the Arctic, China, and Africa. Based on studies of more than 70,000 oil fields and 4.7 million wells, plus new discovery projects, the world's liquid production capacity is projected to grow from about 93 million barrels per day (mpd) in 2010 to about 110 mpd by 2030; that's a 20 percent increase if the projections prove correct.[5]

Where do these figures leave Hubbert's peak oil theory? Some scientists argue that accessible reserves are indeed finite, and that the bell-shaped curve will ultimately prove correct with only minor deviations. In fact, the peak oil theory is still a topic of much controversy; it's fascinating to read the predictions, half-truths, and sheer omissions of current data from websites representing the finite oil theory.[6]

Some of these Internet sites are well-meaning, in that they draw our attention to such issues as environmental risks, national energy preparedness, and a plan of diversity that transitions to renewables and cleaner sources (i.e., natural gas, solar, wind) to stave off possible shortages or planetary harm. But many of the most popular websites also show extreme and even "apocalyptic" bias. Let the reader beware.

Defying Credibility?

Today's proponents of oil and gas exploration frequently argue that Hubbert's predictions defy credibility. For example, in 2010 the U.S. produced 5.6 million barrels of oil per day, an amazing four times more than Hubbert had estimated for the same time period. The U.S. in 2014 pumped 9.6 million barrels per day, rivaling 1970 highs, and surpassed both Saudi Arabia and Russia in oil production in 2014. By 2020, the country will produce 11.6 million barrels a day as it continues to frack dolomite and shale layers in North Dakota, Texas, Colorado, Ohio, and many other locations. Worldwide production should also accelerate, satisfying demand for fuels required for both developed and strongly developing economies.[7] And while predictions are never certain, many analysts believe that the shale boom should last at least until the 2030s, if not thereafter (U.S. natural gas finds through shale are already estimated to last 100 years or more), during which time every country will have the opportunity to develop renewable sources.

Energy historians are quick to point out that Marion Hubbert may have ignored two important factors driving petroleum supply and demand today: economics and innovation. Although Hubbert believed he had accounted accurately for new physical discoveries of oil, he failed to see how petroleum economics, specifically prices for oil and gas, affected output and the willingness to innovate to extract more oil and gas. Moreover, he assumed that he could make an accurate estimate of recoverable resources, when, in fact, the actual amounts of oil and gas trapped in the earth's crust are literally "fluid"—and, practically speaking, unknown.

In fact, a 2006 study from University of California, Berkeley, estimated that the world has used up only *about 5 percent of known technically recoverable oil reserves.*[9] Deepwater drilling (as in the Gulf of Mexico), the Canadian

U.S. CRUDE OIL PRODUCTION VS. HUBBERT CURVE[8]

Historical U.S. crude oil production shows an initial similarity to a Hubbert curve.

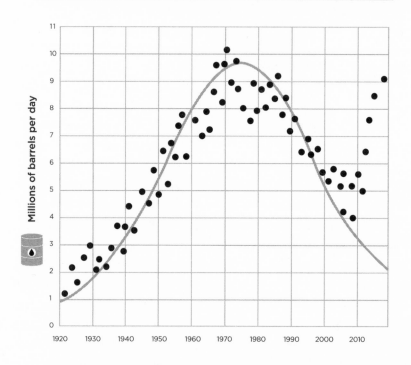

- ● U.S. Production (Source: Energy Information Administration)
- ▬▬ Hubbert Curve

oil sands, and even extraction of oil from shales via hydraulic fracturing in North Dakota are all examples of unconventional oil production.

Petroleum is shifting rapidly to these unconventional sources, as well as to heavy oils laden with bitumen (sourced in Venezuela), augmented oil recovery from conventional wells, synthetic fuels using natural gas or coal as a feedstock, light tight oil shale formations (which require hydraulic fracturing), and also shales used to manufacture synthetic crude oil.

High prices, it turns out, spur both new discovery and technological advancement. As long as prices remain high, they encourage investment and ingenious new ways to increase supply. Supply increases aren't just from new oil fields either, but also from existing ones. Quite often, when a new reserve is discovered, geologists require time to understand it. As time goes on, one reservoir discovery leads to others, including additions to already existing reserves. And since economics determine whether exploration is "worth it," high prices (and alternately, skyrocketing demand, which increases prices) can make a previously unviable resource turn into a recoverable asset.

As prices fall, new technologies are less likely to be funded. And existing technologies are only used if they are cost efficient. More expensive wells and sources go offline, supply decreases, and prices edge up again, once again spurring higher production. Boom and bust, such is the cycle.

Bottom line: Oil and gas production from a combination of unconventional and conventional wells will continue to surge in many parts of the world at least until the mid-twenty-first century. In countries with far-reaching energy policies, though, goals of exploration will include reducing carbon emissions, introducing cleaner forms of energy (e.g., natural gas and renewables), and advancing innovations that help create more choice and the right mix of energy sources for the future. Shale oil and gas will be part of that mix while countries continue to fuel their economies.

SOURCES OF HYDROCARBON FUELS[10]

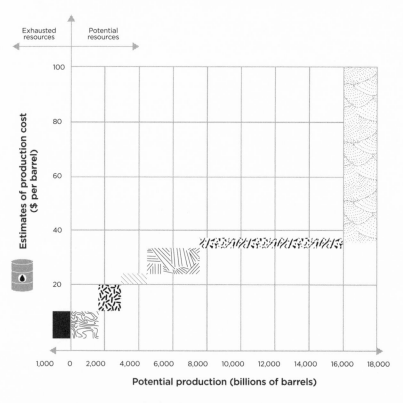

Figure adapted. Original figure available at https://www.e-education.psu.edu/eme801/node/486

PART II

CAN'T WE JUST ALL GET ALONG?

CHAPTER 7

VILIFICATION. LET'S TALK.

He's the lion in winter. He's a voice of conscience. And he's ready to put up his dukes and spar a few rounds with gridlocked congressmen who have pushed the leadership debate in Washington, D.C., to a fractious no-exit.

He's Leon Panetta, twenty-third U.S. Secretary of Defense (2011–2013) and former director of the CIA (2009–2011), perhaps best known for overseeing the military operation that brought down Osama bin Laden. But in a keynote speech at Hart Energy's 6th DUG East energy conference in June 2014, he spoke plainly about energy security and our leadership future.

"All of you in the gas and oil industry are developing energy resources here and worldwide," Panetta began. "I can tell you, as Secretary of Defense, how dependent the security of our nation is on your industry."

Fighting for a Better Life

The U.S. Department of Defense, in fact, is the largest user of energy in this country, consuming roughly 112 million gallons of fuel—$60.4 billion—in 2013 alone. Those numbers are not likely to decrease. "Your mission is the mission of what this country is about: To give our children a better life in the future," Panetta said.

As the son of immigrants who traveled from a poor town in Calabria, Italy, to Monterey, California, before World War II, Panetta learned the values of sacrifice and cooperation while helping in his parents' restaurant. Later he worked in the fields fixing irrigation pipes and harvesting walnuts (which allowed him, as he quipped to his DUG East audience, to prepare "for all the nuts in Washington"). He also watched young men in Monterey training for the World War II battlefields.

"I used to ask my Dad, 'Why would you and Mom travel thousands of miles from the comfort of home to [live] in a strange land?' And I remember my Dad told me, 'Your mother and I believed we could give our children a better life in this country,'" Panetta recalled. "But the dream is just a dream unless you're willing to work at it, to sacrifice, take risks, set goals, have a vision, and fight for what you believe in, and fight to make it happen."

America at the Turning Point

The will to "fight" for American values—national security, immigration reform, education, deficit reduction, among many other issues—is at stake in an America divided and "at the turning point," Panetta said.

According to Panetta, we are governing by crises, combined with fear, which often creates paralysis. For example, a legislator may decide, "I don't have to raise taxes or reduce the budget." Instead, important decisions—and legislation—are just kicked down the alley. "You could operate that way," Panetta said. "But there's a price to be paid; and you lose the trust of the American people in democracy. Trust is everything."

Panetta was worked up, and convincing: "I've been in and out of Washington for over fifty years of public life. . . . The situation in Washington is probably the ugliest I've seen . . . the gridlock and dysfunction is of great concern. And then you add to that a growing mood of somehow withdrawing from the world, not wanting to get involved and not exercising world leadership that this country has always been about. When you put those two together, it raises concerns about what kind of path the U.S. will follow in the twenty-first century."

Panetta, the former director of the Office of Management and Budget, who worked on budgets for every administration since Ronald Reagan, invoked the names of can-do legislators from the past: Mark Hatfield,

Jacob Javits, Everett Dirksen, Hubert Humphrey, Sam Ervin, and Richard Russell Jr., among others—both Republican and Democrat, liberal and conservative. They met in the center to get things done.

"Yes, they fought it out in elections, but when it came to national issues, they worked together to enact landmark legislation. They thought it was good politics," he said. Today, though, "confrontation seems to represent 'better politics.'"

Are We Really Having a Conversation?

They say attitudes trickle down from leadership. For example, in an employee-manager relationship, employees are typically more apt to behave like their managers.

The 2009 National Business Ethics Survey from the Ethics Resource Center, for one, concluded that the actions of top managers drive corporate culture and directly impact outcomes: "We like to believe that, as adults, we make decisions independently and are far beyond succumbing to peer pressure. But social science research tells us that is simply not the case. Study after study confirms it: The vast majority of people act based on the circumstances in their environment and the standards set by their leaders and peers, even if it means compromising their personal moral ideals."[1]

Another such study from the University of Groningen (Netherlands) in 2014 analyzed questionnaires, case studies, and psychological experiments to reach a similar conclusion: Employees in an organization "imitate good behavior in people with higher status."[2]

Does that theory extend to a populace looking up to their politicians? Are the American people more likely to be contentious rather than intelligent in their arguments if they see their leaders doing the same? Certainly, if politicians are behaving the way Panetta suggests—and unfortunately, I think he may be right about the current state of Washington—then abrasive behavior at the governance level *can't be helped.*

Speaking anecdotally, I've personally experienced a great deal of abrasive confrontation when it comes to people "talking" to the energy industry. In fact, I'm repeatedly amazed by the staunch hatred—yes, hatred—that so many have for oil and gas and everyone associated with it. I've even had had a congressman tell me, "It doesn't matter if it makes sense. I can't vote for something an oil company wants."

In response to a recent online post about lifting the crude oil export ban, an issue that I'm specifically passionate about, here are a few of the comments I received:

"This is big oil companies' lies, their pockets will get bigger and taxpayers will get screwed."

"When I hear that a law is holding back the economy, I smell a billionaire rat."

"And I have some oceanfront property for sale in Pennsylvania."

"F*** you and your earth-destroying mentality, a**hole."

To be fair, there were many more comments on the stream that were tamer, but still fairly aggressive and not particularly constructive.

On the flip side, oil and gas companies aren't doing a whole lot to make themselves trustworthy. Sure, they put out propaganda—and yes, a lot of it *is* propaganda—painting fracking as 100-percent clean, or funding blatantly self-serving studies on job and economic benefits.

It's not that there isn't truth in their messaging but that it is so entirely one-sided that it is barely credible.

While busy carefully controlling their message, many oil and gas companies compound the problem by simultaneously shutting out journalists. My own researchers for this book had countless doors shut in their faces—including by some of my own customers—when trying to gain perspectives from those in the industry. Industry members are so afraid of being misquoted that many of them have now stopped talking almost entirely.

Concurrently, fractivists are *loud*.

So what kind of balanced messages are we receiving? What sort of conversation are we really having?

Not a great one.

Conversation vs. Confrontation

The sixteenth-century English philosopher and statesman Francis Bacon wrote in his *Novum Organum,* "The human understanding when it has once adopted an opinion . . . draws all things else to support and agree with it. And though there be a greater number and weight of instances to be found on the other side, yet these it either neglects and despises, or else by some distinction sets aside and rejects, in order that by this great and pernicious predetermination the authority of its former conclusion may remain inviolate."

Basically, you seek out views that agree with yours and ignore information that contradicts your opinion.

Psychological research starting in the 1960s has proven this phenomenon, which is also known as "confirmation bias": our tendency to find and remember information that confirms our own beliefs. Confirmation bias has been found to be strongest when emotionally charged issues or deeply entrenched beliefs are at stake.[3]

Humans take that behavior a step further. If our views are challenged, we will actually begin a methodical process to pick apart the challenge. This act of "logic," where we find a weakness in the other's point and attack it, only serves to strengthen our original opinion. Anything of value in the opposition's opinion is simply ignored.

That's why *confrontation* never works. Each side leaves more convinced than ever that it was correct.

A *conversation,* on the other hand, is what I would like to invite you to have with me. A conversation starts when each person comes to the table with a basic belief that the other person is (a) human, and (b) has an opinion you would like to better understand.

Perhaps more important, a potentially productive conversation is started when we can agree on and work toward common goals.

In the case of energy, I believe our common goals are to develop an energy policy that encourages American energy security, while keeping energy prices balanced, and the environment whole. And I believe if we set our heads together, that goal is completely achievable.

Panetta would agree.

"I believe deeply we could have an America in Renaissance, a strong America in the twenty-first century," Panetta said as part of his DUG East speech. "The fundamentals of our economy are good; we're an economy that has tremendous innovation and creativity."

"We could truly develop energy independence for this country . . . [and] discipline our budget and do what needs to be done on the fiscal side to make sure that we set a strong path in the future."

There are two paths ahead of us, Panetta maintained. The first path requires governance. Elected leaders must work together across the aisle to make "tough decisions" on budgets, taxes, energy, transportation, education, defense, immigration, and human rights.

The second path would see "an America in decline, an America that operates by crisis after crisis . . . an America that is dysfunctional in terms of our ability to govern ourselves, an America unable to protect our most basic freedoms, our economy, and our national security."

Panetta thinks we will choose the first path.

"The fundamental strength of the U.S. doesn't rest in Washington; it rests in the common sense and grit and willingness to fight [of the American people]," he said. "If [leadership] doesn't change from the top down, it will change from the bottom up. . . . People will elect men and women committed to the values of this country."

"All of us are called to action. We will keep fighting for an American renaissance [and] we will keep fighting for an American dream."

I'm not as sure as Panetta, although I'd like to be. I think we *can* change the confrontation. I think we *can* turn it into conversation, but I don't think it's a foregone conclusion.

That will be up to you and me. I'm always on social media like Facebook (@dankeberhart), Twitter (@daneberhart), and LinkedIn (/dankeberhart). I want to talk. So talk to me.

In the meantime, since a book is a bit of a one-sided medium, I'll keep talking. Next, I'm going to talk about energy options, including renewables. If you disagree, you know where to find me.

CHAPTER 8

THE ENERGY MIX:
NO FREE LUNCH

After a brisk autumn hike to Hanging Rock State Park in Stokes County, North Carolina, a group of fifty-something hikers sat down to dinner and began a discussion about fossil fuels, fracking, and climate change. Citing noticeably hotter summers in the Northeast followed by intense cold snaps, drought in the West, rising floodwaters in Miami, superstorms like Sandy and Katrina, and satellite photos of polar icecaps melting at twice the rate that scientists had first predicted, several at the table asked whether the human appetite for burning fossil fuels had already pushed the climate past the tipping point.

"Tell me something seriously," asked one woman named Sheila, a retired special education teacher. "Is there any hope?" Mardi, a dark-haired, confident hiker who sat next to her husband, Hank, an energy engineer asked, "Will we have to start living with less? I mean, maybe not driving to a park seventy-five or a hundred miles away, maybe just taking walks through our own local neighborhoods?

The discussion was passionate. Hal, the wiry hiking leader, a former technical writer, pointed out an invisible challenge in the nation's changing energy mix: "What about the amount of energy you have to *put into* some of these new technologies to get energy out?" he asked. "Lithium batteries in electric cars, for example, take lots of energy to assemble." He added, "What about the human and mechanical resources required to frack oil and gas?"

The group commiserated silently for a moment. Then Hank broke in. "With energy, there is no such thing as a free lunch," he said, smiling broadly beneath a handlebar moustache, as though possessed of an insider's knowledge. "But, yes, there is hope," he continued. "People will rise to the challenge. We're already reducing oil and gasoline consumption, thanks to conservation and more energy-efficient cars. Solar technologies are getting better. Coal-fired plants are being retired in favor of cleaner natural gas. We have buses running on natural gas, and that's happening all over the world," he said. "Humans innovate their way out of the problems. Climate? We'll figure it out."

We'll figure it out. The attitude may sound like cockeyed optimism, but it's not. Throughout recent history, fossil fuels have powered every nation's industrial revolution, turning cities like London, Pittsburgh, Los Angeles, Copsa Mica (Romania), Delhi and Kolkata (India), and Linfeng and Beijing (China), among others, into capitals of soot and lung disease. However, innovative technology and pollution management have, in many cases, produced cleaner energy and quality of life in many world-class cities. That's because "environment quality is essentially a luxury good," contends H. Sterling Burnett, PhD research fellow in energy and environment at The Heartland Institute and managing editor of its *Environment and Climate News.* "The wealthier people are, the more environmental quality they demand," he told my team in an interview. "In the first level of industrial production, environmental quality declines. But market forces eventually catch up and people start to see improvement in the environment."

Growth or Environmental Quality— Either/Or or Both?

When we talk about this energy mix, it seems like it's a conversation in absolutes: We can have *either* economic growth *or* environmental quality. Maybe it's time to switch that dialogue to include the possibility that *both* might be attainable.

Although people generally believe economic growth and environmental quality are inversely related—in other words, growth equates with polluting energy and environmental damage—technological advancement and *rational* stewardship of energy choices can help ensure that quality and growth happen at the same time.

"On a global basis, you have to go through the first hurdle, and that's starting to raise the wealth of people," Burnett said in an interview with my team. For example, 1.2 billion people—roughly 20 percent of the world's population—still live in "energy poverty," without access to modern electricity and all the benefits that accrue such as modern health care, nutrition, and industrial conveniences. As many as 400 million people in India and 550 million in Africa are still without modern electricity.[1] What's more, 2.8 billion people still use solid fuels—wood, charcoal, coal, and dung—for cooking and heating, which causes high levels of indoor pollution, respiratory illnesses, and death, especially among women and children.[2]

But here's the good news. In many parts of the world, affluence and access to affordable energy are rising. For example, as I saw firsthand during a recent visit, Africa is now the world's fastest-growing continent economically, with average GDP growth of 6 percent a year and real income per person increasing 30 percent in the last ten years. Foreign direct investment (FDI) is also booming, life expectancy is up 10 percent, and infant mortality and HIV infections are down. The upshot? Quality of life improvement, energy investments, and environmental cleanup projects all going on at the same time.

"People in Africa are not going to sit by while governments take money from the West (or China, a heavy investor in African infrastructure and energy) and continue to leave them in poverty," Burnett said. "With development, incomes rise, people become wealthier, and markets expand. Environmental quality will improve."

An optimistic view, to be sure, one by an admitted believer in the power of free markets to set things right. But no matter what your belief, whether it's in free markets, strict government energy regulation, or environmental activism, a nation's path toward an *energy mix*—a combination of fuel sources to power current development and future growth—is shaped each day by multiple factors, including global and local energy markets, investment in new infrastructure, and concerns over environmental and human health preservation.

- **Factor number one** is energy markets (both global and local), including pricing for available energy resources. For example, what are the most affordable kinds of energy in a particular location? In developed nations, combinations of oil, natural gas, solar, wind, nuclear, and, to a lesser extent, coal may all be viable options, whereas in parts of industrializing China, coal is cheap and predominant (and polluting). On the other hand, in the most remote parts of Southeast Asia, Africa, and India, rooftop solar installations may be the only kind of power that's both practical and affordable.

- **Factor number two** is investment in new or existing energy infrastructure: pipelines, power plants, oil and gas wells, methane capture systems, recycling, solar and wind farms, hydropower, even biomass. In developing countries, can infrastructure be built to electrify remote areas? In advanced countries, can infrastructure be upgraded to deliver more power with less pollution for lower cost?

- **Factor number three** is the environment. What are the trade-offs to ensure that everyone has adequate, affordable power while minimizing risk to the environment and public health?

Energy trade-offs are complex; most of us, aware of possible dangers to the environment, want a "perfect" energy solution. But even so-called near-perfect solutions such as renewable energy (wind, solar, biomass) also have negatives, as do nuclear and fossil fuels. In other words, there is no such thing as a free lunch.

By this I mean that every fuel source on earth delivers both useful energy and waste. We're talking pollution, unexpected or "collateral" damage to the environment, and possible risks that might involve radioactivity (as in nuclear plants), carbon emissions (fossil fuels), and even damage to wildlife or human health. Even renewable energy sources—wind, solar, hydroelectric, biomass, and, arguably, nuclear power—have engendered controversies.

For example, wind farms have been known to destroy wildlife, especially large birds that inadvertently fly into the windmill blades. Nuclear power, considered by many to be a renewable resource that produces virtually no carbon emissions, has lost favor in Europe and the U.S. because of the fear of nuclear accidents, reactor meltdowns (think Chernobyl, Three Mile Island, and Fukushima), and the potential hazards of nuclear waste. In developing countries, indoor fumes, smoke, and particulates from open-fire cooking kill 1.5 million people a year, according to World Bank reports. In India, toxic chemicals from coal emissions cause lung diseases that reportedly kill 120,000 people a year. And let's not even get started on the vast number of controversies surrounding solar power generation.

Electrification in developing countries is one issue that illustrates the complexity surrounding growth versus environmental quality at any cost. Considering the comparative lack of alternatives in developing countries, is it wise to stop rural electrification projects because the most affordable energy resources include fossil fuels, especially coal, to generate that energy? Advocates of rapid electrification say no. "We need affordable energy and the more we have, the better it is for everyone," said Isaac Orr, a research analyst with the Heartland Institute. As he told my team during an interview in November 2014, "For instance, in the developed world, women now have an 80 percent survival rate from breast cancer, but it's only 40 percent survival in the developing world, and the majority of those deaths are because the societies don't have electrification for modern surgeries and other medical treatments." Orr's message: Whether it's fossil fuels, nuclear, or renewables, the most important issue, first and foremost, is to extend electrification and affordable energy to everyone; that boosts the economy, incomes, and overall access to quality of life.

Energy Sources and Related Information

Energy Source	Barriers	Environmental Impact
Oil, Petroleum	Nonrenewable	Refining and consuming produce air, water, and solid waste pollutants.
Natural Gas	Nonrenewable	Produces fewer pollutants than oil and coal, and less CO_2 but still is not 100 percent clean.
Coal	Nonrenewable	Produces CO_2 and other air, water, and solid waste pollutants.
Biomass: Wood and organic waste, including societal waste	Low energy potential relative to other resources. Slow to grow.	Burning emits CO_2 and other pollutants. Possible toxic by-products from societal waste. Loss of habitat when trees harvested, unless sustainable tree farms.
Hydroelectric	High start-up costs. Influenced by climate and geography.	Destruction of farmlands, dislocation of people, loss of habitat, alteration of stream flows.
Solar Power (Photovoltaics)	High economic cost, particularly in terms of start-up. Dependent on climate and geographical location. Need a storage system for the energy to ensure reliability. Not advanced enough for global use.	Large land use.

Solar Power (Solar Thermal)	Solar energy technology not advanced enough for global use. Dependent on climate and geographical location.	Large land use and degradation. Need for vast amounts of water for cooling.
Geothermal	Technology still undeveloped. Can be geographically dependent.	Disrupts natural geyser activity.
Wind Power	System must be designed to operate reliably at variable rotor speeds. Technology not advanced enough for global societal use.	Aesthetic issues. Needs lots of land. Possible impacts on birds and their migration patterns. Some noise pollution.
Nuclear Fission	Nonrenewable resource U-235 (uranium). Highly technological infrastructure necessary for safe operation. High production cost, due in part to regulations. High water usage for cooling.	By-product highly radioactive and highly toxic. Produces radioactive wastes that have a long lifetime. Technically and politically complex disposal solution. Safety issues in terms of operating a facility with the potential to release radiation to the atmosphere. Public perception problem in terms of radiation and safety issues.
Nuclear Fusion	Technology not yet viable and requires research investment.	Possibility of water pollution high due to radioactive tritium.

Sources:

U.S. Energy Information Administration, *International Energy Annual 1999*, DOE/EIA-0219(99) (Washington, D.C., January 2001).

U.S. Energy Information Administration, *International Energy Outlook 2001*, DOE/EIA-0484(2001) (Washington, D.C., March 2001).

New Directions in Energy

How should any nation choose its specific energy mix to power growth toward the future? And what, indeed, is the right energy mix in light of so many options—including shale oil and gas, renewables, nuclear power, conventional oil and gas, and other sources not yet discovered?

Let's start with the most basic question: What do we use energy for?

Obviously, humans employ multiple energy sources to do useful work: for transportation, industrial products and processes, home and personal applications, and the like. We use both oil and natural gas for cooking, electrical power generation, and for powering cars and trucks (natural gas, considered "cleaner" than oil, is now being used more commonly to power fleet vehicles).

But there are plenty of applications we rarely think about. While lighter forms of refined crude oil are used to power standard internal combustion engines on the road, heavy oil—also known as bunker fuel, which contains high levels of contaminants—is used to power ships. By-products from oil refining are essential for producing plastics, synthetic rubber, chemicals, cosmetics, and lubricants, including waxes, asphalts, and tars. Nearly all pesticides and many fertilizers are composed of oil or oil by-products. Synthetic fibers are also made from petrochemicals, as are paints, detergents, photographic film, and food additives. Special grades of petroleum, combined with additives to prevent sparking, corrosion, or gumming, are used for jet fuel. And with the exception of biodiesel, which is powered primarily from plant waste, diesel fuels are also based on refined oil products generally used in medium- and heavy-duty vehicles requiring power and torque, such as moving vans, garbage trucks, buses, and trains.

Natural gas also has numerous uses. Not only does it account for more than a quarter of the nation's electric power, but it also fuels cleaner transportation for highways and efficient heating and cooking. It provides the raw material for fertilizers and is a component in the manufacture of pharmaceuticals, cosmetics, electronics, plastic toys, and paints. As a heating source to generate steam for industrial applications, natural gas is critical for fueling glass and steel foundries, aluminum and nickel smelters, and factories that produce pulp and paper, plastics and polymers, textiles, and dyes. As a fuel for vehicles on the highway, natural gas can outperform conventional fuels with a higher octane rating, better efficiency, and lower operating costs—all while offering significant reductions in emissions.

Essentially, though, all energy is used in one of four applications:

Heat—47 percent: Heat accounts for almost half the world's final energy consumption. Commercial heating makes up a whopping 80 percent of global consumption. In the average American household, heating represents a full 40 percent of total residential energy costs.[3]

Transportation—27 percent: According to the U.S. Department of Energy, personal vehicles consume almost 60 percent[4] of the energy used for transportation, and transportation is responsible for 28 percent of U.S. greenhouse emissions.[5] More important, the transportation sector accounts for 70 *percent* of U.S. oil consumption.[6]

Electricity—17 percent: In 2013, the United States generated about 4,058 billion kilowatt hours of electricity. About 67 percent of the electricity generated was from fossil fuel (coal, natural gas, and petroleum), with 39 percent attributed to coal.

Non-Energy Use—9 percent: Fuels that are used as feedstocks to make plastic and for power in the manufacturing process account for a small but nonetheless important piece of the energy pie. In 2010, the U.S. used about 191 million barrels of liquid petroleum gases (LPG) and natural gas liquids (NGL) (190 million barrels as feedstock and 1 million barrels as manufacturing fuel) and about 412 billion cubic feet (Bcf) of natural gas (13 Bcf as feedstock and 399 Bcf as manufacturing fuel) to make plastic materials and resins.[7]

But why are we still so heavily reliant on polluting fossil fuels? Given concerns about greenhouse gas emissions, shouldn't we use "cleaner energy" to power our machines and light our homes? Yes, in theory.

But fossil fuels have provided reliable and long-lasting power because of their capacity to store lots of energy—a property known as energy density. Energy density is the amount of energy per unit volume or mass. Energy density for a particular fuel type is often measured in joules or millijoules.

The point is that fossil fuels—coal, oil, and gas—are energy dense. They deliver enough power to electrify entire communities, cities, and states for virtually unlimited time periods. By contrast, burning leaves to generate the same amounts of steam at high temperature and pressure required to drive a conventional power-plant boiler would take whole forests—and the process still wouldn't work efficiently because fallen leaves aren't energy dense, even if you had enough leaves to keep the boiler going.

So solid fossil fuels—the triumvirate of oil, gas, and coal—have become the energy stalwarts for public power generation. Nuclear energy, the energy released by splitting atoms, is infinitely more energy dense than conventional fossil fuels. But nuclear has safety and cost issues. So the "easier" and safer route for industry and civic applications has been—and will likely continue to be—a mix of fossil fuels combined with lesser amounts of renewables and other sources in order to keep our electrical grid humming. Not every fossil fuel is alike, of course, and that is the reason why tweaking the mix of energy-dense sources in each country has become so important.

For more than a century, we burned fossil fuels and didn't care; we didn't do much to control emissions. But now, as the planet confronts the effects of greenhouse gases and climate change, most of us believe that we must choose the cleaner fossil fuels and make them even cleaner through better drilling, filtration, and scrubbing processes. This is where fracking—and the abundance of petroleum liquids and natural gas from fracking—come in. Fracking is changing our energy mix faster than probably any other energy technology on the planet right now.

We'll see how rapidly that mix is changing.

SOURCES OF ENERGY BY USE [8, 9, 10]

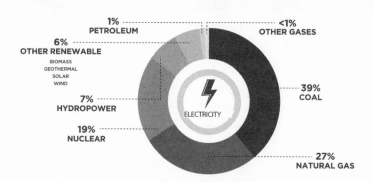

1%
PETROLEUM

<1%
OTHER GASES

6%
OTHER RENEWABLE
BIOMASS
GEOTHERMAL
SOLAR
WIND

39%
COAL

7%
HYDROPOWER

ELECTRICITY

19%
NUCLEAR

27%
NATURAL GAS

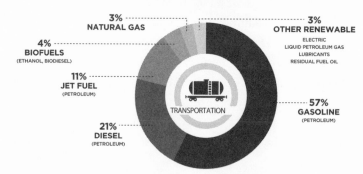

3%
NATURAL GAS

3%
OTHER RENEWABLE
ELECTRIC
LIQUID PETROLEUM GAS
LUBRICANTS
RESIDUAL FUEL OIL

4%
BIOFUELS
(ETHANOL, BIODIESEL)

11%
JET FUEL
(PETROLEUM)

57%
GASOLINE
(PETROLEUM)

TRANSPORTATION

21%
DIESEL
(PETROLEUM)

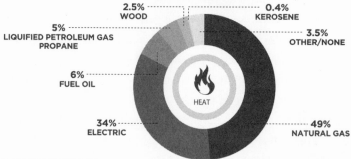

2.5%
WOOD

0.4%
KEROSENE

5%
LIQUIFIED PETROLEUM GAS
PROPANE

3.5%
OTHER/NONE

6%
FUEL OIL

HEAT

34%
ELECTRIC

49%
NATURAL GAS

Due to rounding, data may not total exactly 100%.

Fun Physics Refresher

If we're thinking about using energy to heat a home or generate gigawatts of electrical power used by an entire city, the rule of thumb is *that in order to do useful work, energy must be converted from one form into another.* Work is accomplished when one or more forces—mechanical, chemical, electromagnetic, gravitational, elastic, or radiant energy, among other forms—*move an object over a distance,* whether that object consists of atoms, electrons, or protons, or large objects such as the pistons or crankshafts of a car or a steam turbine assembly.

Think of the chemical energy released when gasoline is burned, for example. Hydrogen and carbon bonds are broken, releasing heat and mechanical energy that power the pistons of the engine.

The radiant energy of sunlight can be captured and converted into useful chemical processes that then convert carbon dioxide and water into sugars—the process we know as photosynthesis.

The thermal energy generated by combusting fossil fuels such as coal, gas, or oil in a power plant will do useful work by undergoing three separate energy conversions. First, thermal energy generated by combustion will produce steam in a pressure boiler; steam turns the blades and shaft of a turbine, producing mechanical energy (a form of kinetic energy—the energy of motion); these, in turn, drive the shaft of a rotary generator, where magnets spin within wire coils to produce electricity.

Power Generation Options

Renewable sources like solar and wind are generally defined as those that are naturally renewed within short time frames. Right now, renewables account for 13 percent of all power generation in the U.S., according to the U.S. Energy Administration.[11] That figure is expected to grow in the future.

Wind power hasn't advanced significantly in recent years or come down in price. But solar, which is being coupled with new methods of energy storage and use in so-called microgrids (electrical transmission grids of limited size) for power distribution, is growing at the rate of 66 percent a year in the U.S.—from less than a gigawatt of power generated a decade ago to 16 gigawatts this year. Moreover, costs of solar modules, labor, and power-plant equipment have been decreasing rapidly—by more than 60 percent since 2011. However, solar still constitutes only a tiny percentage of U.S. energy generation, and most solar projects have required government subsidies.

The future of solar and other renewables will depend on a few key variables, not the least of which is a little problem known as intermittency. (E.g., solar panels generate power only when exposed to sunlight; windmills don't work well in calm air.)

"The big aspect that has held renewable energy back is intermittency. [Renewables are] not as dispatchable as coal or natural gas," said Chad Sachs, CEO of San Francisco's Radian Generations, which provides asset management services to owners of solar projects. He continued, during a November 2014 phone interview, "Wind, solar is free, right? It is not dependent on drilling for more gas or finding more coal. It is always a free resource, unless the government starts taxing weather. And yet, this intermittency has really concerned utilities. It has concerned stability, which is a key and very valuable part of traditional utility service provision."

And the utilities have been vocal in their concern.

As Sachs explained: "There are a couple things that utilities don't like. Utilities are required to deliver power when it's needed. Solar is generating all this power during the middle of the day, so you don't need the utility as much. And it's feeding power into the grid, so the consumption for the utility production and consumption is low during the middle of the day. Then as people start to go home, they turn on their televisions, the load at home goes up, and that's exactly when solar is going down. The sun has now gone down, so now the utilities have to ramp up their dispatchable resources in a more extreme way than they used to.

"Utilities have a base load that they're servicing, which is usually coal and some gas," Sachs added. "In peak situations, utilities are much more expensive to run because they must fire up much faster. The problem is, if in the day, they don't have to run as many gas or coal plants, now they have to turn on more of the peak plants later at night. Does that make it more difficult for them to manage their resources? Well, utilities are telling us at conferences and things like that that it's a challenge. In my opinion, this is a concern that could be tempered with better storage and/ or better management of all the different resources coming in."

In fact, modern ingenuity is spurring technologies that are helping in the development of better battery-storage techniques that address the problem.

"One thing we're starting to see now is an emphasis on storage," Sachs told us. "As you have storage, you might be able to alleviate a fair amount of that need to bring on resources as quickly or in as concentrated a manner. Hopefully that would help utilities get more comfortable that they're not going to have to service volatile swings in the load."

Sachs posed a rhetorical question: "If you can start to store the intermittent energy produced by wind or solar, the question is: Why wouldn't you do it?"

Well, market pricing, weather conditions in local areas, and availability of competitive fuels also remain important factors in any energy mix. While advocates of renewables remain optimistic about future growth, our heavily industrialized society will continue to require fossil-fuel power not only because of its reliability, but also because hydrocarbons in petroleum and natural gas mixtures are essential stuff for building so many other products we need, as well as transportation. Our challenge, then, is to minimize the collateral damage of fossil fuels, reduce carbon emissions, and introduce as many safe practices as we can to keep the environment healthy.

"[Energy advances have] helped drive our carbon pollution to its lowest levels in nearly 20 years. Since 2006, no country on Earth has reduced its total carbon pollution by as much as the United States of America."
—President Obama's Remarks on Climate Change at Georgetown University, June 25, 2013

U.S. coal-fired power plants in 2012 produced roughly 2 billion of the 6.5 billion metric tons of greenhouse gases, including carbon dioxide (the gas implicated in global warming and climate change). By contrast, natural-gas-fired plants, virtually all powered by methane extracted from the nation's abundant shale reserves, produce *half the carbon dioxide emissions of coal per unit of electricity, and 18 percent fewer emissions than oil*. The result? Coal is losing traction rapidly in the U.S. because the Environmental Protection Agency (EPA) has proposed new standards and deep cuts in greenhouse gases from coal-fired power plants. If the EPA standards are fully adopted, thirty-two U.S. coal-fired plants will shut down in the next few years; another thirty-six plants will likely follow, resulting in a significant shortfall in energy that must be made up by a "mix" of other sources.[12]

Who's the winner in electricity generation?

Between natural gas, coal, and renewables, it's currently natural gas—and demand for that fuel type is growing in the U.S., according to the U.S. Energy Information Administration (EIA). "Natural gas is going to be more prevalent for energy generation," Solar Grid Storage's Tom Leyden told my team in a November 2014 interview. "Over the next twenty-five years, there will be plenty of markets for both oil and gas. Coal-fired plants are being shut down [because] they are no longer competitive. With new emissions rules, they can't be the standard."

Even China, which suffers horrific air and water pollution in many regions from unscrubbed coal-fired plants, has agreed to a climate-conscious "peak coal" cap by 2030. The country has committed to ramping up other forms of energy, including renewables and natural gas (some from fracking; most from imports), in order to power a cleaner environment for the future.

Why natural gas? One reason is that natural gas burns cleaner in a power plant than coal, whose high sulfur dioxide content produces acid rain. At the plant, the burning of natural gas produces nitrogen oxides and carbon dioxide but in lower quantities than coal or oil. One drawback to natural gas, however, is that one of its primary components is methane, a greenhouse gas that can be emitted into the air when natural gas is not burned completely. And methane is a very potent greenhouse gas—actually 84 percent more potent than carbon dioxide alone—when it escapes into the atmosphere without complete combustion and capture. Therefore, emissions of methane must be carefully controlled during the drilling and fracking process. On the other hand, sulfur and mercury emissions from burning natural gas are negligible.

The average U.S. emissions rates from natural-gas-fired electrical generation are 1135 lbs/megawatt-hour (MWh) of carbon dioxide, 0.1 lbs/MWh of sulfur dioxide, and 1.7 lbs/MWh of nitrogen oxides.[13] (One MWh is roughly equivalent to the amount of electricity used by 330 homes in one hour.)

Compared to the average air emissions from coal-fired generation, natural gas produces *half as much carbon dioxide, less than a third as many nitrogen oxides, and one percent as many sulfur oxides at the power plant.* That said, the process of extraction, treatment, and transport of the natural gas to the power plant does generate additional emissions, and both state and federal regulations are tightening up on methane emissions standards. Colorado and Wyoming have enacted landmark methane emissions laws. And some energy corporations, among them Chevron, are consciously launching methane capture technologies to recycle lost gases and even pipe them to market as part of a profitable greenhouse gas containment program.

Transportation Options

Petroleum fuel—made from crude oil and liquids from natural gas processing—remains the main source of energy for transportation in the U.S. In 2013, 92 percent of total energy consumed by transportation came from gasoline, diesel fuel, jet fuel, residual fuel oil, and liquid petroleum gases.[14]

Biofuels, an alternative to petroleum fuel, are not a new phenomenon. Ethanol and biodiesel were actually among the first automobile fuels, although gasoline and diesel quickly usurped them. Ethanol is an alcohol fuel made from the sugars found in grains, and biodiesel is a fuel made from vegetable oils, fats, or greases. (It's not science fiction: You *can* power your car with recycled restaurant grease!)

Recent government incentives and mandates have spurred an increase in the use of biofuels, mostly as additives to gasoline and diesel fuel. Virtually all gasoline now sold in the U.S. contains some amount of ethanol. The amount of fuel ethanol added to motor gasoline increased from 1.3 billion gallons in 1995 to 13 billion gallons in 2013. Meanwhile, biodiesel is the fastest-growing alternative fuel in the U.S. Between 2001 and 2013, its consumption increased from 10 million gallons to 1.4 billion gallons.

Ethanol and biodiesel are renewable, cleaner-burning fuels that produce fewer air pollutants than fossil fuels—but they typically carry a higher price tag than petroleum-based fuels. So while biofuels are on the rise, their use remains less than 5 percent of total consumption in the U.S. transportation sector.[15]

Electric power is also on the rise as another alternative fuel source for vehicles—although not without some setbacks. A collaborative study by the U.S. Department of Energy's Office of Electricity Delivery and Energy Reliability and the Pacific Northwest National Laboratory discerned that "off-peak" electricity production and transmission capacity could power 84 percent of vehicles on American roads today if they were all plug-in hybrid electrics. This sounds promising, especially when coupled with the conclusion that the Midwest and East Coast power grids appear to have sufficient off-peak generation, transmission, and distribution capacity to provide for *all* of today's vehicles if they ran on batteries. The bad news is that the West Coast, with a large amount of hydroelectric generation—the Pacific Northwest in particular—has much more limited capacity.[16]

Another stumbling block is that electric vehicles are much more expensive than their petroleum-fueled counterparts. We're talking $6,000 to $10,000 more, mostly due to the cost of the batteries. Breaking even given lower fuel costs, depending on the widely varying prices of gasoline and electricity around the country, could take five to eight years—roughly the lifespan of a current battery.[17]

Heat Options

Natural gas and electric heating are by far the most popular heating choices in American homes, at 49 percent and 34 percent respectively.[18] Overall, however, we're witnessing a downward trend in residential energy consumption, and this reduction is mirrored in heating's portion of that total. In 1993, 53.1 percent of energy consumption was earmarked for home heating; by 2009, this had fallen to 41.5 percent. The drop is attributed to improved equipment, more efficient windows, better insulation, and a population push to warmer climates.[19]

Fuel choice varies significantly by region. Natural gas is the clear choice in the Northeast, Midwest, and West. The South, meanwhile, is primarily heated by electricity. Fuel oil (also known as distillate oil) is virtually untouched outside of the Northeast, while the Midwest and South are essentially the only regions with kerosene heating.[20]

But we're starting to see a change in energy preferences. Electricity has been gaining market share over the other options across the country, thanks in large part to improvements in electric heat pump technology that *moves* heat, instead of creating it from a fuel source, and can deliver up to three times more heat energy than the electrical energy it consumes. A drawback is that heat pumps most often rely on relatively expensive electric resistance heating as the backup when temperatures fall below the effective range of the heat pump.

Why Hydrocarbons Still Rule

The mix of fuel in any particular society is based on historical availability, geological/geographic issues, and even political factors. Although many societies originally relied on such on-the-ground materials as wood or biomass (the detritus of dead animals or plants) to cook food or provide heat, 95 percent of the world's energy requirement today is met by the triumvirate of coal, oil, and natural gas—all of them fossil fuels. These three forms currently store more available, convertible energy than any other current form, although research in nuclear fission and renewables may change that claim within the next century.

Is Nuclear "Renewable"?

Nuclear energy, which some advocates define as "renewable," in fact is a category in limbo these days. While nuclear does not generate hydrocarbons, it is a technology that many environmentalists oppose because of radiation hazards and the costs of building modernized plants. Though nuclear can produce vast amounts of power by splitting atoms (nuclear fission), generating almost no greenhouse gases, the older reactors do produce harmful radioactive waste and rely on finite sources of uranium, which must be disposed of when the fuel is exhausted or "spent."

Moreover, without proper controls, nuclear reactors can experience loss of cooling and subsequent partial-to-complete meltdowns. Although these instances are rare, they're associated with spewing radioactivity for hundreds of miles or leaking radioactive water, causing injury, burns, and even death. Incidents at Three Mile Island (1979), Chernobyl (1986), and the Fukushima Daiichi nuclear plants (2011) have come to define the suspicions about the postwar nuclear era. Both Europe and China, though, are investing in a new generation of nuclear power plants driven by fission of the radioactive heavy metal thorium, considered much safer than uranium-powered plants because of the lack of nuclear waste and better system of controls.

With nearly a hundred sites storing U.S. nuclear waste instead of a central location—although Yucca Mountain near the Nevada-California border was proposed as a deep geological repository for nuclear waste under the 1982 Nuclear Waste Policy Act, continual bureaucratic red tape has been preventing this facility—our country also has had a less-than-optimal system for disposing of nuclear waste. On the other hand, Europe (especially France), recycles nuclear waste and uses it again and again for power generation. America, blessed with more abundant shale oil and gas reserves, appears to be phasing out nuclear power.

WHY PEOPLE ARE FIGHTING SHALE: OF FRACTIVISTS, METHANE EMISSIONS, AND MORAL PANIC

You might call the public debate on fracking "a moral panic."

When it comes to questions of the environment vs. fossil fuels (especially shale development), New York City, Colorado, California, England, France, Bulgaria, and South Africa are becoming epicenters of public anxiety and panic. Many fear that hydraulic fracturing is an outright threat to the moral, social, and environmental fabric of neighborhoods. Lawmakers and fractivists, celebrities and shale barons (so-called "frackmasters"), local communities, politicians, and scientists have been debating—sometimes shouting—about the risks and rewards of this comparatively new shale exploration technology and its effects on planet Earth.

Many see fracking as an assault on environmental and social values or a threat to the public health, safety, and sanity of communities disrupted by noise and drilling machinery. And some assert that the U.S. energy industry should be focusing on renewable sources, not hydrocarbons (which are thought to contribute to climate change), although U.S. efforts reduced carbon dioxide emissions in April 2012 to the lowest levels since 1992. Several complaints about fracking have found their way into Environmental Protection Agency (EPA) reports and well-pad research studies conducted by the National Oceanic and Atmospheric Administration (NOAA), Purdue University, ICF International, and many other institutions. These studies have documented incidents—though relatively rare—of methane gas leakage from well pads and pipelines, groundwater contamination, and seismic activity around shale plays.

The Fracking Debate: Is It More Than Just Rhetoric?

The primary reason for the activity around shale plays is that supplies in U.S. oil and gas wells are being tapped out. Renewables—even vast solar projects in transition—are part of the U.S. energy mix, but not as far along as they eventually will be. Further, the U.S. Energy Information Administration (EIA) forecasts that, by 2035, natural gas-derived electricity will have to roughly double to meet about half the country's electricity needs.

Much of this increase in shale resources comes from advancements in drilling technology. According to Mark Brownstein of the Environmental Defense Fund (EDF), 90 percent of all new oil and gas wells in the nation now employ some form of hydraulic fracturing—and within that, the vast majority of sites are now using horizontal drilling. "The practice of hydraulic fracturing is now the predominant way we are producing oil and gas," Brownstein said in a May 2014 phone discussion with our team. "The question is not whether we drill, but how we do it in ways that minimize risks to health and environment."

But when we spoke with U.S. Senator Cory Gardner (R-CO)—then a member of the House of Representatives—he disagreed with Brownstein's focus on the environmental harm of fracking. "What's a shame are the scare tactics that are being used right now to frighten people away from responsible energy development," Gardner told us in April 2014. "It's irresponsible from an economic point of view, but it's also harmful now—as we've seen—to our allies around the globe who could use American energy to resist reliance on energy from places like Russia."

And so the debate rages on.

Confrontations over fracking have accelerated because of the huge economic and environmental stakes involved. And, as David Spence, professor of law, regulation, and policy at the University of Texas at Austin, has noted, public policy debate appears to seesaw between "cool analysis" and "moral outrage" that obscures the ability to evaluate data rationally and solve complex problems: "The debate over fracking and shale gas production has become polarized very quickly, in part because of the size of the economic and environmental stakes."[1]

This moral outrage is akin to moral panic, a term invented in 1987 by media scholar Stanley Cohen, who defined it as "a condition, episode, person or group of persons [who] become defined as a threat to societal values and interests."[2] In this case, fracking is seen as a disruption to the normal course of community events and as a threat to groundwater safety.

How does moral panic play out in the shale debate? One way is for opponents to exaggerate negative findings. Advocates, likewise, look to overemphasize positive ones.

But the rhetoric attached to the shale debate has become extreme—not at all helpful in increasing public understanding of relative risks and benefits. Mass demonstrations in big cities have galvanized opposition groups. Celebrities like Yoko Ono make speeches, stage news conferences, and produce radio ads attacking the shale oil and gas industry. "Fracking kills," Ono said at a 2013 press conference with other drilling opponents. "And it doesn't just kill us, it kills the land, nature and eventually the whole world."[3]

"Opponents of fracking have generally framed their arguments in moral or ethical terms, calling shale gas production a 'nightmare' that will harm people and the environment," Spence wrote.[4] "The industry's proponents point to the paucity of hard data supporting opponents' claims, dispute the anecdotal evidence opponents cite, and respond with their own exaggerated claims. . . . Meanwhile, systematic research is beginning to build our understanding of the risks associated with shale gas production, though the record is far from complete.

"To me, the most important fracking impacts are all associated with local disruptions: For example, truck traffic, noise, and changes in neighborhood character," Spence maintained. "A lot of the impact that upsets people and motivates local bans comes from intense industrial activity at the well pad. Almost everything else we're talking about—seismic activity, violation of air pollution standards, ground water contaminations—are the exception rather than the rule.

"Fracking has actually gotten ahead of our studies of its impacts," Spence added. "While scientists are filling in the fracking profile study by study and presenting these results circumspectly, public debate has gotten more polarized and shrill."

Environmental Impacts

What has science discovered thus far about fracking? Almost all environmental debate centers on three major issues: 1. groundwater contamination; 2. methane gas emissions; and 3. safe disposal or recycling of millions of gallons of water and chemicals used in fracking. (A fourth issue, seismic activity, is a concern to scientists and citizens in some parts of the country like Ohio and Oklahoma, where drilling and an increase in low-magnitude earthquakes seem to be associated. Investigations are ongoing.)

Issue #1—groundwater contamination: A review article published in *Science* in 2013 and funded by the National Science Foundation investigated what fracking was doing to groundwater supplies. The result? No recorded effect, at least thus far. "There is no irrefutable impact of this industry on surface or ground water quality in Pennsylvania," said Radisav Vidic, a University of Pittsburgh environmental engineer who led the review.[5]

However, in 2009, the northeastern Pennsylvania community of Dimock reported significant methane contamination of groundwater, shortly after Cabot Oil & Gas began drilling for natural gas in the area. Fifteen Dimock families filed a federal lawsuit against Cabot that same year; and the Pennsylvania Department of Environmental Protection ultimately cited Cabot for 130 drilling violations at the Dimock wells, fining the company and ordering it to stop drilling in Susquehanna County communities. Cabot insisted the methane migration in Dimock water wells was naturally occurring. However, the company ultimately settled with ten Dimock families reporting well contamination by paying $4 million in damages. Dimock was quickly identified in the media as "ground zero" of the U.S. fracking debate.[6]

Many factors can influence groundwater contamination, and problems have been sporadically reported in Wyoming, Texas, and Pennsylvania. For example, the influential environmental advocacy website DeSmogBlog in 2013 obtained a copy of an EPA presentation suggesting a clear link between fracking in Dimock and groundwater contamination. The presentation, "Isotech-Stable Isotope Analysis: Determining the Origin of Methane and its Effects on the Aquifer," concluded that methane had migrated up into the aquifers adjoining the Cabot Oil and Gas Gesford 2 well, possibly during the drilling/fracking process started in 2009.

EPA also found arsenic, barium, and manganese, all naturally occurring substances (albeit hazardous in large quantities), "in well water of five households at levels that could present a health concern," according to an EPA desk statement. But the EPA suppressed these findings in 2012 in the wake of President Obama's coming reelection campaign, according to some EPA insiders.

In light of these EPA well tests, Cabot paid for deliveries of freshwater supplies to Dimock-area households for a couple of years but never acknowledged formal responsibility for the problem. EPA followed with an investigation and also paid for water deliveries to nineteen local families beginning in January 2012 and continuing until the investigation ended. But, again, the government agency announced that fracking was not the cause of the water contamination, although some experts involved in the report stated otherwise.

What's the truth?

Both a Yale University study and a Scientific American report on shale oil and gas safety noted that fracking itself, which generally occurs a mile or more beneath the surface, is highly unlikely to actually blast a path to drinking water resources. But if wells aren't properly installed, or if there are cracks in the concrete casings used to seal the main well pipe from the surrounding earth, fracking fluid or methane could leak upward and find its way toward the surface.

Based on 2008–2013 citation records from the Pennsylvania Department of Environment (DEP), for example, roughly 3 percent of all wells drilled in Pennsylvania suffered some kind of faulty construction problem resulting in leaks. Still, Vidic maintained that the DEP does not find evidence of groundwater contamination from methane leaks. And wells in New York State—where no fracking exists—have concentrations of methane similar to those in Pennsylvania where fracking is abundant.

Overall, "we're still trying to understand the risk factors from hydraulic fracturing," said Dr. Anthony Ingraffea, the Dwight C. Baum Professor of Civil and Environmental Engineering at Cornell University. An expert on shale geology, Ingraffea believes that more aggressive renewables development is a "must" to reduce greenhouse gases now and in the future. With current fracturing and horizontal drilling, "the likelihood of there being a serious problem with respect to drinking water contamination is small," he told my team in an April 2014 interview. "It's not negligible, but it's small."

The main conclusion scientists draw from available reports is that checking well casings and construction is paramount to groundwater and air safety. Both the states and the federal government are tightening up on well regulation to assure that leaks are detected and contained.

Issue #2—methane emissions: Methane (CH_4) is a greenhouse gas, 84 percent more potent than carbon dioxide as measured in the first 20 years of release into the atmosphere. Methane can leak right across the shale gas value chain—from well pads to local and interstate pipelines to gas mains to storage tanks and sealed storage pits. But estimates for how much leakage vary significantly, running between 1.5 percent (EPA estimates) to 6 percent or more (Mark Brownstein's guess).

One finding is that, in some shale and coal development regions where drilling has been conducted for decades—or even a century or more—old pipes or weathered concrete casings can act as a conduit for natural gas moving from lower to upper regions. For example, in April 2014, a Purdue University study on methane emissions from shale gas published in *Proceedings of the National Academy of Sciences* showed abnormally high methane levels over a handful of wells in southwestern Pennsylvania.[7]

But the vast majority of wells in the region had little to no emissions. The authors of the study found methane mixtures characteristic of coal-bed gas, not Marcellus gas—which emanates from recently tapped shale fields in Pennsylvania—strongly suggesting that the vented gas had come from old coal beds. Experts evaluating the study indicated that special precautions should be taken to prevent methane escape during vertical and horizontal drilling in these areas. But because the methane sources appear to be extremely limited, the problem can be fixed with stronger gas measurements and containment procedures before, during, and after drilling.

"Once identified, gas leaks in production and transportation systems can be reduced, and there is an economic as well as environmental incentive to do so," *New York Times* commentator Andrew Revkin wrote on the study.[8] Take pneumatic valves in gas pipelines, for example: These actually vent gas as part of their operation and are a big source of methane leakage. But they can be replaced easily with electronic valves.

States like Colorado and Wyoming and parts of Texas have enacted legislation to reduce methane emissions from fracked wells. Further, the EPA has enacted a set of standards to ensure that all of the 11,000 newly fracked wells reduce any leaked emissions by 95 percent by the end of 2015. The techniques for capturing flow-back gas, known as "green completions," are based on known and cost-effective industry practices. About half the fractured wells in the U.S. employ green completions already.

"[Methane leakage] is a solvable problem. We can achieve a 40 percent reduction in methane emissions across the [shale production] system for less than one penny per thousand cubic feet produced," Brownstein told us. "Forty percent reduction opportunities have a net payback to companies; if you're taking steps to minimize emissions, you're saving product. From a societal perspective, none of this is expensive to do."

Issue #3—recycling/disposing of fracked water: Hydraulic fracturing and horizontal drilling require a great deal of water—as much as ten to a hundred times the amount of frack fluid used in conventional drilling—along with chemicals and sand. With Texas and California both experiencing droughts, using water for shale drilling is controversial. A dozen communities in California, for example, have voted to restrict or prohibit hydraulic fracturing in their jurisdictions because of drought and a recent spate of powerful earthquakes. The Western Petroleum Association, an oil and gas industry lobbying group, indicated that a single fracked well consumes 87 percent of the water used by a family of four over a year.

Fracking operations can use 7.5 to 26.6 million liters (1.89 to 6.9 million gallons) of water. Add to the water powerful chemical cocktails (which vary according to the drilling company) using ingredients ranging from grain alcohol to coffee grounds, the danger of toxic spills, large amounts of leftover salt, and even the presence of radioactivity. Tainted water has been located, for example, outside the Marcellus Shale fracking zone deep underground, although more than a mile beneath groundwater supplies. Shallower fracked wells in West Virginia and Wyoming have also contaminated groundwater, according to *Scientific American,* and evidence of contaminants has been showing up in Pennsylvania rivers.[9] Preventing well spills and properly recycling and/or disposing of fracked well water remains paramount.

Because of the geology of the Marcellus Shale, disposal isn't an option, so drilling companies have been increasingly reusing the water in new wells—in fact, 2012 reuse rates in Pennsylvania were 90 percent. Texas is also looking to reform its regulations regarding recycling and disposal, as well as its water usage; at present, companies dispose of fracked water in deep injection wells, although recycling has begun.

In addition, several states have required companies to disclose the chemicals they are using in fracking; the website FracFocus, which is backed by the oil and gas industry, allows anyone to look up specific wells to see what's in the fluid mix. EPA's regulations for green completions will also require companies to use special equipment to separate and capture gas and liquid hydrocarbons in well flow back, helping to reduce waste.

Issue #4—earthquakes: Seismic activity is a concern to scientists and citizens in some parts of the country, where drilling seems to correlate to an increase in tremors. While investigations are ongoing, the general public is certainly aware of the issue—as we discovered at a suburban Houston shopping center.

"All I know is that fracking is a very destructive and dangerous way to retrieve oil," said shopper Robin Weber. "It's causing possible earthquakes and contaminating the water supply totally."

I also posed on Facebook the question of whether fracking causes earthquakes. Earthquakes were a top concern among people who were skeptical of the process. Commenters DeAnna D. and Harold H. both brought up recent earthquakes near drilling sites.

"Earthquakes are caused by this means of getting fuel," DeAnna wrote.

Harold agreed: "You cannot keep causing small earthquakes without triggering a huge one. There is cause and effect. A release of pressure in one spot affects pressure in another spot."

But other commenters were quick to disagree, saying fracking doesn't cause earthquakes or other environmental problems.

Mary Ann K. wrote, "Earthquakes have happened for generations along the Balcones Escarpment in Texas prior to the first well ever drilled. . . . Shale is not solid. It is porous and in layers like slate or mica. The current drilling methods and practices are the safest since the industry began. Our future is in petroleum whether you like it or not. Even wind turbines and solar power use petroleum to be manufactured, in production and in transmission!"

Another commenter, Barry B., said he doesn't believe that fracking creates earthquakes or environmental contamination.

"Fracking does not cause sinkholes or water contamination or earthquakes," he wrote. "Most wells are over two miles down below the water tables. I work in the oil field industry. Contamination is caused by the oil drillers not going by proper procedures."

So, who's right and who's wrong?

The answer—like many things in the fracking debate—is not that simple: According to experts at the U.S. Geological Survey (USGS), there may be some truth in both positions. The USGS has classified the idea of man-made earthquakes as "partially fact." However, the USGS says there are only a few documented locations in the United States where human activity has influenced earthquakes and that, of these ground shakers, most were insignificant.[10]

On its website in 2015, the USGS stated, "The cause was injection of fluids into deep wells for waste disposal and secondary recovery of oil, and the filling of large reservoirs for water supplies. Most of these earth-quakes were minor."[11] Further, USGS notes that the point of origin of an earthquake is typically tens to hundreds of miles underground, and "the scale and force necessary to produce earthquakes are well beyond our daily lives."[12]

Cliff Frohlich, a University of Texas seismologist, agrees with this assessment. At a recent shale-gas drilling conference, he stated that earth-quakes near drilling sites are not caused by fracking but result instead from the disposal of drilling fluids in underground injection wells. And although there have been at least six earthquakes ranging in magnitude from 3.3 to 5.7 on the Richter scale since 2008 in the fracking states of Arkansas, Colorado, Texas, Ohio, and Oklahoma, Frohlich pointed out that, given the amount of oil being produced and how much waste is being disposed of, earthquakes near drilling sites are "very rare." He added that there are 10,000 injection wells in Texas, some in use since the 1930s, that have not caused problems. In other words, fracking and storage alone don't account for the rare occurrences of earthquakes. Frohlich theorized that in cases where earthquakes have occurred, it was likely that the loca-tions were "suitably oriented" near fault lines.

Seismologist Peggy Hellweg of the University of California, Berkley, also knows a thing or two about major earthquakes. The bottom line? She doesn't connect fracking with destructive tremors: "I'm not expecting the Big One to be triggered by this kind of thing."[13]

Fracking Is a Work in Progress

Every industrial activity carries some measure of risk. But the private sector, oil and gas industry leaders, and NGOs (such as the Environmental Defense Fund, the Clean Air Task Force, and the Center for Sustainable Shale Development) are working actively to reduce risk and enforce best practices through cooperative activities.

State laws and regulations about fracking are also important. In addition to environmental concerns, legislative issues are cropping up. Some 450 separate communities across the U.S. are fighting with state regulators over who has the right to block local drilling. Four communities in Colorado have banned it, although a measure to halt fracking statewide hit a wall in November 2014 when the so-called Colorado Right to Local Self-Government Amendment—that would grant local governments the power to ban fracking—failed to make the ballot. On the other hand, New York—one of the four states sitting atop the gas-abundant Marcellus Shale—ultimately decided to ban fracking once and for all in December 2014 after a four-year moratorium on the practice. Governor Andrew Cuomo had delayed making any decision regarding fracking during his first gubernatorial term then upon reelection swiftly moved his state away from the option.

Despite these bans, it's notable that the country is actually divided about shale development—pretty equally. A recent Pew research study found that 47 percent oppose additional hydraulic fracturing, while 41 percent are in favor of it and 12 percent don't know.[14] The question remains how shale hydraulic fracturing and other forms of energy development, including renewables, will affect the economic and environmental picture of our society long-term.

The jury is out.

Attention to science—not myth mongering—is critical to finding common-sense energy solutions. "Many of the risks [of shale fracturing] can be addressed through appropriate operating practices and best practices, and that's what we're trying to do," said Susan LeGros, president of the Center for Sustainable Shale Development in Pittsburgh. LeGros told my team in a May 2014 phone conversation that the center is working with four major energy partners—Shell, Chevron, EQT, and Consol—along with several environmental NGOs to define a fifteen-point certification process for fracked wells in the Appalachian basin (Pennsylvania, West Virginia, and eastern Ohio)—the region that perhaps represents the epicenter for the fracking debates because it currently has both a thriving oil and gas industry *and* a particularly vocal opposition.

Society accepts some level of risk with all industrial activity. "We don't ban cars or electricity, even though people are sometimes harmed by those activities," Spence pointed out. "The challenge for regulators is to minimize the probability of harm and of human error, and to balance the benefits of this form of energy production against its risks."

CHAPTER 10

REGULATIONS: CAN'T LIVE WITH 'EM, CAN'T LIVE WITHOUT 'EM

On a bitterly cold Friday night at the University of Wisconsin, the icy wind off Lake Mendota sends chills through even the most warmly dressed party seekers. From the TKE fraternity house, notable for its modern facade in the midst of Tudor and Colonial Revival buildings, come the strains of one of the most fitting drinking songs imaginable in a state known as much for its breweries as for its cheese and fan-owned football team, the Green Bay Packers: "In Heaven There Is No Beer."

"In heaven, there is no beer/ That's why we drink it here/ And when we're gone from here/ Our friends will be drinking all the beer."

Badgers may not drink all the beer, but they do drink a lot—some 36.2 gallons of the foamy, fermented beverage per capita per year, according to the Beer Institute. The Wisconsin Historical Society says that records of the state's earliest breweries date back to the 1830s territorial era.

Now you're wondering: Aside from barrels, what can beer possibly have in common with oil? Is there any plausible connection between keg tapping and fracking?

Why, yes, there is: Germany.

The advent of Wisconsin breweries—think iconic names such as Schlitz, Pabst, Blatz, and Miller—harks back to the settlement of German immigrants in the state. Those pioneers brought with them not only the knowledge of German brewing techniques but also a fierce determination to maintain their cultural identity.

Likewise, the German beer-making community is fiercely determined to maintain the quality of its product. And one way to do that is by fighting the possibility of fracking under German soil.

The nation gets a third each of its natural gas and oil (and a quarter of its coal) from Russia, not the most collegial of purveyors. But despite Germany's increasingly urgent need for diversity in its energy sources, drilling for shale gas there remains under an unlimited ban. The nation's beer industry is among those actively working to keep the prohibition in place.

Why? Well, as anyone who's had exposure to beer advertising knows, it takes great water to make great-tasting beer. And great water is what the German brewers are trying to protect. Fracking, the *braumeisters'* federation contends, could "reduce or even completely eliminate the security of the water supply."[1] And that would be in conflict with a beer purity law called the *Reinheitsgebot*, which was adopted in 1516 and mandated that beer can contain only three ingredients: water, barley, and hops.

The brewers argue that anything else that might turn up in the water used for beer-making—say, fracking chemicals—is strictly verboten.

Admittedly, hauling out an antiquated law like the *Reinheitsgebot* to keep fracking at bay seems like a stretch, and it's a strategy not likely to be attempted in the U.S.—although a Pennsylvania resident recently posted a question online about whether fracking had anything to do with the fact that her bottle of Yuengling, the state's much-loved local beer, tasted different. (She was assured that it did not.)

Smoke on the Water

Compared to Germany's food and beverage purity law, the history of water regulation in the U.S. is about as shallow as the Ogallala Aquifer, which provides drinking water to more than 1.8 million people in eight mid-central states. At just fifty feet below the surface in some places, the Ogallala isn't very deep at all. Neither, actually, is our national commitment to clean water: The most significant laws are less than fifty years old. In fact, recorded legislation only goes back to 1899's spottily enforced Rivers and Harbors Act, intended to curb the dumping of refuse into the country's waterways. It wasn't really until the late 1960s that the health and societal effects of water pollution seeped completely into the American consciousness.

Of course, a river catching on fire has a way of opening both eyes and minds—which is exactly what happened on June 22, 1969.

Around noon on that second day of summer, oil-coated debris on the industrial Cuyahoga River at Cleveland, Ohio, was ignited by sparks from a passing train and burst into flames. Although the fire was out in less than a half-hour, the incident received widespread media attention, enflaming the passions of an increasingly eco-aware public as well as local, state, and national legislators. (Interestingly, it was later revealed that the dramatic photograph accompanying most accounts of the 1969 blaze was actually from a larger, deadly inferno on the Cuyahoga River some seventeen years earlier. The Cuyahoga had, in fact, burned at least eleven other times; river fires weren't all that unusual in the U.S. in the late nineteenth and early twentieth centuries.)

Almost immediately, environmental laws began to fall into place like a well-trained regiment. In less than six months, the National Environment Protection Act (NEPA) was signed into law. Within a year, NEPA had spawned the Environmental Protection Agency (EPA), which has been shaping both debate and policy around clean air, water, and land, climate change, and human health ever since. The EPA quickly put forth the groundbreaking grandfather of all water-pollution rules, 1972's Clean Water Act, which was summarily approved by Congress. Two years later, the Safe Water Drinking Act (SWDA) authorized EPA to set national health-based standards for drinking water to protect against both naturally occurring and man-made contaminants.

Oversight or Overlooked?

It would seem that SWDA regulations would be a boon to fracking opponents. But the fact is, fracking is exempted from SWDA regulations. In what may seem extreme irony, the exclusion is thanks to the EPA itself.

To understand how that came about, rewind to 1997—about a decade before the first volley in the oil and gas shale revolution. That's when the U.S. Court of Appeals for the 11th Circuit (Florida, Georgia, and Alabama), which had decided that fracking for coal-bed methane production should be regulated under SDWA, pulled the EPA into the fray.

Charged with examining hazards to drinking water sources related to coal-bed methane fracking, the agency concluded in 2004 that unless diesel fuel was being used, there was "no unequivocal evidence" that hydraulic fracturing presented a health risk. No national oversight was necessary, the EPA said, adding that fracturing fluids aren't necessarily hazardous in and of themselves and can't travel far underground.

A year later, based upon the EPA's statement, the Energy Policy Act of 2005 explicitly excluded from the SDWA the injection of fluids (except diesel fuel) and propping agents used for hydraulic fracturing purposes. In essence, this made complaints about hydraulic fracturing and its associate fluids beyond the purview of the SDWA.[2]

Some critics maintain that the EPA's influential declaration calling fracking safe severely constrained attempts at further regulation. Even one of the study's three main authors seemed unsure that the agency had made the right call.

In a 2008 interview that's still finding traction among media outlets, EPA hydrogeologist Jeffrey Jollie cautioned that the study focused solely on the effects of hydraulic fracturing on drinking water in coal-bed methane deposits. That means its results can't necessarily be extrapolated to shale drilling, which occurs in geologic formations deep underground. "It was never intended to be a broad, sweeping study," Jollie told ProPublica reporter Abrahm Lustgarten. "I don't think we ever characterized it that way."[3]

Jollie wasn't alone in his unease. According to the Union of Concerned Scientists, several EPA scientists challenged the study's methodology and questioned the impartiality of the expert panel that reviewed its findings. No doubt, those misgivings provide ammunition to fracking opponents.

But to date, the EPA stands firm on the conclusions from its 2004 study, in no small part because it's still conducting additional research.

According to a personal email to our team from EPA spokesperson Kelsey Maloney, the agency is working to capture the "state of the science" in its "Study of the Potential Impacts of Hydraulic Fracturing for Oil and Gas on Drinking Water Resources." Maloney noted that the study reflects a "careful and intensive review and synthesis of existing scientific literature, EPA research results, and ongoing stakeholder input." Although a "Progress Report" was issued in 2012, Maloney said it "didn't provide the information or the synthesis necessary to draw conclusions or to answer the study questions."

Since 2005, congressional attempts to repeal SWDA's fracking exemption have died in committee. An updated version is currently languishing in both the Senate and the House.

It's All About the Base

In the decade since the EPA's 2004 assertion that fracking is safe, dozens of troubling reports cite pollutants in water wells near natural gas fields. Although culpability hasn't been established, the prime suspect is high-pressure frack fluid, a mixture injected into rock formations to help oil and gas flow.

The only thing is, frack fluid is mostly simple H_2O.

According to the industry-backed online chemical disclosure registry FracFocus, water makes up anywhere from 98 to 99.2 percent of fracturing fluid. The rest is a small volume of sand and additives intended to boost production.

Drilling companies haven't been required to disclose the exact nature of their frack fluids, and many haven't wanted to, saying that the precise nature and concentrations of the additives they use constitute trade secrets. Even the EPA doesn't know exactly what's in drilling fluids.

Last year, the EPA announced its intention to use the Toxic Substances Control Act (TSCA) to require oil-field services companies to provide information about the health and safety of the chemicals used in fracking. Not only have no rules been made so far, according to Bloomberg

Business, the agency has taken the unusual step of saying it may decide to stop short of rules and use incentives or voluntary steps as an alternative.

But some companies are proactively opting for full disclosure. In August 2014, oil-field services company Baker Hughes began posting on FracFocus every single one of the chemicals in its drilling fluids, eliminating any mystery.

Little Blue Legislative Pills

If the federal government appears impotent when it comes to fracking laws, with a recent pair of legislative "little blue pills," it might seem that the feds are getting their mojo back. As part of its commitment to addressing climate change, the Obama administration has been fairly determined in its efforts to regulate pollutants released into the air by oil and gas operations.

With the 2015 Clean Air Act (CAA) final rules, there are now federal regulations restricting the amount of smog- and soot-forming pollutants that can be released as wells transition from drilling to production. The new limits are expected to have a significant impact, yielding a nearly 95 percent reduction in emissions of volatile organic compounds from more than 11,000 hydraulically fractured gas wells each year.[4] The EPA maintains that this reduction would result primarily from capturing natural gas that currently escapes into the air. In a sort of backhanded bonus for energy companies, they will be allowed to make that gas available for sale.[5]

The CAA directive should also reduce cancer-causing air toxins and cut methane emissions. Methane, a key constituent of natural gas, is a potent greenhouse gas whose global warming potential, according to the EPA, is more than twenty-five times higher than that of carbon dioxide. Although the oil and gas industry's voluntary actions have already reduced methane emissions 16 percent since 1990, they were expected to increase by about 25 percent over the next decade without further regulation.[6]

In addition, in March 2015 the Bureau of Land Management (BLM) at long last issued a final rule governing fracking on federal and American Indian lands that was more than four years in the making. Intended to "protect public health and the environment during and after hydraulic fracturing operations,"[7] according to assistant secretary for land and minerals management Janice Schneider, the new BLM rule is chiefly concerned with:

- Ensuring the protection of groundwater supplies
- Public disclosure of fracking chemicals through FracFocus
- Standards for interim storage of recovered waste fluids from hydraulic fracturing
- Lowering the risk of cross-well contamination with chemicals and fluids used in the fracturing operation

Leave It to the States

"The government has a broad agenda: It includes economic development, but it also includes the environment, international commitments, and alliances . . . so the government role is never easy," historian Jay Hakes told us in May 2014. "The federal government has to represent both states that are mainly consuming states and states that are mainly producing states. So that's why our policy often appears to be incoherent, because in some sense it is incoherent." Given that, perhaps we should consider that one-size-fits-all federal mandates don't make sense when it comes to energy production. Instead, individual states might be the best regulators for their own lands.

Critics of the 2015 BLM standards concerning fracking point out that the new rule largely duplicates the work the states already do, with only some slight changes. (A provision in the Energy Policy Act of 2005 gave states the exclusive right to regulate fracking on state and private lands; the BLM regulates public and American Indian lands.) Detractors suggest that the BLM mandates won't solve any issues related to fracking that persist under state law. What's more, global legal firm Baker-Hostetler pointed out that the BLM failed to show even one incident that the new federal rules would ban that isn't already well-covered by an existing state rule.

Oops.

Not only does the BLM rule have its detractors, it also has its litigants—namely, the states of Wyoming and North Dakota, who've filed a lawsuit against it. They contend that the rule is unlawful in part because it interferes with their own regulations around fracking. They also contend that it's in conflict with the federal SWDA.

As North Dakota attorney general Wayne Stenehjem asserted, "Our rules are very robust, very stringent, and we enforce them."[8]

David Spence, who co-directs the University of Texas at Austin's Energy Management and Innovation Center (EMIC), agrees that when it comes to fracking, the states have been doing the regulatory heavy lifting. Citing a University of Tulsa survey, Spence said that some states give their environmental regulatory agency authority over fracking, while others regulate through their oil and gas commission's well-permitting process.

Others promote enhancing states' authority because of the uniqueness of the individual shale plays. With unconventional drilling and production hardly a cookie-cutter proposition—fracking in California, with its shallow, less water-intensive wells, is much different than it is in North Dakota, where drilling can extend nearly two miles underground—one-size-fits-all regulations aren't terribly appropriate.

We spoke in April 2014 with U.S. Senator Cory Gardner (R-CO), who is a strong supporter of giving states the ultimate control: "We know that fracking can be done safely, but we also know that we have to do it in a responsible manner, and that's where strong regulations are key. I believe those strong regulations come from the states, though, who know the geology of the state far better than any bureaucrat in

Washington, D.C., ever could. That's where we have to turn for strong environmental protections."

What's more, only a few of the risks of shale-gas production—methane leakage, for example—extend beyond state lines. In addition, states have been overseeing natural gas development for decades, making them more experienced with permitting and oversight than anyone. As *The Wall Street Journal* suggested, "Both the benefits and the costs of fracking fall mostly on states and local communities. States gain the most from added jobs and tax revenue; they face the truck traffic, noise, pollution risks and rapid industrial growth. Consequently, states are in the best position to figure out how best to balance fracking's costs and benefits."[9]

Today, many oil and gas companies are saying, "Enough is enough!" when it comes to additional external control. Ahead of the EPA's potential amendments to the Toxic Substances Control Act, the American Petroleum Institute, American Fuel & Petrochemical Manufacturers, and the American Chemistry Council have all told the agency that shale development is safe, sufficiently regulated, and doesn't require additional intervention.

That's not likely to be the end of it, of course.

Daniel Fiorino, director of the Center for Environmental Policy at American University's School of Public Affairs, predicted that the Republican takeover in 2014 of many state legislatures may make the battles between environmentalists and commerce, science, and ideology even more pitched.[10]

Perhaps the Germans are right. Maybe it is less complicated and more productive to strip away the geological layers of modern legislation and simply refer back to a 500-year-old decree to regulate fracking. Or maybe the U.S. tug-of-war between the federal government and the states will eventually wind down, with the states asserting their rightful claim to regulate fracking activities.

All we know is that this isn't an issue to be settled easily over a couple of steins of beer.

Subsidizing Big, Bad Oil

American policymakers, starting at the top, have the potential to disrupt the pace of a transition to natural gas by limiting the nation's ability to reap the rewards of shale gas development. Analysts caution that restrictive regulations could even impede the manufacturing renaissance enabled through the lower cost of natural gas.

Some of the most detrimental government actions underway involve tax policies on the oil and gas industry. Among these are calls to repeal legitimate tax treatments bandied about by politicos and news media alike as "tax subsidies." Truth be told, tax treatments for the oil and gas sector outlined in the federal tax code are no different than those afforded other manufacturing segments—but unlike mining, automotive, food, or other industries, oil and gas faces continual, substantial efforts to repeal some of its tax treatments.

Jay Hakes, the author of *A Declaration of Energy Independence* (Wiley, 2008) and onetime administrator of the nonpartisan Energy Information Administration, expounded in a May 2014 phone interview with my team that the basis for this belief stems from a misunderstanding. "For a very long time, the oil industry had the oil depletion allowance, which was a special tax that benefited the industry," Hakes told us. "Going back to Truman through the 1970s, people crusaded against that, and it was done away with in the 1970s. A lot of people are acting like the old depletion tax is there, even though it's been gone for forty years."

Taxpayers are duped into thinking that *we* foot the bill for oil and gas subsidies, as if the industry is on the government dole. Nothing could be further from the truth. Oil and gas companies, like all businesses, are allowed to deduct their expenses for salaries and equipment they purchase. But the government has a history of applying some of those treatments differently when dealing with the oil and gas industry.

Just take the often-misunderstood intangible drilling cost (IDC), a financial incentive written into the U.S. tax code that has somehow become seen as a subsidy. Intangibles include everything except the actual drilling equipment: labor, chemicals, mud, grease, etc. This category constitutes a huge cost component in oil-well drilling, combining to account for 65–80 percent of the total cost of any drilling project. IDC is 100-percent deductible during the first year of a drilling operation.[11]

Or consider percentage depletion, the oil and gas industry's version of depreciation deduction for the energy reserves in the ground. Every industry is allowed a depreciation deduction on its assets, but the government repealed the percentage depletion allowance for all the integrated oil companies in 1975. As a result, this one segment of U.S. industry has been denied the same tax deductions available to other industries for forty years.

We could argue that this move to eliminate "subsidies" is another way of increasing taxes on oil and gas companies. Not only is it unfair to single out one industry, particularly one that has been a major job creator and one where nine million people are gainfully employed, but it's a move that could lead to workforce reduction and serious economic repercussions.

PART III

BOOM OR BUST. DISTINCTLY AMERICA.

CHAPTER 11

THE WIZARDS OF MARCELLUS

To Dave Spigelmyer, president of the Marcellus Shale Coalition, drilling natural gas wells into the Marcellus Shale has paid off like a grand bet—something like putting your money down on the top race horse or plunking down $100K in a college fund for a brilliant child. The Marcellus has changed our outlook for natural gas supply from a period of scarcity to one of affordability and abundance.

"There are nearly 8,000 unconventional (shale) wells in Pennsylvania today," Spigelmyer told us. He chuckles a little. "Well bores are like children, with different yields and personalities."

Hearing him talk this way reminded us of Forrest Gump and his box of chocolates. Before the fracturing actually begins two miles below, you don't know exactly what you're going to get.

It's not that shale development companies know nothing about what lies beneath. But even with all the new geoseismic detection techniques—the laser-guided drilling technology, the use of sonar and sensors to detect the shape and contour of shale formations—there is always some uncertainty about how much a well will ultimately produce and for how long.

In early December 2014, we toured several Marcellus natural gas well sites with Spigelmyer in Washington County, Pennsylvania. Standing on the McMaster well pad built by Range Resources roughly ten months prior, we saw the activities of drilling multiple horizontal wells to reach hundreds of acres from this one location.

The pad was quiet—surprisingly so. Despite the flow of gas coming up through a series of nested steel pipes, despite the monitoring equipment, gas-collection tanks, control and vapor-elimination systems, along with machines, derricks, and wellheads that look like a giant Rube Goldberg contraption, all we heard was the sound of voices muffled by wind.

During our visit, the energy workers were performing multiple tasks, including the separation and recycling of drilling mud in large Dumpster-size containers filled with corn husks (a natural drying agent). Spigelmyer and a tour guide told us that the drilling mud (a corn oil– or salt-based lubricant) returns to the surface for recirculation when drilling the horizontal portion of the well. Once hydraulic fracturing of the well is completed, any produced water on the site is filtered, recycled, and reused.

"Fracking is a five-day process in the approximately thirty-five-year life of a Marcellus well," Spigelmyer said. "When I speak to folks, especially reporters, it's helpful for them to understand that fracking is not about driving a truck to a well site or laying a pipe. It's a completion process— the last process of injecting sand, water, and chemicals to release the gas from solid rock." Today an average Marcellus well may take twenty or twenty-five days to drill.

Spigelmyer also said that the chemicals used in a fracturing job are composed of an antimicrobial agent, a friction reducer, and a scale inhibitor to prevent pipe corrosion. Range Resources was the first company in the Marcellus to voluntarily disclose its frack chemicals, which it did both on its own website in 2010 and subsequently on the nationally recognized FracFocus website, which is now the required disclosure resource in fourteen states, including Pennsylvania.

The tour guide pointed out that the chosen fluids for each job are 99.9 percent water and sand, with the rest being common additives that most people encounter in everyday life. Some of the additives are even biodegradable.

Range Resources is now operating 500 unconventional wells and 5,000 conventional ones in Pennsylvania. The company is one of roughly 70 operating in the Marcellus today to extract both "dry gas" (mostly composed of methane; these wells are concentrated in northeastern Pennsylvania) and "wet gas," a salubrious mixture of natural gas and liquids known as NGLs or condensate. Wet gas is the primary product of the wells we saw in southwestern Pennsylvania. The liquids include many types of hydrocarbon compounds—ethane, butane, isobutane, pentane, hexane, and propane—which are used for many industrial applications such as chemicals, pharmaceuticals, fertilizer, steel, lighter fluids, and propellants.

Marcellus is the largest natural gas shale production basin in the U.S. today. It provides 25 percent of all U.S. natural gas needs. The shale play has been so productive since 2008 that a map of Pennsylvania's unconventional wells today makes the Commonwealth look like a pincushion. The ten most productive wells in Pennsylvania are concentrated in Susquehanna County, in the northeast. But other big gas- and liquid-producing counties include Bradford, Lycoming, Wyoming, Butler, Beaver, Washington, and Greene counties, among others.

The Local Tour

At the McMaster pad site, engineers in the drilling rig's control center were monitoring the six horizontally drilled wells that will extract gas from shale beds located more than a mile beneath our feet. We walked on a gravel pad filled with pipes and metal storage trailers. The wellheads were quite close to each other—no more than twenty feet apart. Spigelmyer spoke about their yield—the billions and even trillions of cubic feet of natural gas released through hydraulic fracturing these days—as though he were talking about his own two children.

Born and raised in Clearfield County, Pennsylvania, Spigelmyer described himself as a "local boy" who speaks with foreign oil dignitaries who come from afar to witness the shale gas miracle happening here. A government-relations expert, Spigelmyer has spent his entire career in energy. He's a former vice president of Chesapeake Energy's Appalachia division, holding similar posts at Dominion Resources, National Fuel Gas, and EQT. During our visit, he showed us completed natural gas well pads that appeared incredibly pristine. We drove in a truck up a winding paved road through farmland until we arrived at a leveled four-acre finished well pad populated by a few silo-size storage tanks painted green, a couple of wellhead pipes (also green) sticking out from the ground with big round valves attached to them, and an auto shutoff "panic" button assembly a few yards away that anyone can press in case of emergency. (This one was painted red and separated from the wellhead pipes by yellow guardrails.) Almost all the gas pipes here—which move gas from the Marcellus Shale bed 6,500 feet below the surface to a remote telemetry station—were invisible, buried in the ground. In fact, there was very little equipment and piping left on the site at all.

Spigelmyer reminded us that fracking wasn't really responsible for the great advances in shale discovery here. "Fracturing isn't new. It's been going on in one form or another since the 1940s. What *is* new are the amazing advances in turning a drill bit and drill pipe horizontally," he continued. "That's what has really revolutionized shale production."

The horizontal drilling technique happens deep underground. Yet it allows a tiny footprint on top, where four to eight well bores can be drilled only fifteen to twenty-five feet apart on a central "square" inside the well pad. Actually, the wells reach out in a fan-like configuration beneath the earth's surface. They target a shale bed with remarkable accuracy, extending through miles of shale using drilling machinery and a series of "laterals"—pipes that extend the well's reach as far as 640 to 1,280 acres (one to two square miles per pad). In energy operator speak, that's less than 1 percent surface disturbance per square mile.

Drilling operators penetrate the shale bed using a series of thick, scabbard-like horizontal laterals and steel pipes. When the drilling is complete and the casings are installed both vertically and horizontally underground, the configuration of these laterals resembles two menorahs or two sets of pitchfork tines welded back to back. The most important feature, though, is that drilling vertically 5,000 to 8,000 feet, followed by turning the drill horizontally thousands of feet more, actually allows the well to access huge volumes of shale gas without disturbing the ground above. The underground configuration maximizes yield while producing far less environmental impact than conventional, vertical drilling. And this is especially true because companies in Pennsylvania have been under pressure, pardon the pun, to refine their methods to ensure that natural gas development can coincide with the environment and everyday life.

A Good-News, Bad-News Scenario?

Washington County, Pennsylvania, has no doubt benefited from the shale boom. The oil and gas industry has created jobs, jobs, jobs! And that has been a boon to the local economy.

So how can that be a bad thing?

In researching the region, we have noticed that businesses in the Washington County area are having a hard time attracting and retaining workers, losing them to higher-paying jobs in the oil field. Sure enough, Jeff Kotula, president of the Washington County Chamber of Commerce, confirmed these findings.

"The Marcellus Shale play has had a tremendous positive impact on Washington County's economy over the past decade. Our county leads the Greater Pittsburgh Region in terms of well activity, economic expansion, and the corresponding job creation that is following the growth of the natural gas industry. However, the high-quality, high-paying jobs the energy industry is creating caused an initial competition for skilled workers among our employers, especially in fields such as welding, machining, and other skilled trades," Kotula conceded in a May 2014 interview with my team.

"To alleviate some of this competition, the business community, county government, and energy industry—working together—collaborated to identify and invest in new opportunities that would train the additional workforce needed to meet both the continuing employment requirements of our indigenous employers as well as the new positions being created by the energy industry. While there will always be a demand for highly skilled workers in any field, we have to continually invest in new training programs to insure our Washington County companies have the quality workforce they need to continue their business growth and thus create new jobs for our residents."

An Incredible Journey

The Marcellus, a rich organic black shale about 380 million years old, is now counted among the largest shale gas plays in the world, a giant formation spanning West Virginia, Ohio, Pennsylvania, and the southern tier of New York State. The play holds at least 500 trillion cubic feet of gas, according to Penn State estimates. The Utica Shale, thousands of feet beneath Marcellus, may contain even more gas; shale energy companies are just beginning to plumb its lower depths.

Our location for the tour, Washington County, is especially famous for liquids-rich mixtures of hydrocarbons that can be "cracked" and separated by using cryogenic (freezing) processes to extract pure chemical streams. The liquids and gases—including ethanes (used to make polyethylene and other plastics), butanes, and isobutanes—are then shipped by rail from a gas-processing plant in Houston, Pennsylvania, to major pipelines that cross the state.

Shale activity in the region now yields an annual 4 trillion cubic feet of natural gas. If you add gas production from eastern Ohio, West Virginia, and Pennsylvania, the yield exceeds 5.3 trillion cubic feet annually or *roughly 25 percent of America's natural gas supply*. Moreover, the volumes of Marcellus gas are rising. Almost all of the new production today comes from shale gas and advances in horizontal drilling. New mapping techniques and better geological data have allowed the major energy players in southwestern Pennsylvania, like Range Resources, XTO, Noble, Chevron, EQT, Rice, Southwestern, Rex Energy, CNX Gas, and Vantage, to shrink the time needed to complete a well pad from fifty days to as little as twenty days. Reductions in cost and time have allowed the companies to remain competitive despite plummeting energy prices and stiff competition.

"It's been an incredible journey," Spigelmyer reflected. "In 2008 we produced a quarter of the *state's* gas supply at 180 billion cubic feet a year. We thought maybe we could be natural gas independent in Pennsylvania by 2014. We hit that target in late 2010. We're producing so much natural gas today that I can't imagine the need for importing any of it in Pennsylvania going forward."

And, yes, shale gas wells are like children, he said. The wells need care, constant monitoring, and significant up-front investment—as much as an average of $7 million per well, according to Spigelmyer. Range Resources was the first company to successfully drill a shale well in the Marcellus back in 2004. Many of those early test wells are still producing today.

Even though no one can predict exactly how much gas each well will yield, an energy company always hedges its bets by conducting extensive 3D geoseismic measurements before deciding to kick off a project. A single well permit fee is $5,000. In the "old days," a well permit cost $100. Prospective sites today require surface and subsurface mapping, arranging and securing land leases from farmers along with royalty payments, and then hiring various subcontractors to begin the drilling process. Preparation includes pipes and erosion and sedimentation controls to prevent runoff damage and water containment, trapping, and filtration. Various environmental subcontractors proactively clean and monitor the site with filtration systems designed for "zero vapor" capture. Well-pad liners catch any water or potential spills on site. And every location has remote telemetry, safety valves, gas tanks, and thousands of steel pipes and concrete well casings, along with horizontal (lateral) drilling motor assemblies and pipes that can bend 1 to 2 degrees progressively until a single well bore literally reaches "sideways" anywhere from 10,000 to 17,000 feet.

The guide showed us marked pipes that are used to develop the lateral extensions after the horizontal drilling is completed.

It's difficult to imagine a drill being able to turn 90 degrees more than a mile underground. But Spigelmyer used a pencil analogy: "If you take one pencil, you can bend it a little," he said. "But if you take a hundred pencils, you can actually make a circle out of them. Same for a 30-foot piece of static drill pipe: You can bend it a little, but if you extend many of them in a long line across a mile, you can make a perfect horizontal bend."

For the wells we visited, Range Resources employs a two-rig system. Before the big drilling rig arrived to develop the horizontal portions of the well, the company had a smaller rig drilling and casing the vertical top-hole portion of the well. Each top hole defines the vertical portion of all shale wells. Drilling contractors then install a series of steel well casings, each one smaller in diameter than the next, fitted and then cemented in place like a large, extended telescope of many pieces. The goal is to prevent gas leaks, isolating the well bore (the end point of the lateral pipe) from the surrounding ground and water table. On average, more than 3 million pounds of steel and concrete are used in a single well.

- In the first drilling stages, three different size pipes are cemented in place inside the largest 24-inch conductor casing that extends from the pad surface to thirty to one hundred feet below ground.
- This is followed by a 20-inch casing that reaches another 200 to 500 feet, intended to bypass and protect the water table from the wall.
- The next layer is a 13⅜-inch "mine casing" that drills down another 1,000 feet, isolating the well bore from existing coal seams.
- The last string installed by the smaller, air rig is the 9⅝-inch casing that is installed to a depth called the "kickoff point," or the point at which horizontal rig operators will begin the directional drilling process. (To visualize this, refer back to chapter 2, Figure 2.1. "How Fracking Works.")

All three layers are cemented into place. Then the smaller rig moves off site, and the larger horizontal drilling rig begins its work. The drill bit snakes a mile vertically underground, then begins its horizontal turn at the kickoff point about 1,000 to 1,200 feet above the actual shale bed, because it takes roughly that length to turn the bit horizontally.

Once the drilling is complete and the drill bit removed, operators install the final production casing of 5½ inches in diameter, which extends to the remaining vertical depth, plus the length of the laterals.

When all of the pipes are cemented and set, the hydraulic fracturing can begin. Each well is completed in stages, starting at the toe of the well bore and working out towards the heel (i.e., the vertical portion). The actual fracturing process—pumping water, sand, salts, and other chemicals down the well to fracture the shale to release gas—lasts only two to five days. (Spigelmyer said there is discussion of a beneficial reuse, allowing salt from shale operations to melt ice on area roadways. The abundant snowfall in the previous winter of 2014 left the Pittsburgh region with a salt shortage.)

Meanwhile, the fracturing water that returns through the wellhead is filtered and recycled for use in other wells. Range's well pad has a double liner during operations to prevent any water or chemical leaks from getting into the groundwater, and filtered water is kept in lined reservoirs until it can be used again.

"Given the general public sensitivity toward fracturing, the practice now is to filter and recycle all the water," Spigelmyer said. "Companies like Range have every incentive to run an environmentally sound operation. In fact, I actually think fracking is a 'green' thing."

How can fracking be green?

In a lot of ways. First, natural gas is cleaner and produces far fewer emissions when used as an energy source and combusted. Second, fracking accelerates America's economy and ability to stand apart from other less environmentally strict oil-producing nations. "Everyone I meet today believes the entire shale development process is all about fracking," Spigelmyer explained. "It's not. It's about American energy security. Technical improvements have allowed us to produce gas from much vaster amounts of acreage and from a single well pad with less surface disruption."

Long Life to the Well

How long will these new "unconventional" wells last? When will they peak? When will they tap out? What's the average? Though some critics have claimed that certain individual wells have been tapped out in less than a decade, the new Marcellus wells could last for several decades to half a century.

"This is a pretty young field; most of the gas wells here have only been drilled and fractured since 2008 or later," Spigelmyer said. "What we've seen so far is that the decline curve is a little less steep than the historic

Appalachian vertical well, where roughly half of production occurs in the first twenty-four months. The fractured wells are expected to produce for many decades. Some of the hydraulically fractured wells have yielded more than 1 million cubic feet of wet gas per day. The technology is so recent that long-term production data isn't available.

"The Renz No. 1 Well, for example, the first in this area, has lasted ten years so far. I haven't heard of anyone having to plug the wells after six to eight years of operation," Spigelmyer said.

The Marcellus, now counted among the most productive shale gas plays in North America and the world, actually dwarfs the Texas Barnett Shale that was successfully tapped first. Mitchell Energy successfully fractured the first unconventional shale well in the late 1990s in the Barnett Shale. But as former Mitchell geologist Dan Steward reminded my team in a separate conversation in Spring 2014, "Keep in mind: It was industry as a whole, not just Mitchell. The U.S. Department of Energy and the Gas Research Institute were funneling money into other companies, as well, for doing large fracks—Mitchell was just one of them, and the first one was, in fact, the Cotton Valley Limestone. It just so happened that George Mitchell was the first to take what industry and the government were trying to do and apply it to shales." Because of the work of these shale pioneers, the Barnett now produces roughly 5 percent of all U.S. natural gas.

Amazingly, the Marcellus in Pennsylvania produces five times that much.

Natural gas production in the Pennsylvanian commonwealth increased by 72 percent from 2011 to 2012 alone, the biggest jump out of all the major gas-producing states. Shale development has created an estimated 30,000-plus jobs directly related to the energy-extraction process, and another 170,000 or more jobs because of the upstream and downstream supply chain. The numbers could push much higher if Pennsylvania and surrounding states fully develop the Marcellus.[1]

In addition, there are geopolitical benefits few people outside the local community can see. "I don't know if any of you hear enough about this, but in this community, you see signs that say Drill a Well, Bring a Soldier Home," Spigelmyer noted. "Yet every time you Google 'fracturing' you see signs saying 'Stop Fracking Now.' This is a community whose economic activity grows all the time, and there are signs like Drill a Well, Bring a Soldier Home that never see the light of day anywhere else."

So what's the connection between wells and soldiers?

"We have soldiers abroad protecting the free flow supply of oil. However, if we have energy security here at home through shale development, we can bring a soldier home from overseas," Spigelmyer explained.

New Opportunities, Growing as Fast as a Child

Certainly some issues remain unresolved in the Marcellus, such as the pushback from opponents over development. In New York, opponents have blocked the ability to use hydraulic fracturing as a well completion technique. As such, policies such as those adopted in New York fuel the debate in other regions. In Pennsylvania, debate continues about the prospects for additional taxes—companies already pay a 3.1 percent "impact fee," which is a euphemism for a tax.

In addition, the sheer drop in prices for gas and oil has set the shale energy industry on a roller coaster. No one knows the outcome, but competition and a glut of energy can squeeze producers and result in rig reductions (already seen in Marcellus in early 2015) and delay or cancellation of new projects.

Spigelmyer wasn't terribly worried. "This winter, the price of natural gas for consumers is around $10 per million cubic feet. That's half of what it was in 2008," he said. "Actually, the prices could be good for everyone because we now are truly competitive in our energy prices compared with anyone else, and that's already encouraging new growth in major manufacturing here.

"We're going to see new opportunities in manufacturing: steel, glass, plastics, chemicals, fertilizers, powdered metals, pharmaceuticals, all dependent on using affordable and abundant natural gas. Foreign investors are already showing up from Japan and China," he continued.

"I spoke the other day at Clarion University, and the head of the Jefferson County Economic Development Authority said he *never* expected to see a rural county like Jefferson hosting foreign investors who are visiting for possible manufacturing ventures. It's incredible. We have an opportunity today to generate enormous numbers of manufacturing jobs right here at home if we get this opportunity right."

Dave Spigelmyer on Shale Development, Gas Prices, and International Competition—December 2, 2014

As president of the Pittsburgh-based Marcellus Shale Coalition (MSC), the region's largest shale energy trade association, David Spigelmyer represents some 300 member companies. Working closely with legislators, regulators, international visitors, and the civic community, Spigelmyer is a champion of shale development, economic growth, and environmental safety in the Appalachian region. He was a public service major at Penn State University and later worked for National Fuel Gas in Buffalo, CNG (bought by Dominion Resources), EQT, and as vice president of Chesapeake Energy Corporation's Appalachia division.

An avid outdoorsman, he said he favors any energy source that can be developed in an environmentally responsible fashion, brings jobs, and can be used safely. Spigelmyer was instrumental in the MSC's founding in 2008. Working closely on association standards of conduct and development of its guiding principles with Tom Ridge, former Pennsylvania governor and first U.S. Secretary of Homeland Security, Spigelmyer has served as the MSC's chairman, vice-chairman, and lead of its legislative committee. He's also a spokesman for a Pennsylvania he loves, and though he avows no expertise in international energy relations, he was outspoken about current issues we share here.

Q: How has shale energy development affected our international out-look for energy imports?

A: The liquids produced in shale here have had a significant impact on world oil and gas supplies and prices. We've moved from 57 percent dependency on foreign oil sources to 43 percent, and the numbers are dropping quickly. The same holds true for natural gas. We're now seeing the effects at the pump. Oil has dropped to below $45/barrel, and natural gas in 2008 was $13.71 at the wellhead and nearly $20 per thousand cubic feet delivered to consumers. Today it's less than half that. The Marcellus is already providing 25 percent of America's gas needs. We're going to top 5.3 trillion cubic feet in the Marcellus region, including West Virginia, Ohio, and Pennsylvania. It's incredible. In '08 we produced only a quarter of the state's gas supply at 180 billion cubic feet. Today we produce 4 trillion cubic feet alone in Pennsylvania. And then there's the Utica Shale that we're only beginning to explore.

Q: You sound happy.

A: It's an incredible journey.

Q: But energy prices are dropping so fast. OPEC this past December decided not to pull back on production—apparently with some motivation to drive out U.S. shale producers by making energy so cheap it would not pay for them to operate. And there has been so much opposition at home to shale development.

A: The story doesn't get told very often, but you'd think the American public would be more astute when countries like the United Arab Emirates (UAE) and Venezuela fund [anti-fracturing] movies like *Gasland* to create skepticism about shale. These countries' motivation is to vilify U.S. operations and stop the activity.

Q: Did the UAE and Venezuela actually do that?

A: Yes.

Q: Have you heard of any companies that will have to stop drilling projects because of the costs and declining energy prices?

A: It's a huge investment absolutely; the average cost of a well in Pennsylvania is about $7 million. Some companies have reduced their drilling and fracking rig numbers since 2012. We had 140 rigs in 2012, and we've lost about 60 rigs from pricing pressure.

Q: But how can these companies continue?

A: This area in southwest Pennsylvania is a liquids-rich region under significant pricing pressure. Marcellus is a 380-million-year-old stack shale formation. It produces natural gas and liquids, primarily ethane, pentane, butane, isobutane, propane, and hexane. It's a wet gas play, and it's remained lucrative even at low prices.

Q: How far can oil and gas companies be stretched? Halliburton, for example, lost $23 billion this quarter in value because of dropping energy prices. Many believe, and certainly the folks at Canary believe, that Americans should push to open up our oil and gas markets for exporting abroad.

A: It would help our country's geopolitical position, and you're going to see more of that debate. Though some of the public is skeptical about exports—they believe it's going to push our oil and gas products overseas and increase prices here—well, I don't want to be naïve; there could be a little bit of a price increase, but there's so much gas on the market today that big price jumps are unlikely anytime soon. We're producing 16 billion cubic feet a day of gas, and we're so far ahead of where anyone expected us to be.

Q: Where is Marcellus gas being shipped?

A: The Cove Point project off the coast of Maryland is probably the closest point of delivery for Marcellus gas. It's capable of processing a billion to 1.5 billion cubic feet a day. But that's less than 5 percent of the [local] natural gas that could go that way. Exporting gas really wouldn't strap the market for supply. I think exports make perfect sense.

Q: Have natural gas and liquids infrastructure projects been going on a long time?

A: You bet. Many of southwestern Pennsylvania's liquids have been targeted for transportation into the Pennsylvania Mariner East Pipeline. Northeastern Pennsylvania dry gas has been tagged for transportation into Williams/Transco's Atlantic Sunrise Project, and there's pressure to find available markets. Right now we need capacity to move the volume of gas, and we have a significant shortage of pipelines available. There's currently a "spot reduction," or basis differential that shaves up to $2 off the Henry Hub price (today $3) per thousand cubic feet. Companies are taking a $2 haircut on gas commodity sales, plus another 60 cents to gather the gas. Consequently, much of the Marcellus gas today is being sold at $1 to $1.50 per thousand cubic feet.

Q: Really low. Can they still afford to do that?

A: People are trying to hold acreage, and if you're in a really good gas production area, the volume can make up for it in production. That's why there has been a battle in Pennsylvania about taxes. It's tight right now. And I've been adamant about the fact that you should allow an energy industry foundation to be built first here before you put additional taxes on it.

Q: Do you think Congress will liberalize and expedite permits for liquefied natural gas (LNG) exports and build terminals to process them faster? These terminals are said to cost $10 billion each, and there's been a real lag in the approval process for gas exports.

A: Some of the LNG terminals are already built. For example, we have gas terminals in the U.S. set up for imports, but these facilities can be turned around to accommodate LNG processing *for exports*. Cove Point was an import facility in order to supply additional gas to Washington, D.C., and Baltimore. They can turn this process around [for export], but the D.C., Baltimore, and Philadelphia regions are still dependent on gas from the Gulf Coast and Midwest. That's because the original pipeline infrastructure was set up from south to north.

Q: So what can be done about it?

A: We're working on that now. By 2020, roughly one-third of our gas will be moving north to south instead of south to north.

Q: How much have we reduced our natural gas imports?

A: I don't have a direct figure on that, but we were taking as much as 3 trillion cubic feet of gas out of Canada. Now we're producing so much natural gas that I can't imagine importing it—unless there is a niche market that doesn't have the pipeline infrastructure to get gas to it.

Q: So will Congress really liberalize the export rules for both oil and gas?

A: I think there will be a fight, but we are a capitalist society, and we should be able to open markets that strengthen our geopolitical standing as a nation and create jobs.

Q: What about international energy competition, especially from Russia? Their economy isn't doing well now: inflation, devaluation of the ruble, European sanctions for aggression in Ukraine.

A: Vladimir Putin has an extraordinary amount of power. But, unfortunately, you've got to fight fire with fire. And we (our nation) must get an appetite to fight fire with fire. That's where energy comes into play. I think the Ukrainian situation will be a driver in this. Putin has been able to wield such control over the energy market over there. But with an open supply of energy coming from the U.S. and a robust energy export market, we can change that dynamic pretty quickly.

We have an opportunity today to generate enormous numbers of manufacturing jobs if we get it right. A short time ago, I was given the opportunity to discuss energy production with Dr. Mohammed Bin Hamed Al Rumhy, the minister of oil and gas from Oman. Minister Ruhmy was educated at Oklahoma State, and he discussed his personal role in the Middle East peace process. He's working especially hard to broker a much softer dialogue between Iran and the U.S. Al Rumhy said, "If I'm not successful, the Middle East loses because your group is moving so quickly into an energy leadership position. You guys have been the leaders in horizontal shale development, and we're trying to learn from you!" It's been a real eye opener.

CHAPTER 12

BOOM! WORKING GIRL TRICKONOMICS AND OTHER SHADY SPOTS

Pan to Williston, North Dakota, the poster city for shale's ability to catapult a lagging state economy from thirty-eighth to first, in terms of per-capita gross domestic product (GDP).[1]

The year was 2013. Local headlines in the *Williston Herald* read "Looking Ahead to the Limitless Possibilities of a New Year" (December 29, 2012) and "Sales Tax Collections Dip, Still Lead State" (July 19, 2013). Further afield, the *Bismarck Tribune* had no dearth of good news to report: "Oil Contributed $30.4B to State's Economy" (March 13, 2013); "Budget Surplus Estimate Keeps Growing (June 18, 2013); and "Beulah, Watford City Ranked in Top 10 Cities for Young Families" (December 11, 2013). Even the venerated *Wall Street Journal* paid attention to this once-sleepy frontier 2,000 miles away: "In North Dakota, a Burst of Energy: State Undergoes Refining Renaissance Fueled by Sharp Rise in Oil Production" (April 10, 2013).

The oil was flowing, and the Bakken region was booming. Rough-and-ready workers flocked to North Dakota for its promises of hard work and high wages. They weren't disappointed, and they settled in for the long haul, dollar signs dominating their dreams. But despite the abundance of oil to be extracted and the barrels of money to be made, not everyone in the Bakken was wearing rose-colored glasses.

"An Oil Town Where Men are Many, and Women are Hounded"
The New York Times, January 15, 2013

The female population was one segment—albeit a small one—of this society that encountered some negatives to the Bakken boom. Amid a mass influx of mostly men into once-stagnant towns such as Williston, women suddenly became scarce—and so did many of the men's sex lives.

The result? Single, available females (and maybe even some who were not so available) became a coveted commodity in this town, especially in the eyes of the hordes of workers who trekked to Williston to capture their own piece of the Bakken bounty.

With a population that swelled by more than 127% between 2010 and 2012,[2] Williston definitely qualifies as a boomtown. But it seems there wasn't enough "boom boom" going on to satisfy the male energy suffusing Williston, which was benefiting and, in some ways, breaking under the strain of the sudden and massive oil and gas production brought on by the Bakken.

The population census revealed that, in 2011, 58 percent of people in North Dakota ages eighteen to thirty-five were men, but the Bakken area boasted an even more lopsided man-to-woman ratio. Even the official count of 1.6 men for every woman didn't tell the whole sad story. That figure only represents those who reported the state as their permanent residence, which many of the short-term oil labor and construction workers didn't do.[3] In fact, some estimates put the male-to-female ratio at nearly 2 to 1.

A love story in the making for the ladies? Hardly.

It meant that even a routine trip to the local Walmart often turned into an exercise in exasperation. Women reported being followed, repeatedly and aggressively propositioned and even harassed while trying to buy groceries. Many began to limit their shopping to daylight hours and to avoid the local nightlife scene.

Heidi McCormick could relate. She moved with her family to Williston from Spokane Valley, Washington, in 2009, when her husband landed a job with a local company that heats water to aid the drilling process. Although she was never personally harassed or had problems with men, her daughter experienced a scare in—you guessed it—Walmart.

"She was followed by a group of about four or five men two years ago when she was sixteen," McCormick related in a May 2014 personal interview with my team.

Her daughter quickly sought out her boyfriend, who was in another part of the store, and the men scattered. But that incident, along with the 2012 kidnapping and killing of teacher Sherry Arnold by oil-field workers in nearby Montana, put McCormick and others on their guard and spurred her to obtain a concealed weapons permit.

"Everyone was freaked out about that," she said.

Both McCormick and her daughter began carrying pepper spray, and McCormick kept a gun in her purse—just in case. Fortunately, she never had cause to use it.

This situation wasn't limited to newcomers. In a *New York Times* report, lifelong Williston resident Megan Dye, twenty-eight, lamented how her life has changed because of the shale boom. "So many people look at you like you're a piece of meat," she said. "It's disgusting."[4]

The shortage of women spelled opportunity for some savvy entrepreneurs in the sex industry. Looking to cash in on the sex-starved drillers, professional strippers and escorts began routinely flying in from Las Vegas for one night at a time, quickly scoring a large payday.

The testosterone-loaded small town also began experiencing its share of bar fights. Nightly brawls, an influx of "working girls," and a rapidly changing landscape—the scene seems strangely reminiscent of another time in American history, one also fraught with lawlessness and debauchery and marked by rapid change. Williston, North Dakota, looked to be the Wild West of the twenty-first century.

"Sushi, Craft Beer and $5 Coffee Come to North Dakota"
CNBC, November 15, 2013

If you based your impression of North Dakota solely on the snow-covered scenes in the quirky murder mystery movie *Fargo*, the image brought to mind would be accurate, if not even a little bit charitable.

In this place where the thermometer struggles to rally above two degrees in January, cities like Fargo are the exception. Most of the landscape is vast and unsettled, with snow-drenched white expanses of pressing nothingness stretching for miles. Ghost towns are real here. They're not just long-gone realities in the pages of books; instead, they're something you can actually drive through and observe beyond your car window.

But panning back through our 2013 retrospective of newspaper headlines, we see that, as the epicenter of U.S. shale development, tundralike North Dakota had become one of the nation's hottest areas for both job and population growth. Parts of North Dakota had changed and developed so much that they were hardly recognizable compared to only a decade before.

In Williston in 2013, you could eat at Basil, the new Asian fusion restaurant that barely accommodated the crush of patrons who came to sip the sake and sample the sushi. Afterward, you might visit the Williston Brewing Company, where beer connoisseurs—or wannabes—tried out one of the forty specialty beers on tap or any of the eighty bottled brews. The caffeine-deprived could also grab a fancy latte at Boomtown Babes Espresso, a hot-pink drive-through coffee kiosk that typically boasts a line of waiting customers. This was vastly different from what you could experience in Williston just a few years earlier.

After the fusion feast and a couple of brews or a late-night java, it would be about time to make your way back home. But where was home?

At the boom's beginning, the flood of workers who couldn't find room at the local hotels spilled out into the town, with thousands living in RVs in makeshift campgrounds. At times, even some of Canary's employees slept in their cars or in tents pitched along the side of the road.

And then many laborers found their way into "man camps." These crop-housing options sprouted up in communities around shale country as temporary solutions to the severe housing crunch caused by the inundation of workers pouring in.

"Man camps" have sprung up all over shale country to meet the skyrocketing demand for housing.

Turns out, these man camps have been far from temporary. These housing arrangements are still one of the only options for many oil-field workers. And conditions in these camps vary widely. Researchers at the University of North Dakota have revealed that some have amenities like catering and recreation activities, while others don't even have regular access to power and water.[5]

Nathan Nider lived for three months in cramped quarters in a company-sponsored man camp in Watford City, near Williston. That was about as much as he could take.

"When I first got up here [in 2010] I swore the devil lived in Watford

City," he told my team in a personal interview in May 2014. "I witnessed thefts, crime, drug use, and a lot of drinking. I saw guys get in fights over toilet paper, and I heard about a guy pulling out a gun on his [longtime friend and roommate] over who was going to wash the dishes. And who policed that? There was no security and nothing that was going to stop anything that was happening."

Hailing from Kansas, Nider first arrived in North Dakota to take a job as a truck driver, bringing his wife and four children with him. He now works as a district casing manager for a different company. Initially, he worked two jobs and averaged about three hours of sleep a night in the man camp while his family lived in a rented home two and a half hours away.

He said problems in man camps are inevitable and widespread, and until the housing supply can satisfy the intense demand, he doesn't anticipate the situation getting any better.

"First and foremost, there are so many different types of people, they're all money-hungry, and everybody comes up on their last dollar. It's unreal," he said. "Beds are strewn everywhere, clothes are on the floor, there's no furniture, it's dirty, and there's no comfort whatsoever. It's just raw."

Nider said these types of conditions don't lend themselves to the kind of decompression and relaxation these men crave after working long, grueling hours.

"You have guys who are fatigued and irritated, and they have no place to release their frustration, so it creates a lot of anxiety," he said.

Despite the rough conditions Nider suffered initially, he said if he had to do it all again he would.

"Looking back it was all worth it."

"Williston, ND, Oil Boom Means Rents as High as New York City's"
AOL Real Estate, January 14, 2013

In addition to man camps and roadside tents, many oil-field workers made their homes in campers and trailers parked in the Williston Walmart. Problems soon followed, and store officials were forced to respond.

The mega-retailer eventually resorted to ordering them off the property or risk having their vehicles towed. According to flyers Walmart distributed in 2012, the long-term squatters were causing "safety, noise, litter, and property-damage problems."[6] Those using the parking lot as their home base were told they had one day to leave. The move worked, and the parking lot was soon cleared—but it also ruffled feathers in the process. Some oil-field workers pulled their patronage of Walmart: If their vehicles had to go elsewhere, so would their money.

With so many issues resulting from these man camps and people's natural wish to settle into long-term housing, developers began scrambling to cash in. As a result, homes for the house-hungry popped up like popcorn in North Dakota, where the real estate industry expanded by 9 percent between 2007 and 2012.[7]

But despite the need and the desire to build, housing developers have found that's not always enough to get the job done. Construction efforts have been thwarted as supplies have become scarce in the midst of the boom. Even basics like concrete have proven hard to come by. Plus, it's difficult to find enough workers to complete the housing developments quickly enough—and if workers come from another area, then they need somewhere to live, too.

In mid-2013, it was reported that six new housing units were built every day in Williston, but North Dakota state economist Nancy Hodur reported that 14,000 new units were still needed.[8] This high demand and low supply created a seller's market, causing housing prices to skyrocket.

Nathan Nider had strong words for the apartment and home prices he's seen in his adopted state: "There is no justice when it comes to what people are charging up here."

"An Oil Boom Takes a Toll on Health Care"
The New York Times, January 27, 2013

Housing isn't the only industry that struggles to keep up with the exploding population of a boomtown. Health care struggles, too.

Waiting in an emergency room is an exercise in patience anywhere, but people in Williston in 2013 couldn't be blamed if their patience began wearing thin. The city's only hospital saw emergency room visits increase 50 percent in a year and was witnessing average wait times of at least two hours. Overworked hospital staffers were forced to turn away 30 percent of patients seeking medical services each day because there simply weren't enough health-care providers.[9]

Heidi McCormick, the gun-toting Williston newbie, said that a couple of clinics, in addition to the city's one hospital, served the sick. But, she said, receiving timely preventative care was still a challenge.

"You have a better chance of being squeezed in if you are a patient of record, but they do have spots reserved for emergencies," she said. "These spots fill up fast, so you have to call first thing in the morning."

Schools were packed as well, as more and more oil-field workers have relocated their families to North Dakota and taken up permanent residence. Viola LaFontaine, superintendent for Williston's public schools, reported in 2014 that the past few years had seen an increase of more than 1,000 students. Seventy percent of those students were in elementary school. Williston was the fastest-growing public school district in the state and badly in need of more teachers and new facilities.[10]

And then there's the traffic—and other infrastructure problems. The local budget hasn't been able to cover all the expenses needed to keep up with the escalating population. Williston's new infrastructure demands in 2013, just to keep up with the influx of Bakken oil workers, was running into the neighborhood of $625 million,[11] with improvements needed at the airport, on roads, in water supplies, and for other basic facilities. In fact, the city's wastewater treatment facility was even reaching capacity—without these upgrades (at price tags upward of $100 million), the city considered the need to halt building permits and restrict further development.

"Showing Williston the Money"
Williston Herald, September 23, 2014

Of course, there's an upside to all these growing pains: money.

People flocked to North Dakota in 2013 and are still streaming in today because there are good-paying jobs—plenty of them—and not just in the oil patch! With all the labor going to the oil industry, other segments have found attractive ways to lure staffers.

Registered nurses, for example, are scoring bonuses up to $5,000 up front when they sign on the dotted line. The local Walmart also resorted to offering up $17/hour paychecks in its attempt to secure lasting employees. That makes the Williston store the highest-paying Walmart in the country.[12] Fast food has followed suit. The town's Hardee's franchise offers up to $15/hour,[13] while the local McDonald's upped the ante even more: full medical benefits and a $300 signing bonus to staffers.[14]

All that money flying around leads to one of the biggest pros of a shale boomtown: a big boost to the local economy. Because Americans are known more for their spending sprees than their saving habits, it's likely that 95 percent of each individual windfall will find its way back into the marketplace. And although those dollars represent just a fraction of all consumer spending, they matter—and they add to overall economic growth.

What's more, those dollars are mobile. With these propped-up paychecks comes more spending power and, in the case of workers relocating to boomtowns to earn heftier salaries, it stands to reason that those dollars will travel. Think of the "working girl" who makes her fast money in Williston but then heads back to Las Vegas, where she buys her groceries, fills up her gas tank, or even does a little gambling. Think of the young nurse who heads north to work in the medical field but returns home regularly, meeting friends to shop or dining in restaurants with family she hasn't seen in several months.

"U.S. Oil Notches Record Growth: Rise in Production Is World's Largest; Fueled by Fracking"
The Wall Street Journal, June 12, 2013

An industry's "employment multiplier" measures the contribution that its jobs make to the economy; the larger the multiplier, the greater the ripple effect of support jobs and residual economic benefits across the broader economy. Returning to 2013 in Williston, North Dakota, we see that the oil-and-gas employment multiplier surpassed finance, construction, and many manufacturing sectors. In fact, the unconventional oil and gas industry was projected to support 3.3 million jobs by 2020 and 3.9 million just five years later.[15]

Those jobs aren't just in the oil industry. They're created on three fronts: direct (e.g., at oil exploration companies), indirect (e.g., in supply industries), and induced. That last category includes positions in consumer goods and services that increase to meet the demand of the new directly employed workers, like the restaurant server who takes the order of the driller with income to spend.

Since the Great Recession of 2008, employment has surged the most among direct jobs in states with shale production. For example, Texas, Pennsylvania, California, Louisiana, and Colorado all added tens of thousands of jobs linked to shale development: Texas (where shale development has created 575,000 jobs to date); Pennsylvania (102,600 jobs); California (96,500 jobs); Louisiana (78,900 jobs); and Colorado (77,600 jobs).

It's hard to imagine any other single industry contributing more than that.

Shale's employment multiplier in 2013 could be seen in nonproducing states that sold goods and services involved in shale's supply chain. For example, New Jersey–based Linde, the world's largest industrial gas company, added hundreds of new jobs to reach employment of more than 1,000—a far cry from what appeared to be its imminent closure ten years

WHEN THE OIL AND GAS INDUSTRY BOOMS, OTHERS FOLLOW

Industries across the board experience indirect and induced growth from shale.

Manufacturing
Costs decline from lower natural gas prices and increased demand for goods

Railroads
Increase in shipments of crude oil

Construction
Building of new roads, drilling infrastructure, housing, commercial space, and airports

Professional Services
Banks, financial services, and law firms expanding to meet new local demands

State Treasury
Increased state tax revenue from more workers with higher wages

Airline Industry
Regional airport expansions and increased passenger load

Real Estate
Greater demand for home ownership

Hospitality
Fully booked hotels, new properties constructed

Trucking
Increase in shipments of crude oil and supplies for local industry

ago.[16] Other states with high numbers of indirect and induced jobs were Illinois (38,600 jobs), Michigan (37,800 jobs), Missouri (37,700 jobs), and Florida (36,500 jobs).[17]

What's more, the supply chain associated with shale production—which creates the indirect jobs—is based almost entirely in the U.S. Fracking technology showcases some of the best domestic intellectual capital—it became a widespread industry practice here years before it was used in other areas of the world. As a result, many of the specialized equipment, machinery, and tools required for the procedure have been designed and manufactured right here in the United States. That means that even states that aren't participating in shale extraction can benefit financially.

A 2013 study from the Federal Reserve Bank of Minneapolis[18] shows this Bakken "ripple effect" well. The researchers aimed to find out if North Dakota's shale oil activity influenced employment and wages even farther afield than the Bakken's immediate vicinity. Did the massive shale play's good fortune seep into neighboring counties or even to adjoining states?

To assess the Bakken effect, the bank plotted data in 100-mile concentric circles moving away from the twelve counties that comprise the shale region's core. At first blush, the results don't seem like much of a surprise: The closer to the Bakken, the greater the benefit in terms of higher wages and lower unemployment.

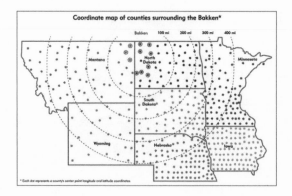

But closer inspection reveals a more gripping story. Even workers living 100–400 miles away from the Bakken's core faced a brighter economic picture of higher wages and better employment prospects than U.S. employees as a whole.

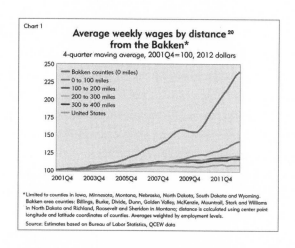

Chart 1

Average weekly wages by distance [20] from the Bakken*

4-quarter moving average, 2001Q4=100, 2012 dollars

— Bakken counties (0 miles)
— 0 to 100 miles
— 100 to 200 miles
— 200 to 300 miles
— 300 to 400 miles
— United States

*Limited to counties in Iowa, Minnesota, Montana, Nebraska, North Dakota, South Dakota and Wyoming. Bakken area counties: Billings, Burke, Divide, Dunn, Golden Valley, McKenzie, Mountrail, Stark and Williams in North Dakota and Richland, Roosevelt and Sheridan in Montana; distance is calculated using center point longitude and latitude coordinates of counties. Averages weighted by employment levels.

Source: Estimates based on Bureau of Labor Statistics, QCEW data

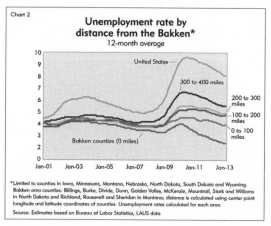

Chart 2

Unemployment rate by distance from the Bakken*

12-month average

United States

300 to 400 miles

200 to 300 miles

100 to 200 miles

0 to 100 miles

Bakken counties (0 miles)

*Limited to counties in Iowa, Minnesota, Montana, Nebraska, North Dakota, South Dakota and Wyoming. Bakken area counties: Billings, Burke, Divide, Dunn, Golden Valley, McKenzie, Mountrail, Stark and Williams in North Dakota and Richland, Roosevelt and Sheridan in Montana; distance is calculated using center point longitude and latitude coordinates of counties. Unemployment rates calculated for each area.

Source: Estimates based on Bureau of Labor Statistics, LAUS data

This ripple effect was true not only for North Dakota's Bakken but for other shale plays, as well, like Pennsylvania's Marcellus.

There is no doubt that the Keystone State benefited from an abundance of drilling, but even residents living in cities far from the shale fields played their own roles in the industry and saw dollar-boosting results in the process.

Two towns near Pittsburgh, Pennsylvania, couldn't boast of oil and gas gushers, but they did produce their own type of gushers that the energy industry needs. The towns sold more than 300 million gallons of essential water to CONSOL Energy for use at their fracking sites. As a result of this arrangement, money coming into the township's municipal water authorities not only kept water rates stable for residential customers but also provided funds for needed water-line and sewer improvements.[21]

For what may be the most compelling example yet of shale's ability to spread economic goodness, look to Arizona's real estate market. Although it's 1,500 miles from the Bakken and nowhere near any other direct shale activity, Arizona's housing industry has gotten an unexpected boost from North Dakota's oil bonanza. Because 2013 home prices in Phoenix and other cities were still low, North Dakotans whose businesses or land were purchased by oil and gas companies began heading south to warmer climates. In fact, a suburban Phoenix real estate agent originally from Minot, North Dakota, reported selling eight homes to former North Dakotans.

And there are dozens of other shales covering a wide expanse of the U.S. that began generating their own multiplier effects.

Back in 2013, experts expected this trickle effect to continue well into the future. IHS, a provider of market and economic information, extrapolated that household disposable income from increased activity in the shale value chain should reach $2,000 by 2015. Looking farther down the road to 2025, the organization predicted household gains of more than $3,500 per year.[22]

2013 Snapshot of Shale's "Ripple Effect"

State	Main Shale Plays	Local Benefits as of 2013
Alabama	Floyd-Neal/ Conasauga	Alabama's energy prices were 5 percent lower than the national average, due to its considerable conventional and unconventional natural gas reserves, numerous oil refineries within the state lines, and proximity to the Gulf of Mexico. Its three refineries increased the state's oil production by 35 percent in the last two years.
Alaska	North Slope	While the region's supply of easy-to-recover oil has dwindled in recent years, the U.S. Geological Survey estimated that the North Slope's shale rock could hold as much as 2 billion barrels of recoverable oil (the second-biggest deposit of unconventional crude after North Dakota's Bakken and more than Texas's Eagle Ford) and 80 trillion cubic feet of gas (the fourth-largest gas-shale deposit in the country).
Arkansas	Fayetteville	Oil and gas jobs in the state rose 120 percent from 2004 to 2008 and were paying better than average. The 36,000 unconventional sector jobs in Arkansas created in 2010 were projected to swell to 54,000 by 2015 and 80,000 by 2035.
Colorado	Niobrara, Green River	In 2012, oil and gas contributed $29.6 billion to the state's economy and $3.8 billion in employee income to Colorado households. Oil and gas also added 110,000 high-paying jobs. Production increases drove the state's natural gas prices to historical lows, dropping average Colorado household energy costs to 23 percent less than the national average.
Illinois	New Albany	A range of economic outcomes could benefit Illinois through expanded natural gas production, with the most conservative estimates of 1,000-plus jobs and $1 billion-plus in economic impact.
Indiana	New Albany	Indiana could host ten or more new chemical industry projects, due to competitive prices of natural gas.

Continued

State	Main Shale Plays	Local Benefits as of 2013
Kansas	Excello-Mulky, Mississippian Lime	Unconventionals amounted to just 3.8 percent of the state total, but their proliferation could bring investments into the billions of dollars and thousands of jobs to Kansas over the next twenty to thirty years.
Kentucky	Big Sandy, New Albany	Proposed transportation fuel projects such as the Bluegrass Pipeline, with a projected capacity of 200,000 barrels a day, would stimulate Kentucky's centrally located economy and encourage more investments through shale-friendly policies.
Louisiana	Haynesville	Energy activities brought in $7 billion to the state and created 57,000 jobs in 2009 alone, and the state announced $50 billion capital investment in 2012–13. The 81,000 jobs created in 2010 were expected to increase to 125,000 jobs by 2015 and to 200,000 jobs by 2035.
Michigan	Antrim	In 2010, the Antrim was the thirteenth-largest natural gas producer in the U.S., with an average estimated ultimate recovery (EUR) of 0.28 billion cubic feet per well and 19.9 trillion cubic feet of technically recoverable gas.
Mississippi	Floyd-Neal/ Conasauga, Tuscaloosa Marine	Although much is unproven, the state has prospects for economic quantities of shale oil as recovery techniques continue to improve. Shale-friendly legislation has encouraged many major drillers to set up operations.
Montana	Bakken	Higher individual income tax collections led to a budget surplus of $102.4 million for fiscal 2013, nearly 25 percent more than estimated.
Nebraska	Niobrara	Horizontal drilling interest in Nebraska has increased over the past five years due to the state's flexible permitting process and less restrictive regulatory environment than its neighbors.
New Mexico	Avalon/Bone Springs, Lewis	Energy operations grew from less than 1 percent of total state employment in 2000 to 4 percent in 2011. Oil and gas extraction's share in the state GDP was 5.1 percent in 2010.

State	Main Shale Plays	Local Benefits as of 2013
North Dakota	Bakken	By 2013, North Dakota had the nation's highest state GDP per capita (29 percent above the national average), highest per-capita GDP increase (13.4 percent), highest population growth (4 percent in just two years), and lowest unemployment rate (3.2 percent statewide, 1.8 percent in the Bakken). Shale development was credited with adding 20,000 temporary drilling jobs, 12,000 temporary infrastructure jobs, and 2,000–3,000 permanent jobs each year. In 2013, wages in the Bakken for all industries were up 40 percent from 2009.
Ohio	Marcellus, Utica	Shale development has generated $900 million in state and local government revenue. In 2012 alone, shale added $4.1 billion to Ohio's gross state product, produced $2.5 billion of labor income, and saw 20 percent higher sales tax revenues in the shale regions than in 2011.
Oklahoma	Fayetteville, Woodford	Oklahoma's unconventional energy sector generated 28,000 jobs in 2010. This number was projected to hit 42,000 jobs by 2015 and 69,000 jobs by 2035.
Pennsylvania	Marcellus, Utica	As of Q2 2013, new shale jobs were up 35 percent compared to 2010; by 2020, Marcellus could support more than 211,000 fracking jobs across the state. Pennsylvania oil-field workers' salaries averaged $25,000 more than the overall state average.
South Dakota	Bakken	South Dakota manufacturing, modular home construction, and professional services industries benefited substantially from the Bakken boom, filling in the gaps where North Dakota firms are overwhelmed.
Texas	Barnett, Eagle Ford, Granite Wash, Haynesville, Permian Basin (Cline, Wolfcamp), Woodford	In May 2013, Texas accounted for 34.5 percent of all U.S. oil production. In August 2013, seven of Forbes's top ten "best cities for future job growth" were in Texas. In 2012 alone, the economic impact from the Eagle Ford was $61 billion from 116,000 jobs created, $1.2 billion in state tax revenues, and $1 billion-plus in municipal tax revenues. The Cline's total economic impact across an eleven-county region was projected at $30 billion annually.

Continued

State	Main Shale Plays	Local Benefits as of 2013
Utah	Mancos	As of 2013, Utah expected substantial expansion to bring in $10 billion in capital investments and $5 billion in taxes and royalties over the next decade, as well as 36,500 new jobs by 2015 and 51,000 jobs by 2035.
Virginia	Big Sandy, Marcellus	Although Virginia produces relatively small amounts of shale gas, its proximity to high-producing neighbors has boosted its energy economy.
West Virginia	Marcellus, Utica	Average income for Wheeling residents rose by 3.1 percent from 2012 to 2013; 1 percent job growth and 2 percent per-capita income growth was likely each year until 2018. West Virginia's shale energy development has already supported 12,000 extraction jobs and generated $280 million in state and local revenue. In 2012 alone, shale added $1.6 billion to the gross state product and $794 million in labor income.
Wyoming	Hilliard-Baxter-Mancos, Niobrara	Unconventional energy development in Wyoming generated 35,000 jobs in 2010 and was expected to produce 48,000 jobs by 2015 and 79,000 jobs by 2035.

Americans Benefit from Tax Revenue

Of course, when individual incomes go up, so do taxes paid to state treasuries. In 2013 North Dakota, for example, the state's coffers were swollen with a billion-dollar budget surplus—and were expected to increase even more given a tripling in the number of taxpayers reporting adjusted gross income exceeding $1 million.

But that's nothing compared to the amount of money that the energy industry was spending on development. In 2012, spending on drilling, completion, facilities, and gathering systems reached $87.3 billion. That figure was expected to more than double by 2020 (to $172.5 billion) and more than quadruple by 2035, when it should reach $353.1 billion. Overall, between 2012 and 2035, the energy industry was projecting investments of more than $5.1 trillion in energy development in the United States.[23]

During the same twenty-two-year period, the increased production of goods and services related to continued shale development could contribute as much as $475 billion to GDP. Tax revenue would also expand: Per the 2012 projections, the cumulative tax contribution from the oil and gas revolution would surpass $2.5 trillion by 2035.[24] About half of that would go to the federal government, which might consider this source as it struggles to develop long-term strategies for reducing the national debt.

It's undeniable that the U.S. economy has benefited from shale production—just like any other industry that creates many jobs and spends a lot of money. And even those citizens who didn't personally feel the positive ramification through the jobs, wages, and indirect spending of shale production were benefiting from the many taxes sent back into the state and federal governments.

A Renaissance in U.S. Manufacturing?

The early years of the twenty-first century dealt a life-threatening blow to U.S. manufacturing, if not exactly a nail in the coffin. Long a key traded sector in the American economy, manufacturing simply seemed to hit a wall.

Hobbled by overseas outfits that could do the same work with lower labor expenses, American factories began to close left and right. The situation was exacerbated by the U.S. recession that began in 2007 and spread, plaguelike, from coast to coast. In the first decade of the 2000s, domestic manufacturing employment shrank from 17.3 million to 11.4 million.[25] In other words, more than one third of the total number of manufacturing jobs disappeared—a figure that represents the worst job loss rate in U.S. history. Yes, even worse than the Great Depression!

In fact, by 2010, the death knell seemed to be ringing for America's global manufacturing dominance. That was the year that China surpassed the U.S. as the world's largest manufacturing nation in terms of output, producing goods worth $1.92 trillion compared to our $1.86 trillion.[26]

But a funny thing happened on the way to the morgue: The patient stirred to life again. Although it helped that the nation was emerging from its overall economic depths, many experts maintain that American manufacturing was resuscitated by the abundance of cheap natural gas and growing oil production flowing from U.S. shale.

There's a name for the practice of bringing U.S. manufacturing and services back home: It's called reshoring, and Harry Moser is an expert on it.

Moser, founder and president of the not-for-profit Reshoring Initiative, gave us some striking insight about how lower-priced natural gas from shale is influencing the trend. Natural gas is used both directly as a fuel itself and to generate power for industrial applications, primarily as a source for electricity. Moser pointed out that natural gas had already become more important, as old coal plants were being shuttered in response to EPA regulations. But with natural gas prices continuing to fall, energy costs are a shrinking line item on manufacturers' total operating budgets. This is especially meaningful for energy-intensive industries like steel and glass manufacturing.

And while energy-intensive industries are experiencing the biggest savings, the advantages of lower natural gas prices are being felt across the board, Moser said, although for industries like machining, stamping, and assembly, energy represents only 1 to 2 percent of total manufacturing costs.

Moser estimates that about 150 companies have reshored, or moved positions from overseas to the U.S., since 2010. This has contributed about 80,000 jobs—or 15 percent of the total manufacturing jobs added.

"Natural gas is an accepted and proven advantage," Moser told us. "It's having a real and sizable impact. When manufacturers are considering sites for their facilities, they want to tick off energy with stable availability and low price."

With falling energy prices making U.S. manufacturing cheaper, it's no surprise that enterprises from around the world are looking to get in on the opportunity, too. As a result, the U.S. is becoming more attractive as an investment destination for foreign companies.

Or as Moser summed it up: "It's a good time to be in manufacturing."

Shifting Oil Sands

Fast-forward to today.

All these facts about the shale boom still hold true, and the prognosis is still favorable. As of this writing in mid-2015, BP had just released *Energy Outlook 2035*[27], reporting that U.S. oil production growth in 2014 (roughly 1.5 million barrels per day) was the largest in U.S. history—primarily as a result of our shale boom. This increase ranks *among the largest the world has ever seen,* surpassed only by Saudi Arabia.

BP goes on to forecast that 2015 will be the year that North America switches its status from net importer to net exporter of energy, as the increase in tight oil production couples with declining demand. And even better news: The U.S. is still on the path to becoming energy self-sufficient by the 2030s. Thanks to a span of high oil prices that urged producers to push the boundaries of technology, recovery of unconventional resources considerably boosted U.S. production and transformed the global energy market.

But this is, after all, the oil business, full of nasty little surprises and inevitable roller coasters. The falling price of oil that began with OPEC's Thanksgiving 2014 meeting has caused many to wonder how much longer the positive prognosis will be the case. Headlines have changed a bit since 2013. Whereas just a couple years ago, they read "Shale Boom Spurs Rapid Job Growth" (Fox Business, August 2013), now they look more like "The Shale Slowdown Is Here" (*Business Insider*, February 2015).

We are left to wonder: What will happen to the economic bounty that the shale revolution promised us in 2013?

What does it look like when oil towns slow down? What happens to the jobs? What becomes of the tax revenues? Where does the boom (or the "boom boom") go after a bust? And are we really fixing to find out?

Or do we take heart in sentiments like Thomas Miller's March 2015 piece on OilPrice.com, "Three Reasons Why US Shale Isn't Going Anywhere"?[28] "There is still an abundance of oil and gas to be extracted, with ample incentive to figure out the most efficient ways to develop it."

Do we instead lean on the sage wisdom of Bob Dudley, BP group chief executive, who reminds us that "Today's turbulence is a return to business-as-usual"?[29]

CHAPTER 13

HOW OPEC PLAYS DICE
WITH THE UNIVERSE

Joseph Nye doesn't look like much of a gambler.

The historian, diplomat, and former dean of Harvard University's John F. Kennedy School of Government appears every bit as distinguished as his resume might suggest. But when we spoke with him early in 2014, on an afternoon when he had rushed home from his office to beat an impending New England blizzard, Nye was willing to wager on how OPEC might respond to the global oil glut, much of it coming from American shale.

He bet that top OPEC exporter Saudi Arabia would do everything it could to preserve its own market share, even if that hurt other OPEC members—in particular the kingdom's religious and political opponent, Iran, and cash-strapped Venezuela, which needs higher oil prices to keep from defaulting on its debt.

"If the Saudis were to decide to cut back on production, then essentially they could make a scarcity in markets that could help OPEC," Nye said. "But I don't think the Saudis are about to do that because, if you look at the revolutionary situation in the Middle East, they want to have a lot of walking-around money."

In the weeks before OPEC's Thanksgiving 2014 meeting in Vienna, that kind of thinking may have made Nye something of an outlier. At the time, demand for OPEC oil had been predicted to drop sharply; as such, the market was forecasting that Saudi Arabia would shave output to buoy the price per barrel. It's customary wisdom that, because their state budgets depend on oil revenues, OPEC countries need high prices. In the case of Saudi Arabia, Nye said, oil generates 92 percent of the nation's budget. When crude reached its $100-plus per barrel peak last year, it was empirical evidence of Riyadh's influence. As energy economist Ed Hirs told us in August 2014, "Oil is $100 per barrel because the Saudis and OPEC want it that price. That's how the Saudis balance their budget—they work backwards from how much money they need to the price of oil that will support their budget."

But, as it turned out, Nye's hunch was correct.

Know When to Hold 'Em

Although prices were already softening because of the oversupply of crude, Saudi Arabia announced at OPEC's meeting in November 2014 that it refused to cut back on production. Instead, the kingdom signaled it was willing to accept depressed prices now in order to protect its market share long-term—assuming, as *Bloomberg View* columnist A. Gary Shilling wrote, that the Saudis "can withstand low prices for longer than their financially weaker competitors, who will have to cut production first as pumping becomes uneconomical."[1]

The Saudi decision sent crude oil prices into a freefall as fast and blustery as a Boston snowstorm. The price of West Texas Intermediate (WTI) crude oil, which had already lost more than 31 percent of its value between June and November 26, 2014, tumbled another 10 percent the very day after OPEC met.[2] The oft-touted notion that Saudi Arabia had lost its position as global oil's price-setting swing producer was abruptly discarded.

This isn't the first instance of OPEC playing dice with the universe; the cartel has used its energy to manipulate the market multiple times. In 1986, for example, Saudi Arabia manufactured an American oil bust by flooding the market just as U.S. production was increasing. In less than four months, oil prices plunged 67 percent, to just above $10 a barrel. It took nearly twenty-five years for American production to rebound.

Even earlier, in 1973, OPEC used oil to draw the world into the Middle East conflict, with the Arab Oil Embargo giving rise to long lines of cars circling futilely around gas stations whose tanks were empty.

This time, at least, OPEC has created a pain *not* felt at the pump: Since the cartel's confab, American drivers have been enjoying some of the lowest gas prices in years.

But the sting is being felt deeply among American shale producers. As prices have dipped below the level necessary to sustain production at some of the more expensive tight oil projects, the hurt is being reflected in idled rigs, lost jobs, and shrinking capital budgets.

For example, in mid-February 2015, the U.S. rig count was experiencing an eleven-week dive, reaching a low not seen since 2010. In the space of just two months—December 2014 and January 2015—some 300 U.S. rigs went offline.[3]

Is the end of the assault in sight? Not yet, said Raymond James investment-banking analyst Praveen Narra. Narra told the *Houston Chronicle* in December 2014 that as many as 550 drilling rigs may have to "sit on the sidelines" for the near future.[4] And given the fact that shale oil investment has also been heading downward—in recent months, more than $150 billion worth of energy projects have been put on hold—that future looks pretty uncertain.

What does seem undeniable is that, with their November decision, the Saudis were attempting to break the back of fracking with a swift and decisive scheme to rout marginal shale producers and stem production from others. By squeezing out the competition, analysts said, OPEC could capture greater market share and grow revenues from emerging economies such as China and India, while also allowing oil prices to inch back to the $80 or $90 per barrel mark.

Speaking to CNBC, former Wells Fargo CEO Richard Kovachevich called OPEC's refusal to cut oil production in the midst of dropping prices "an attack against U.S. companies using hydraulic fracturing to extract oil."[5]

Though less brazen, Jamie Webster, an IHS analyst, expressed a similar view: "The faster you bring the price down, the quicker you will have a response from U.S. production—that is the expectation and the hope. I cannot recall a time when several members were actively pushing the price down in both word and deed."[6]

But this isn't just a fight between OPEC and American oil, Afshin Molavi contends. In an opinion piece for the English edition of *Al Arabiya*, Molavi, a senior fellow and director of the Global Emerging and Growth Markets Initiative at Johns Hopkins University School of Advanced International Studies, wrote that OPEC's decision was also intended to scare off any potential Chinese or Indian fracking starts: "[This is] a battle between OPEC and future shale. Because what is most dangerous to the future of OPEC is not U.S. production, but a world in which China, India, and Europe all begin their own fracking revolution."[7]

Whether Molavi is right or not, the Saudi strategy seems to have legs: in February 2015, *The Wall Street Journal* reported that the call for OPEC oil already was up. The cartel's monthly oil market report estimated that demand will grow to 29.2 million barrels a day during 2015. Not only does that represent a 100,000-barrel-per-day increase over last year, it reverses OPEC's earlier forecast that demand for its oil would actually decline by 300,000 barrels per day this year.[8]

But here's the funny thing: Despite rising OPEC output, lower crude prices, fewer rigs, and significant job losses, the Energy Information Administration (EIA) forecasts that U.S. oil production will grow in 2015, too. We're expected to add 670,000 new barrels per day to the global marketplace. That's 82 percent of the world's total anticipated growth.

Shifting Demand and the Price of Oil

As of early 2015, energy prices were still in free fall. While low oil costs have helped relieve "pain at the pump" for oil-consuming nations like the U.S. and Japan, major oil-producing economies like Russia, Iran, Venezuela, and Nigeria are suffering. Each of these countries is highly dependent on oil revenues to keep its economy afloat, and a continuation of the current oil price slide is likely to cause political instability, inflation, and high unemployment. At this writing in mid-2015, Russia is facing severe devaluation of the ruble. GDP is dropping into negative territory in Iran. Venezuela's economy is expected to shrink 3 percent this year alone. And Nigeria's energy tax revenues are sagging.

Let's first consider Russia, which is coming up a big loser. With a devalued ruble and 17 percent interest rates, consumers are rushing to stores to buy washing machines and cars rather than saving their cash. Revenue related to the sale of oil and natural gas accounts for about half the country's budget, and Moscow loses about $2 billion in revenues for every dollar decline in the price of oil. As expected, Russia has cut its growth forecast for 2015. The World Bank is even less optimistic, projecting that the Russian economy will shrink by at least 0.7 percent this year if oil prices remain where they are.

Ironically, even though recession is likely, Russia refuses to cut production, worried that would decrease its market share and invite competition.

OPEC has also decreed not to cut production. Estimates by the EIA suggest that the price decline will cost all twelve OPEC members a total of $257 billion in lost revenue this year. Member countries most exposed to lower oil prices will be hurt the most. That would include Iran, which needs a break-even price of $143/barrel to balance its budget, and cash-strapped Venezuela, which, as mentioned, teeters on the brink of default.

Even before the OPEC decision, Iran was reeling from sanctions over its nuclear program. Not only did export revenue decline 30 percent, but the nation's oil and gas fields were virtually closed to investment. As a result, Iran's access to technology that could boost output and offset its high break-even price was severely limited.

Venezuela is an interesting case. The nation is one of the world's largest oil exporters, but even before the price of oil started to slide, it was in dire financial straits. Inflation is a staggering 60 percent, and the economy is rapidly headed for recession. Because of fuel subsidies, Venezuela enjoys some of the world's cheapest gas. Cutting subsidies would help the economy, but the government refuses to do so. Analysts today say that Venezuela has a 93 percent chance of defaulting on its debt over the next five years.

Looking toward Africa, lower oil prices are especially hurting the resource-rich nation of Nigeria, the continent's biggest oil producer. Although Nigeria is experiencing growth in other areas of the economy, energy sales account for up to 80 percent of all government revenue. You can imagine what a 50 percent reduction in oil prices means for the country's coffers. Albert Goldson, executive director of New York City–based Indo-Brazilian Associates LLC, a boutique global advisory firm and think tank, gave us equally dire statistics when we communicated with him in October 2014: "Militants and black marketers, often with government connections, siphon off as much as 20 percent of Nigeria's oil production."

Who's Winning with Lower Oil Prices?

There are some winners emerging from the low-price scenario, however. Take China, for example, which has overtaken the U.S. as the largest consumer of energy and is set to become the world's largest net importer of oil. Lower prices mean a boost to its slowing economy. And they give the nation more leverage over key supplier Russia, which desperately needs to keep its customers happy and preserve all the energy income it can. As long as crude prices stay low, China has an upper hand in its negotiations for Russian oil.

Or consider India, which imports 75 percent of its oil. Falling prices are helping to ease a current account deficit. If prices stay low, the cost of India's fuel subsidies could decrease by $2.5 billion this year alone.

Of course, U.S. shale producers are hurting. In fact, according to the *Daily Kos*, at $50.04/barrel—the price of oil on January 6, 2015—thirty-seven out of thirty-eight shale oil fields are operating at a loss.[9]

But if we have so much oil, why does OPEC still matter? Here is the kicker: No matter how much oil we have, crude oil is always bought and sold on a world market basis; it's considered a fungible (interchangeable) commodity. Unlike natural gas, petroleum is not priced simply by regional availability. When there is more of it available for sale than there is demand, then buyers can shop around for lower prices.

Global supply and demand is the primary driver of crude oil prices.

We're all part of an interconnected economic web of energy consumers and suppliers—a network that keeps us entangled with suppliers who may not necessarily have our best interests at heart. Or, as Yale economist William Nordhouse has suggested, when it comes to oil, the world is like a bathtub. Producing nations are the faucets, Nordhouse said, introducing oil into the inventory. Consuming nations are the drains, drawing oil out.

It doesn't matter whether the faucets and drains are labeled "U.S.," "Russia," or "Denmark," Nordhouse told an audience at the International Energy Workshop in 2009. The price and quantity of oil in the world market is determined by the sum of demands and supplies and the level of total inventory.

When rapidly growing countries such as China and India increase demand, for example, world oil prices rise. Conversely, when those nations consume less, prices can go down.

The result: Having oil helps us shield the world (and ourselves) from oil price spikes, since we can produce more in times when supply is down. Consider these recent examples:

- *A North Sea pipeline leak in January 2013:* This shut down operations and caused a backlog of oil from nine offshore production platforms. A similar outage in the past would likely have caused escalating oil prices, but that day prices fell.

- *2011–2015 sanctions on Iran:* This joint effort of the U.S. and the European Union led to a daily reduction of 1 million barrels of Iranian crude from the international market, but the drop had little lasting impact on prices—an outcome that would have been practically unthinkable a few years ago before the U.S. shale gale. Because of our increased oil supply, we were able to implement these sanctions without worrying about our oil supply. "Iran's often-threatened military action to block oil shipments via the Strait of Hormuz no longer carries the same menace," a *New York Sun* column proclaimed. "To be sure if it ever happens it will push prices up in the short term, but the move's largest victims will be the Persian Gulf oil producers themselves, namely Saudi Arabia, Kuwait, the UAE, Qatar and Iran itself, who will be deprived from the single resource accounting for 90 percent of their income."[10]

- *Summer 2013 coup d'etat in Egypt:* The unrest in Egypt led to higher oil prices (from the low $90s to more than $100/barrel) in the U.S. by early July, impeded oil shipments through the Suez Canal and the Sumed pipeline, and coincided with a drop in the U.S. oil inventory as a result of transportation issues. Such a triple whammy in the past would have escalated gasoline prices at the pump, but the impact was much less than it could have been because of the reserves of domestic fuel, with production enhanced by the shale revolution, that counteracted the "international hysteria" over the Egyptian situation.

So, our supply helps keep prices from spiking, but unfortunately it does nothing to keep prices from falling. If OPEC keeps supply sky-high, we're vulnerable.

Do we have options? Is it really a doomsday scenario for shale energy? Will we ever be able to cut OPEC out?

Pricing Volatility and Energy "Independence"

"The term 'energy independence' refers to supply—or not having to rely on someone else for oil and gas—but you also need to consider economics," said Jorge Piñon, director of the Latin American and Caribbean Energy Program in the Jackson School of Geosciences at the University of Texas at Austin. As he told my team in a September 2014 phone conversation, "Economic independence cannot be achieved because of the volatility of the price of oil."

These days, the term "energy independence" reflects a naïveté that arises from substantive misunderstandings of the concept. The ability to produce oil in sufficient quantities does not spell independence since our country still buys and sells petroleum in the world marketplace. "Talk to the people on the street—not experts—and you'll get many interpretations," Piñon continued. "People need to understand that while Western countries may be wealthy with oil and may become more self-sufficient, the price of domestic oil will still be impacted by events taking places thousands of miles away in the Middle East. [Such events] will increase market volatility and affect the global economy. U.S. geopolitical interests in the Middle East are not going to go away, no matter how self-sufficient the nation is in producing oil."

Claire Casey is the managing director for the international advisory firm Garten Rothkopf. When we spoke with her in April 2014, she agreed that there is a serious misunderstanding surrounding these concepts: "There is an unwillingness to acknowledge that we are part of a global market, and that we will remain part of a global market—and that there are benefits associated with that. Do we want that marketplace to have greater flexibility? Do we want to be less dependent on specific producers? Absolutely."

News about renewable energy sources such as solar and wind may also be confusing the issue. "Early in the current administration, the White House made a statement that renewable energy resources were going to lessen dependence on Middle East oil," Piñon reminded us. However, "solar and wind primarily contribute energy to the electric power sector. In the U.S., less than 1 percent of electricity is generated by oil. These alternatives don't power automobiles. Increased electric generation via renewable sources is, of course, good. But to connect that to the assumption that we will reduce consumption of Middle East oil is totally incorrect."

CHAPTER 14

SHOULD WE BE WORRIED?

Logan Moore, the founding president of Marlin Oilfield Divers, which services oil companies in the Gulf of Mexico region, noticed a slowdown in his business in mid-January 2015. Marlin Oil Divers is based in Houma, Louisiana. They handle all kinds of oil-field needs, such as new installations (e.g., burying pipe in the seabed), and field maintenance and repair. Moore points out that 99 percent of the (mostly conventional) oil companies he services—twenty-two in all—are (in their own words) "not spending any money that's not essential to current production."

"We've lowered our rates, and we've laid people off," he told my team during a conversation in early 2015. "We used to do 1,400 to 1,500 offshore work days a year. That's over 100 a month. Right now, we haven't lost any clients, but with what's going on with this oil price drop, we're down to ten or twelve jobs a month, from over a hundred. You can do the math. Real simple."

With prices so low, some experts cite the possibility that shale oil may not be worth pursuing much longer. Wells that are producing oil or gas right now are extraordinarily profitable, yes, because most of the costs have already been sunk. As Bruno Gremez, co-founder CT&F Consulting pointed out, "Rig count in the United States seems to be decreasing, but production levels have remained steady."[1] However, the output of shale wells declines rapidly in the first year—by 60 percent to 70 percent. Within a handful of years—Geology.com estimates six years, depending on the well—we can expect this oil will stop flowing so prolifically.

What then? No one can say exactly how low prices have to fall before exploration for and drilling of shale becomes truly unprofitable. That's because costs vary quite wildly from place to place. Wells produce different mixes of oil and gas (gas sells for less); transport costs vary (it is cheap to pipe oil from the Eagle Ford play in Texas, but expensive to shift it by train out of the Bakken formation in North Dakota), and so on.

Clearly, OPEC is hoping that U.S. shale producers will eventually be driven out of business since shale is more expensive to extract than Saudi or Kuwaiti oil. However, U.S. shale oil developers in different areas of the country have been able to use technological advances to extract tight oil for less money per barrel, with break-even prices ranging from the mid-$30s to more than $70/barrel. "If oil stays below $60 per barrel, some U.S. companies will cancel or scale back shale drilling (a number of big companies are already pulling out of Texas's Permian Basin for now). But other drillers may try to cut their costs, grit it out, and keep drilling. It really varies from company to company," maintains Kier Yorke, Director of Financial Sales Services at SinusIridum, a London-based technology and financial services company.[2]

Some say a profit can still be made at $25/barrel, which would mean production might never stop entirely.

Bound and Determined

It's not inevitable that resource extraction booms end in disaster. These days, "busts" are called contractions, or retarding cycles, or slowdowns. With good governance and stewardship from local and state governments, wealth can realistically be maintained over the long term: Sensible regulation, structured funds for the revenue gained, and thoughtful investment in infrastructure are all that is generally needed.

Ben Morton is a partner at Mendelawitz Morton, an Australian law firm in a very large mining town that has survived and grown through at least a hundred years of boom-and-bust cycles. He observes that when there is a price downturn, many of his private-sector clients "need to reconstruct their business, sell assets, or undertake some form of creditor negotiation." But the town doesn't disappear, as he noted in a February 2015 email to our team. A bust permits a period of appraisal and thoughtful planning. And when commodity prices "kick in again, then suddenly everyone will come out to play."

Whether you call it a retarding cycle, or a contraction, or a plain old bust, it's no longer necessarily anything to fear. Each bust of the cycle can create the base for the next boom. Demand always returns . . . eventually.

Right now, the industry as a whole seems like it is shrinking, and some experts wonder if the bust of the 1980s will repeat itself: Between November 1985 and March 1986, the price of crude plunged by 67 percent. Between June 2014 and today, crude prices have fallen by almost the same difference, and some say that prices could well head lower.[3]

Although oil prices trend upwards from their 2015 lows, they remain about half what they were in June 2014. And the uptick isn't necessarily a positive sign for U.S. drillers, as it reflects the fact that lower oil prices forced shale oil producers to cut supplies along with their spending. Considering that in December 2014, Saudi Arabia's oil minister, Ali al-Naimi, told the Middle East Economic Survey that OPEC wouldn't cut production even if oil falls to $20/barrel, the structural floor may still be out of sight.

Logan Moore, for one, is concerned. He described his peers in the oil-field service sector, "I've got a lot of good friends in this business that are twice as old as me, got gray hair, and have made fortunes and lost fortune two and three times. They've never been as concerned as they are now. A lot of people are afraid oil is going to make another dip and go even lower."

In the 1980s, scores of companies disappeared over almost five years of depressed prices. But while conventional oil fueled the eighties, unconventional (shale) oil is powering the U.S. now—so there are big differences between the oilscape of the eighties and the oilscape of today.

First, shale's faster. Shale oil's investment cycle is shorter than conventional oil production. Shale can ramp up quickly. New wells can be brought online in weeks rather than years.

Second, shale oil is cheaper to extract. An expensive land well now costs $10 million, compared with the billions needed to drill offshore wells and build associated infrastructure.

Third, we know where the oil is. The tight oil business is about deposits people have known about for decades but could not afford to extract. Josh Stein, a Texas attorney and self-described oilman, once told us, "Shale is entering only a temporary slowdown. There's too much money to be made and too much oil still out there."

All of this means that shale oil is much more responsive to prices than conventional oil. Some economists think this could turn America into a swing producer, helping to moderate the booms and busts of the global market.

There are also some analysts who think that OPEC's risky business might actually backfire in the long run.

The *Motley Fool* writer Travis Hoium called OPEC's approach a "dangerous game" based on anticipating future energy consumption.[4]

"(OPEC) may be able to squeeze out marginal players in the oil market today, increasing their market share in the future," Hoium said. "But if the oil market begins to shrink long-term and it then owns a larger share of a smaller pie, it'll come out on the losing end of this battle.

"(In 2015) alone, the EIA predicts that OPEC will lose out on $257 billion in revenue because of low oil prices and it'll need to make that up in the future for the strategy to be a success," he added.

Morgan Stanley also sees holes in OPEC's tactics. The investment firm has suggested that an intensifying survival-of-the-fittest mentality may actually be positioning shale drillers for even greater success going forward: "Lower prices may only force U.S. producers and service companies to innovate even faster, pushing down the cost of production and lifting overall non-OPEC supply potential."[5]

Even now, the impact of innovation is reverberating in American oil fields. One reason production continues to grow as rig count drops is that exploration, drilling, and extraction have all become more efficient. Current break-even costs for 90 percent of the new wells in the Bakken range from just $29/barrel to $41/barrel, down from about $75/barrel only three years ago.[6] (It's important to note that, because most of the costs associated with shale wells are up front—drilling and fracking—it doesn't cost much to keep collecting the oil being produced.)

To some, like Citigroup's head of global commodity research Edward Morse, this indicates that the U.S. has "broken OPEC's ability to manipulate the market."

"It looks exceedingly unlikely for OPEC to return to its old way of doing business," Morse wrote in a research report.[7] "While many analysts have seen in past market crises 'the end of OPEC,' this time around might well be different."

The world will not end with this latest readjustment. But the world as we know it will certainly change and rebalance—and most likely for the better, as more non-OPEC countries continue to produce and become more energy secure and independent on their own.

We know that shale oil and gas development has been a major job creator and boost to the American economy since the 2007–2009 recession. In shale energy states, employment is up 40 percent in the oil and gas fields, and as of this writing in mid-2015, a million jobs were expected to be created in the next two years, along with as many as 100 factories (built with both American and foreign investment) providing infrastructure such as pipelines, servicing equipment, and drilling rigs. But that was before the big oil price drop in late 2014. So it's hard to say exactly how many jobs and factories will be gained or lost thanks to global market gyrations.

Prophets of doom (among them Goldman Sachs, the same company that invested billions in shaky credit default swaps, producing the U.S. subprime mortgage crisis and stock market crash of 2008) profess that a sustained oil crash throughout 2015 could result in the cancellation of $1 trillion in new energy investments. Norway's Rystad Energy, a consulting firm, claims that 800 global oil and gas projects will be delayed or canceled if oil prices remain low or suppressed throughout 2015.

But here's the good news. Even with these gloomy short-term predictions, something important and ultimately beneficial is taking place.

What we are really seeing, besides a primarily U.S.-induced oil supply shock worldwide, is an important rebalancing and readjustment of the Global Energy Security System (GESS), a concept describing the totality of global energy markets, pricing, and availability of resources rather than a focus on national or regional energy economies. U.S. energy analysts believe that GESS is critical to achieving more stable energy markets and economies of the near future. For example, we've seen that shale discovery has allowed the U.S. to drastically reduce its energy dependence on the few oil and gas monopolies (e.g., OPEC) that have acted with myopic self-interest in the past. U.S. imports of liquid fuels, including crude oil and petroleum products, recently dropped to about 6 million barrels per day, about half the peak levels of more than 12 million barrels per day between 2004 to 2007, with self-sufficiency in North America projected around 2030 or earlier, according to energy policymakers and analysts Jan H. Kalicki and David L. Goldwyn, who edited *Energy and Security: Strategies for a World in Transition* (Woodrow Wilson Center Press, 2013). The U.S., which in the past also acted myopically by failing to plan for adequate energy supplies, technologies, and patterns of production and consumption, now has taken an entirely different tack, ushering in a stunning new era of abundance and energy diversification. These changes are affecting world markets and global prices of energy—and we have only begun to see how the rebalancing will play out.

In the words of Raymond Tanter, in a February 2014 email to our team, "The rest of the world relies on American policing efforts. Look at the deteriorating situation in Syria: Although President Obama would like to refrain from arming the rebels; they are policy-forcing events propelling him to decide in favor of doing so and much more if arms alone are not dispositive."

And he should know. As president of the American Committee on Human Rights, president of the Iran Policy Committee Publishing, and associate fellow with the Washington Institute for Near East Policy, Tanter has vast experience with these topics. But despite this interconnectedness, he seems to agree that the shale revolution has far-reaching repercussions across the entire globe: "Despite interdependence, the United States remains the only true global power, whose comparative energy sufficiency over time is bound to have huge effects on the rest of the world."

Tanter also told us that he doesn't foresee a time when the U.S. will lessen its military presence around the world—either in the interest of our own security or the security of our trading partners and allies—"because energy is only one of the drivers of American policy." In addition, he believes it's doubtful that the we will ever step back from international relations to focus more on domestic policy, because of prior commitments to nations with which America has shared values.

Even Logan Moore of Marlin Oilfield Divers agreed that shale is a national treasure. "Shale oil hasn't necessarily been a good thing for my personal business because when my clients drill for a barrel of shale oil, they're not drilling for the [conventional] oil that they need my help with," said Moore. But shale oil has been a good thing for the country. It has definitely been a good thing for the country."

Thanks mostly to private initiative, the U.S. is leveraging breakthroughs in shale oil and gas production, deepwater resource development, and energy-efficiency measures as never before. Analysts Jan H. Kalicki and David L. Goldwyn call these developments The New Energy Pivot.[8] I call it the Switch.

The Switch signifies a turn of affairs that will create greater oil and gas market stability, more options for moving and diversifying energy channels and partnerships worldwide and also for producing lasting benefits for the U.S. and its immediate energy alliances and partners (think Canada, which now provides 32 percent of all the oil the U.S. imports).

Here's how Kalicki and Goldwyn describe it:

"Remarkably, the United States and its partners are at a pivot point in history where they can diversify dramatically global supplies of oil and gas, lessen the potential of Middle East instability to shock the global economy, reduce greenhouse gas (GHG) emissions more quickly, and enable the United States—for a change—to use energy as a powerful and positive tool of foreign policy."[9]

The Switch swings the energy picture around in new directions that were inconceivable as recently as 2008.

OPEC is scared, and it should be. Could Saudi's refusal to curtail production be a last act of desperate defiance against an inevitable shift in worldwide power generation? These current price dives and rises may indeed usher in the end of one era and the beginning of another; traditional global and regional energy scions are losing their power. OPEC was once the cartel that determined world oil prices. Today, North America, Norway, Russia, and Brazil have become substantial players with real influence over global supplies and prices. By the same token, Soviet, then Russian gas production once dominated the Eurasian gas marketplace. Now, traditional customers in Western Europe and Asia are diversifying sources of supply, looking to alternate foreign and domestic suppliers, even suppliers in the U.S. and Caspian Sea countries, to create a truly competitive global gas market that resists the price fixing of kingpins and monopolies.

Most analysts believe fossil fuels will constitute 80 percent of the global energy mix at least until 2035. But now, say Kalicki and Goldwyn, "the United States has the power to enhance its own security and shift the energy balance of power strongly to its advantage by leveraging U.S. technology, U.S. markets, and the U.S. role as guardian of the world's sea lanes—shared, in the future, one hopes, with other like-minded powers— to create a more interdependent, stable, and climate-friendly system."[10]

It's true: If Americans can execute the energy switch deftly, and with enthusiastic cooperation among stakeholders and constituents, a globalized energy security system and alternate energy marketplace can flourish in ways we never thought possible.

Will this switch happen? Only if the U.S. commits to four major changes. The first change is to actively assist allies in developing their own energy sources and technologies, enhancing security and diversifying supplies to allow for free international energy trade in open markets.

Next, the U.S. needs to adopt energy policies that continuously build on our technological advancements in shale discovery, deepwater exploration, carbon emissions capture, renewables, and economic and security incentives to protect our energy industry and increase cooperation across borders.

Third, we need a comprehensive energy strategy that tells the world we are ready to practice what we preach. We need to lift the crude oil export ban, allowing the U.S. to trade crude on the free market. We need to support LNG exports and amend policies to allow us to sell to friendly countries in need such as Ukraine.

Finally, we need to invest in the single most important asset that has allowed us to come first to market with shale energy: We need to invest in our own oil and gas infrastructure, including the Keystone XL pipeline.

PART IV

PRACTICE WHAT WE PREACH

CHAPTER 15

LET'S TALK CRUDE

OPEC continues to twirl the global energy market like a top. But the axis is shifting, thanks to the extra spin from the U.S. shale revolution. The U.S. Energy Information Agency (EIA) projects that America will pump more than 3 million barrels of new petroleum and other liquid fuels per day between 2012 and 2020—principally from light tight oil.[1]

As a major proponent for international free trade, the U.S. is heavily involved in exports of all kinds. But when it comes to energy, the U.S. does not rank among the export leaders.

Yes, you read that correctly.

Even while the U.S. is currently producing more oil than Saudi Arabia. . . . Even while the state of North Dakota is now producing more oil than Libya. . . . Even while U.S. crude oil production has reached its highest point in twenty-six years (and is pushing our domestic refineries to their capacity limits). . . . Even while our country is on track to hit the highest level of oil production our country has seen since 1972, the U.S. actually prohibits the sale of most of our domestically produced crude oil abroad.

Waiter, There's a Ban in My Alphabet Soup!

This ban on exporting crude oil was a reaction to price shocks that accompanied the Arab Oil Embargo of 1973.

While the embargo itself lasted less than a year, its repercussions hound us today. In fact, some regard the embargo as the first event since the Great Depression to have a persistent economic effect on our nation. Overnight, we said goodbye to cheap gas and perceived security, and hello to justified paranoia and loss of control. And the government's reaction was a flurry of hurriedly penned legislation in an attempt to desperately convince the American people that we still managed our own energy security.

The ban is a complex recipe of "alphabet soup." Although often discussed as if it were a single piece of legislation, the moratorium is not actually a single law, but rather a collection of laws and residential documents that together provide authority to ban crude oil exports from the U.S. The main laws that make the ban possible—the Energy Policy and Conservation Act (EPCA) of 1975 and the Export Administration Act (EAA) of 1979—were put into place as a direct response to the embargo.

The EPCA essentially bans U.S. crude oil exports to all countries except Canada. It does this by giving the president the power to restrict exports of fuels, materials, and equipment for producing energy, including:

- petroleum products
- coal
- natural gas
- petrochemical feed stocks
- equipment for exploration
- production, refining, and transportation of energy supplies

The EPCA also puts the Department of Commerce in charge of issuing licenses to anyone who wants to export crude oil. The export of refined products (such as gasoline, diesel, and jet fuel) is not restricted.

The EAA provides legal authority to the president to control all U.S. exports—including oil—for "reasons of national security, foreign policy, and/or short supply." In order to keep the export controls in place when the EAA expired in 1994, President Bill Clinton declared a national emergency under the International Emergency Economic Powers Act (IEEPA).

The IEEPA allows the president to "investigate, regulate, or prohibit any transactions in foreign exchange." Every president since Clinton has followed suit in order to maintain the ban on crude oil exports.

The legislation was originally implemented to keep scarce energy resources safe at home to make our country stronger and safer and more self-reliant—a sound, smart move during the terrifyingly eye-opening energy shortage of the 1970s. But times have changed in the four decades since then, leaving the ban tantamount to a self-imposed embargo that forbids us from fully participating in the global crude oil markets. The ban now serves to keep us dependent upon other oil producers—some of whom have not been exactly friendly—because of a key element to our energy story: refineries.

Refineries take a hazardous but nearly useless material—hence the name "crude" oil—and turn it into valuable refined products like gasoline, diesel and jet fuel, petrochemicals, Styrofoam, and many other important materials. Refineries are absolutely critical to the oil and gas industry—yet they're often overlooked and misunderstood. And in today's energy market, they're saddled with (at least!) three major obstacles.

Refining Obstacle 1: No Fountain of Youth Here

Famed author George Orwell once wrote, "At fifty, everyone has the face he deserves."

The same could be said for a majority of U.S. refineries: They're at least that old—and just as set in their ways. Many of these complex industrial behemoths were built a hundred years ago. Even the newest large-capacity refinery is somewhat of a relic, dating all the way back to the Carter administration.

The first refinery actually came before commercialized oil drilling—we're talking way back in the 1840s. Granted, that plant didn't even come close to the image of today's massive refineries: It consisted of a single still in the middle of downtown Pittsburgh. Today's more modern U.S. refineries—which are actually somewhat vintage, the newest having been built in 1976—are large industrial complexes where refiners continue to tweak their processes as they learn how to become more efficient. But, aside from their size, the actual refineries themselves have, for the most part, remained strikingly unchanged.

The shale energy boom is creating a surge in oil production—and therefore in refining needs as well. This unprecedented expansion is pushing U.S. refineries to their limits. In 1982, the earliest year for which the EIA has data, our 301 operable refineries produced 17.9 million barrels of oil per day. Today there are only 149 refineries, but they produce 17.4 million barrels—less than in 1982, but more than any year since then.[2]

The EIA estimates that the gap between refinery capacity and consumption—the same issue that is overtaxing today's refineries—is expected only to widen over time. In fact, the EIA projects that by 2020, consumption will increase 19.2 percent, while at the same time capacity will grow just 9.4 percent. This means that refining capacity will be only 100,000 barrels a day more in 2020 than it was in 1981.[3]

That's a very underwhelming expectation, especially given the forecasts from the shale boom.

Under most circumstances, there's nothing wrong with senescence; unfortunately for the process of refining today, middle age is the bellwether of disaster. As a result of this soaring capacity, the fewer U.S. refineries are running flat out at full stride, overtaxing their aging facilities. A decade ago, they operated at a comfortable 70 percent capacity; today, the rate often exceeds 90 percent. The facilities weren't designed to run at that level, and to do so increases the risk of recurring equipment failures, fires, explosions, or chemical releases.

Refining Obstacle 2:
Bureaucratic Red Tape Abounds

With aging refineries subject to less-than-ideal production efficiencies and potentially devastating equipment failures, it would seem that building shiny new refineries would be the logical solution to bridge the gap.

OPERATIONAL U.S. REFINERIES

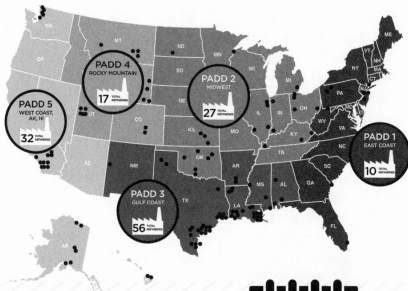

PADD 4
ROCKY MOUNTAIN
17 TOTAL REFINERIES

PADD 5
WEST COAST, AK, HI
32 TOTAL REFINERIES

PADD 2
MIDWEST
27 TOTAL REFINERIES

PADD 1
EAST COAST
10 TOTAL REFINERIES

PADD 3
GULF COAST
56 TOTAL REFINERIES

142

In total, there are 142 operational petroleum refineries in the United States.

1976

The last new complex refinery was built in 1976, over 38 years ago.

PADD: Petroleum Administration for Defense District (U.S. Department of Energy)

Not so fast. Building new refineries is a vastly expensive, time-consuming undertaking.

For those who argue that we should do some value-added processing to our unrefined, unprocessed products—to support local jobs and let us export higher-value products like diesel and jet fuel and gasoline—Thomas Tunstall, research director for the Institute for Economic Development at the University of Texas at San Antonio, plays devil's advocate. When my team sat down with him in October 2014 for a conversation on the topic, he raised some counterpoints to that line of thinking.

"One of the problems with that is that if we could instantly build refineries, that might be a way to address the issue. But the reality is that I don't think a *new* refinery has been built in the U.S. since 1976 because of the onerous regulatory hurdles that have to be overcome," said Tunstall. "Instead what's happened is that existing refineries have expanded. But the ones on the Gulf Coast were designed for the heavier crudes. To repurpose them for the lighter crudes is a fairly substantial investment and takes years to complete."

Consider Phoenix-based Arizona Clean Fuels Yuma, hoping to build what would be the first new refinery in the U.S. since 1976. Initial plans called for daily refining capacity of 150,000 barrels of crude oil and 1.8 million gallons of other petroleum-based materials, with output including gasoline, jet fuel, propane, and diesel fuel.[4] The project price tag? A cool $4 billion.[5]

And taking on expenses is just the beginning. There's a lot of red tape to navigate afterward.

With today's regulations, it would cost upward of $100 million and two to four years of engineering, regulatory review, and approval just to get started—even before any concrete's been poured or pipe's been laid. As a result, it could take a decade or more for a new, high-capacity refinery to come online.

Glenn McGinnis, CEO of Arizona Clean Fuels Yuma, is recognized as a global industry expert in areas of refinery design, development, and operations. But even his level of experience likely didn't prepare him for the delays that have plagued this project. The first steps—permit applications to build near Mobile, Arizona—began seventeen years ago, in 1998. Five years later, as the company believed it was wrapping up its permit application, the state belatedly determined that Mobile was part of the area around Phoenix that was out of compliance with standards for the smog-forming pollutant ozone, which meant that the facility would have to be built in Yuma instead. The final permit was issued in April 2005—seven years after the company started the permitting process—but there's still no refinery. It's a bad sign that the company's online Press Room web page, which proclaims "Refinery still moving forward," hasn't been updated since 2009. And *U.S. News & World Report* noted back in 2011 that "financing has reportedly brought that project to a standstill."[6]

Strict environmental requirements are one of the biggest hoops that possible refiners must jump through before building. Refineries have found it neither easy nor economical to comply with regulations. In fact, the strict regulations of the federal Clean Air Act amendment of 1990 are likely a main reason why U.S. refineries now total half what they were in the 1980s.

Refining Obstacle 3: Do You Take Your Crude Light and Sweet or Heavy and Sour?

To top off old age and red tape, the shale boom itself is throwing yet another curveball: Many refineries aren't configured to process the *type* of oil that pumps prolifically from the shale plays and constitutes the majority of the production spike.

Types of crudes? That's right, not all oil is created equal.

If you've ever been baffled by the names and choices of brews on a coffeehouse menu board, you might find the variety of crude oils extracted from the ground an equally mind-boggling experience, only without the caffeine kick afterward. Crudes vary in color, from clear to tar black; in viscosity (or thickness), from watery to almost solid; and in quality (components that make up the crude, which include sulfur, heavy metals, waxes, water, and mercury). In addition to those characteristics, the crude classification system could make even a coffeehouse barista's head spin.

Different types of crude oil yield a different mix of products. The economic viability of a refinery depends on the type and quality of crude (known as a crude slate) it can obtain and process, the complexity of the refining equipment (refinery configuration), and the type and quality of products produced (product slate) to meet market demand.

Light, sweet crudes—à la shale oil—have a higher proportion of the light molecules used to make premium fuels like gasoline and naphtha (a liquid hydrocarbon mixture). Heavy, sour crudes—imported from, say, Venezuela and Saudi Arabia—have a higher proportion of molecules that can only be used to make diesel fuel or residual fuels oils that are sold at a discount to ships or power producers. They are also more difficult to refine, requiring intensive processing using catalytic cracking and coking units.

Most of the light sweet infrastructure is moving crude into the U.S. Gulf Coast, where refineries had invested in complex configurations that allowed them to use cheaper feedstock of imported heavy sours in order to produce the large quantities of gasoline to satisfy American demand. This means that companies in North Dakota and Texas that are producing lighter, sweeter crudes can't find enough refiners to process it.

So if building a rash of new refineries isn't a likely solution to our capacity woes, what about retrofitting current configurations for light, sweet crude?

For the U.S. to use all of the oil it produces now, more domestic refineries would have to make costly investments in distillation towers, furnaces, heat exchangers, and downstream conversion units to enable them to handle more light oil. This expensive choice is frustrating for refiners who already devoted large capital expenditures to increasing capacity for imported heavy sour crude. In the 1990s and 2000s, a number of U.S. refineries already made substantial investments in coking units, in anticipation of more medium- and heavy-grade feedstock. They're not financially motivated to make yet another round of changes unless the sweet light grades are guaranteed to stay at a significant discount over the long term—and with the billions of dollars it could cost, they're not ready to make that bet.

Still, Ed Hirs, managing director of Hillhouse Resources, expects more refiners to go in that direction.

"A refinery is an industrial complex, and they can all be varied to a certain extent to adjust to the grade and quality of the crude oil input. Most refineries are configured for one type of feedstock or another—there's no question about that—but they all have the ability to reconfigure on a short-term or long-term basis for different types of feedstock," Hirs told my team in our September 2014 conversation. "The issue is what's the more economical decision for that particular refinery. They all want to operate at the lowest cost possible."

While refineries hem and haw—and no immediately apparent solution appears in sight—we still have a glut at home. Granted, it's complicated to configure a refinery to work with so much variability. But the shale boom is prompting many companies to respond anyway, showing that the perennially sluggish refinery sector is finally stepping up.

Breaching the Ban

A few exceptions over the years have allowed the export of *some* domestic oil. Such exceptions include crude produced in Alaska's Cook Inlet, oil that travels through the Trans-Alaskan Pipeline, oil sourced from certain fields in California, and oil shipped to our strong energy ally Canada for domestic consumption.

During May 2014, the amount of crude exported amounted to just 8.938 million barrels, or about 296,000 barrels per day (nearly all of it headed to our northerly neighbor).[7] But exports the next month jumped to about 390,000 barrels per day—meaning that we exported more crude that month than OPEC member Ecuador. This increase of some 35 percent over May's daily tally also represented the highest U.S. export total since the 1950s.[8]

Is Canada suddenly thirstier than ever for our oil?

Actually, the export gains are the result of another slight fissure in the ban that is allowing more crude to leave the U.S. for foreign shores. Not all forms of crude, mind you, but condensate, a gas that condenses into an ultralight oil that refiners blend with heavier crudes to make them easier to refine. Condensate is tapped from shale formations in abundance—to the tune of some 750,000 barrels per day. But because so much of the present U.S. oil boom involves light oil, there's not a lot of heavy oil to add it to. In addition, many U.S. refineries aren't configured to process condensate. With U.S. refineries already running close to capacity, they simply can't ramp up to absorb all the light oil and condensate that's being produced.

Garten Rothkopf's Claire Casey explained to our team in September 2014 that it makes a lot of sense for us to export condensate: "In this case, the thing that's building up in the U.S. market is condensate. We do not have a productive use for it—because our infrastructure is not based around this as a feedstock—and we could export it to economies that *do* have a productive use for it, and it would be a win-win."

This makes condensate a prime candidate for selling abroad. And in June 2014, the Commerce Department allowed operators in Texas's Eagle Ford oil play, including Pioneer Natural Resources and Enterprise Products Partners, to do just that. The Commerce Department agreed with the firms' position that, because condensate is minimally processed through stabilization and distillation, it's not technically crude oil but a refined product—which should exempt it from the ban.

And as Tunstall reminded us, "The U.S. can export *refined* products without restriction. Even natural gas can be exported to countries we have a Free Trade Agreement with. So it's really just crude oil. Even there, you see condensate splitters (sort of a subset of full-blown refineries) being put in place to process condensate, and after that's done, that qualifies as a refined product."

Sure, these semantics might just be a keen way of redefining crude. And, sure, they apply only to condensate: The determination doesn't signal that the federal export ban in its entirety will be lifted any time soon.

LIFT THE CRUDE OIL EXPORT BAN

"...Forbidding the export of U.S. crude violates the principle of free trade."
— Margo Thorning, Senior Vice President and Chief Economist, American Council for Capital Formation

"The reality is that until someone steps in to change the game, OPEC will do everything in its power to weaken the market and dominate competitors. That someone can and should be the United States... Our country's energy abundance is a strong geopolitical tool, and it's time for the policymakers in Washington D.C., to demand that we use this opportunity to our strategic advantage when it comes to facing down oppressive and authoritarian regimes like Russia and Venezuela. By doing so, we provide our friends and allies around the world with an alternative source of oil while creating jobs and opportunity here at home."
— David J. Porter, Commissioner, Railroad Commission of Texas

The crude oil export ban is a popular topic amongst experts, including political leaders, corporations, think tanks, and the press.

Whether in favor of lifting the ban or keeping it in place, everyone is talking about crude.

"Permitting the exports of oil will actually reduce the price of gasoline."
— Larry Summers, former Director of the White House National Economic Council for Economic Policy, Obama Administration

"It is in America's national security interest to leverage our nation's energy boom to reduce the dependence of our allies on the natural resources of Vladimir Putin's Russia."
— Sen. John McCain, R-AZ

"Like free trade in general, selling American oil overseas would be good for our economy. It would make the oil market more efficient, encourage a build-out of the U.S. energy network and stabilize prices over time for consumers ... Congress should have lifted the ban years ago ... Today, however, the government has no reason to keep holding back one of the nation's most promising industries."
— The Chicago Tribune

"By all logic, we should be working to sustain the oil boom. We aren't, and therein lies a classic example of how good policy is held hostage to bad politics and public relations."
— Robert J. Samuelson, Columnist, The Washington Post

"Together, we can send a strong signal to the world that the United States is ready to lead on energy, the environment, and trade. Lifting the ban will help create jobs, boost the economy, and keep our production at record levels."
— Sen. Lisa Murkowski, R-AK

"The antiquated policy that we're talking about today didn't have a lot of logic after we deregulated oil. And it has even less logic in the dangerous world that we live in today... We have an opportunity to say to our allies — whether it's Japan or Europe—don't worry about whether somebody is going to hold you hostage because we've got your back. But we can't have their back if we don't have the ability to export our crude oil. The bottom line is that the restriction against exports of crude oil makes no sense, absolutely none."
— Sen. Heidi Heitkamp, D-ND

"We're sort of driving down the road with the windows open and hundred-dollar bills flying out the window for no reason."
— James LeBas, Economist, Texas Oil and Gas Association

"We export cars, we export everything. But we don't export energy. Why? Because the law prohibits it. So the law needs to be changed."
— Rep. Ted Poe, R-TX

"The world needs the crude."
— Ryan Lance, Chairman and CEO, ConocoPhillips

"It's as if we own the world's biggest bank vault but misplaced the key... Let's lift that export ban and have America shaping the market price in our own interest."
— Andy Karsner, CEO, Manifest Energy LLC

"The 1970s-era policy restricting crude oil exports — a vestige from a price controls system that ended in 1981 — is a remnant from another time."
— Daniel Yergin, Vice Chairman, IHS

KEEP THE CRUDE OIL EXPORT BAN IN PLACE

"Lifting the crude oil export ban means Big Oil will export oil until the world price and the American price are the same. We should keep American oil in America just as we have for the last 40 years."

— Sen. Robert Melendez, D-NJ

"Lifting the crude oil export ban would harm U.S. refineries and workers... Oil companies that engage in exploration and production would reap huge profits at the expense of their refining units that have to buy oil on the open market. Also harmed would be independent refiners that do not engage in oil exploration... The reasons for not ending the crude oil export ban are obvious... Congress and the administration should not even be considering incremental legislation that would lift the ban in stages."

— Gary Beevers, International Vice President, United Steelworkers

"Eroding the crude oil export ban in place for more than 40 years is incredibly controversial. At a time when the nation has made a commitment to reduce climate-warming emissions and the renewable energy sector is going gangbusters in job creation, U.S. energy policy should reject any measure that encourages more drilling and more production of highly polluting crude oil."

— Patti Goldman, Managing Attorney, Northwest regional office, Earthjustice

"Crude exports on the part of a country that imports nearly half of its crude oil requirements are, in our view, very unlikely to improve energy security or advance national interest, as we will simply make ourselves more dependent upon crude oil imports as we export our own crude."

— Michael C. Jennings, President and CEO, HollyFrontier Corp.

"Lifting the oil export ban will raise prices for U.S. refiners... The math is simple on this action: Removing export ban = higher oil prices = higher gasoline prices - angry voters."

— Thomas O'Malley, Executive Chairman, PBF Energy

"Selling crude oil at a higher price on the world market would pad the bank accounts of oil companies, but it could also raise gasoline prices at home and increase our imports. To protect the pocketbooks of families and businesses and maintain our energy security, we should keep American oil here at home."

— Daniel J. Weiss, Senior Vice President of Campaigns, League of Conservation Voters; former Senior Fellow and Director of Climate Strategy Center, American Progress

"As the United States enjoys a boom in oil production, common sense dictates that the oil should remain at home, providing American refinery jobs and reducing the nation's reliance upon oil imports... Lifting a ban on exports would be a bad idea for the United States, both economically and environmentally."

— The Columbian

"In order to play its part in meeting global climate goals, it is imperative that the United States maintains the ban on crude oil exports and does everything it can to decrease, rather than increase, the global pool of fossil fuel reserves that are exploited."

— Oil Change International

"With all of the increased production coming from controversial fracking techniques, lifting the ban not only would raise gasoline prices for U.S. families, but would create bigger environmental headaches."

— Tyson Slocum, Director, Public Citizen Energy Program

"If we lift the ban on crude oil exports, we will export both our oil and the jobs and economic activity associated with refining that oil."

— Brad Markell, Executive Director— Industrial Union Council, AFL-CIO

"The Middle East is in turmoil. Gas prices are sky-high in the middle of driving season. And we still import millions of barrels of oil a day. Exporting our crude oil is not the answer for anyone but oil companies."

— Sen. Ed Markey, D-MA

But these baby steps could lead to breaching the barrier entirely.

And cracks in the export barrier are appearing. In addition to the shift enabling these increased condensate exports, another portent was visible at the end of September 2014: supermajor ConocoPhillips shipped the first cargo of Alaska North Slope crude to Asia in more than ten years.

Don't Fix What Ain't Broke

A debate is raging over what to do about these cracks. The U.S. appears to be at a fork in the road, legislatively speaking: One direction perpetuates the status quo, while the other sends us down the path toward crude export.

Continuing with the status quo might be the easy choice. In fact, many politicians, economists, scholars, and environmental activists contend that the current system prohibiting crude export absolutely *is not* broken. Their conclusions encourage maintaining the ban in perpetuity—or at least, in some opinions, until we have fully analyzed all the potential ramifications and studied every possible outcome.

Many U.S. refiners also resolutely oppose lifting the ban over concerns that the profits they're seeing from the shale gale will be lost if exported oil goes to refineries overseas.

Without question, refiners have been some of the biggest beneficiaries of the shale boom. The flood of U.S. oil has dropped the price of West Texas Intermediate (WTI, the U.S. crude oil benchmark), making it cheaper for refineries to buy feedstock. But the price refiners command for their finished products isn't linked to WTI; instead, it's tied to more expensive Brent crude (the global benchmark). With the gap between WTI and Brent widening, refineries have been buying low and selling high in recent years, reaping significant financial rewards they don't want to lose.

If the U.S. banishes the export ban, domestic refiners would have to compete with the entire world market. Without boundaries, U.S. oil producers will have the luxury of selling to the highest bidder. As a result, the price American refiners will pay for crude will likely increase, causing profit margins to shrink.

Free the Flow

Doug Sheridan, founder and managing director of Houston's Energy-Point Research, understands the refiners' point of view. But it rankles him, to say the least. When we spoke with this twenty-year veteran of the oil and gas industry in September 2014, he pointed out that many of the refineries objecting to the idea of a crude oil ban reversal are located in the northeastern U.S. To him, their opposition—backed by political leaders—is akin to one region of the country hampering the economic opportunities of another: "It's a case of nonhydrocarbon-producing regions telling the hydrocarbon-producing states what we can and can't do with our assets."

"Boston is a technology center, but you don't see anyone telling them not to export their technology," Sheridan expanded on his stance. "It's like Texans telling Detroit not to sell their pickup trucks overseas because we need them all."

Stephen Brown, visiting fellow at Resources for the Future and director of the Center for Business and Economic Research at Lee Business School of the University of Nevada, offers another counterargument for these doubtful refiners. As he told my team in an October 2014 interview, "Repealing the export ban will make refinery options a lot more efficient throughout the world, particularly in the Western Hemisphere."

And other export advocates see lifting the ban as not just a question of economic benefit, but of national identity—a means of lengthening America's reach as a reborn energy superpower, extending the benefits of greater supplies, and diversifying resources worldwide.

Tom Ridge, former governor of Pennsylvania and first U.S. Director of Homeland Security, is a strong advocate for energy exports. In an exclusive interview with my team in September 2014, Ridge insisted that U.S. energy exports should be part of an "energy-smart, all-in" national policy, a key to cementing global relationships and increasing world supplies while lowering prices of multiple energy sources, not just oil and gas. Free U.S. energy trade would also mean greater security for the U.S. and our allies, placing energy "buffers" in zones that are at the mercy of unstable and even hostile suppliers.

Remember Russia shutting off the tap to Ukrainian gas, again and again?

"You do not want to rely on certain sources of energy from unreliable and unstable countries," Ridge said. "As the Russians have demonstrated now: You don't have to have as large an army if you can control the energy of potential adversaries."

And in this parley, Ridge is certainly not a lone wolf.

"Recent analysis confirms lifting the export ban would spur economic growth and create hundreds of thousands of additional jobs, while at the same time lowering prices at the pump. It would also diversify the world oil supply—strengthening our energy security and giving us more leverage in foreign policy matters," senior lawmaker Representative Joe Barton (R-TX) told us in a September 2014 email. "The U.S. has long been committed to free trade and open markets; it's time we practice what we preach when it comes to energy."

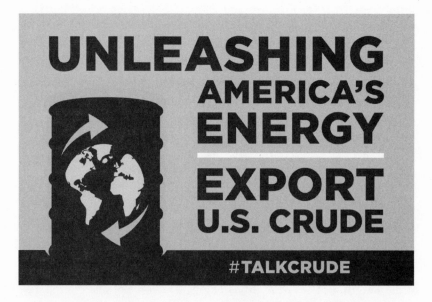

Canary, LLC, supports a repeal of the crude oil export ban, launching an online campaign to petition the government to consider this action and encouraging followers of "#TALKCRUDE" on social media.

MAKE YOUR VOICE HEARD

HELP UNLEASH AMERICA'S ENERGY

SIGN THE PETITION

LIFT THE CRUDE OIL EXPORT BAN

At the EIA's annual energy conference in July 2014, John R. Auers, executive vice president of Turner, Mason & Co. Consulting Engineers, Dallas, said the day will come when our crude production exceeds refinery capacity to the point that prices will become heavily discounted to comparable overseas grades. When that happens, producers will stop increasing production, drying up our supply of light crude and making us more reliant on foreign exports.[9]

Daniel Yergin, the noted author, agreed. "The rationales for a crude oil export ban are gone, but the ban is still in place," Yergin remarked at the July 2014 EIA Conference in Washington D.C. "Lifting the ban on crude oil exports would signal the U.S. government's commitment to global markets and energy security. The U.S. has preached to other countries for decades about the need for free flow of resources. How can we say to Japan that it can't import any of our LNG but must not buy Iran's oil?"[10]

A Bolstered Economy

Export proponents back their arguments with some impressive statistics, from lower gas prices to greater employment opportunities to overall improvements to the U.S. economy.

Because of the issues we've discussed surrounding U.S. refinery configuration for heavy and sour grades from the Middle East and South America, the flood of light and sweet blends coming out of domestic shale plays has built up supply gluts. The upshot is a plunge in domestic crude prices, making producers desperate to unload their oil to international refiners who not only will pay a higher price for it, but are better are equipped to handle it.

If the crude oil export ban is lifted, producers will be able to sell their oil on international markets at a higher price, and the global supply of crude will increase.

The result? Even lower U.S. gas prices—to the tune of a $5.8 billion annual reduction in consumer fuel costs from 2015 to 2035, according to ICF International and Ensys Energy.[11]

It's a win-win. Energy producers get to sell their energy to the global market. Consumers continue to enjoy reduced gas prices due to ample global supply.

When U.S. oil producers can fetch higher prices on international markets, loosening export restrictions should make domestic oil production more profitable. This would lead to an increase in exploration and production activities throughout the U.S., creating hundreds of thousands of new jobs in drilling, production, and transportation—as well as in industries that are indirectly affected by oil and gas operations.

Bernard Weinstein of the Maguire Energy Institute maintained that, for every oil and gas extraction job, seven others manifest in energy-related services.[12] Likewise, international consulting firm IHS recently concluded that the resulting increase in production activities from lifting the export ban could add anywhere from 394,000 to 859,000 new jobs to the U.S. economy between 2016 and 2030.[13]

In addition to lower gas prices for American drivers and more jobs across the nation, expanding crude exports would also reduce the country's long-time trade deficit by as much as $22 billion by 2020.[14] The trade deficit has already experienced a decline in recent years as overall U.S. exports have increased. Now at its lowest level since 2009, the trade deficit could dive even lower with expanding exports. EIA data evidences this potential: "Since 2009, exports of petroleum and petroleum products have played a growing role in reducing the overall merchandise trade deficit."[15]

Let's say that our illustrious leaders in Washington just can't come to a decision—that politicians remain at loggerheads, locking horns instead of legislating—and the ban remains in place. Crude production will continue to increase, and with refining capacity stretched to the limit, a domestic surplus in the not so distant future is a very realistic possibility.

Great, right?

While the idea of having "too much" oil *seems* like a good thing, its negative impact on domestic production would likely reverberate throughout the U.S. economy. As an excess of light crude builds up, domestic oil prices will fall—and if they fall too far, optimization of shale plays will become unprofitable and production will taper off. If this happens, all the benefits that come from expanding crude exports would be jeopardized: Jobs would be cut, foreign investment in shale production would decline, the trade deficit would increase, and the U.S. would miss out on the opportunity to use its abundant supply of energy to help American consumers and bolster its waning economy.

And analysts caution that, the longer the export ban stays in place, the more negative an effect it will have on the U.S. economy.

Renewed Security

But there's more to the export story than just strengthening our economy. With exports of refined petrochemical products like diesel, condensate, and LNG rising—and imports of crude oil falling—many industry experts say that the future of energy security in the U.S. is stronger than it has ever been.

Expanding our exports not only keeps our shale producers in business by providing them more of a marketplace. Broadening our marketplace will also strengthen our national energy security by maximizing the scope of the production boom and boosting American economic power that forms the basis of U.S. national power and global influence.

Consider the geopolitical maneuvering that would be possible. Exporting to our trade partners currently being held hostage by unfriendly suppliers would create a stabilizing effect the world over. Reliable U.S. oil exports could go far to lessen global security threats. The flexibility to export our crude could also address supply disruptions as we shift oil rents away from less-than-reliable suppliers.

Consider Stephen's informed opinion. He admitted to my team during our October 2014 conversation a certain sympathy for the opposing view that shipping out our own oil and bringing in oil from other countries reduces our national security—but he still doesn't agree with that idea. "The fact is that we're in a global oil market—even if we don't import oil from an unstable country like Venezuela, all the prices of oil are going to move in concert with any movements created by a disruption of production from Venezuela. I have sympathy with it being a security issue, but I think it's misinformed."

One other thing to consider is, for lack of a better term, "saving face." As one of the world's economic superpowers, the U.S. is boldly vocal in encouraging others to adopt a free-market society. We are up in arms, for example, over China's mineral export restrictions. They don't export certain minerals that they use in watches, protecting them as "natural resources." But how different is their stance than our refusal to export our shale resources?

"Do we want to be producing all of our energy at home and not engaging in that global marketplace?" Garten Rothkopf's Claire Casey asked us rhetorically. "No. It would mean resource nationalism in a way that we point fingers at other countries for engaging in."

Rescinding the crude oil export ban would stake our claim as an international energy role model—and might encourage other economies to follow our example. Of course, the world energy market remains tumultuous. No amount of "new oil" on the scene will really change the ups and downs of the cyclical commodity—but a spate of U.S. product could act as a stabilizing force for both prices and relationships the world over.

Importers Cheer for Reform

Mounting pressure on Washington is coming from energy trade partners—current and potential—who are seeking their own stability. Voices from all corners of the world entreat U.S. to ship our crude overseas.

Japan, for one, would love to see a regular provision of our resources. After the Fukushima Daiichi nuclear reactor disaster in March 2011, the country was forced to turn to alternative energy sources. Heavily dependent on the Middle East for its crude oil imports, Japan brought in 84 percent of its crude oil from this region in 2014.[16] But the Japanese are also keen to geographically diversify their supply sources. As soon as the U.S. green-lighted ultralight condensate exports, Japan jumped at the chance: In late 2014, the country became one of the first to import U.S. ultralight.

Likewise, South Korea is enthusiastically pursuing our ultralight crude. President Park Geun-hye told a delegation of U.S. representatives from the House Energy Committee that she hoped Congress would indeed find a solution to enable U.S. condensate exports to enter her country. In addition, one of South Korea's leading refiners chimed in to encourage the U.S. to permit exports.

Another foreign dignitary added his voice to the debate. In September 2014, Ukrainian president Petro Poroshenko flew to Washington to appeal for military and energy assistance in the wake of Russia's Gazprom shutting off Ukraine's gas earlier that summer.

And as any energy disruptions to Ukraine mean disruptions throughout Europe, surrounding countries have tried to diversify in recent years, actively seeking U.S. oil and gas to help ease their dependence on Russian energy. In July 2014, for example, the *Washington Post* leaked a secret document showing that the European Union is pressing the U.S. to lift its ban on crude oil exports as part of a "sweeping trade and investment deal" that could equal $4.7 trillion if completed.[17]

Even with predictable delays of implementation and supply, a U.S. crude export program would also deliver to our energy-consumer allies a powerful tool to counter monopoly supplier aggression.

A Matter of Psychology

Even with all the data supporting the benefits, Claire Casey of Garten Rothkopf cautioned that getting the American populace to truly buy into broad crude exports is going to be a convoluted process because it goes against the rhetoric that we've embraced for the last forty years concerning our quest for energy independence to combat oil price shocks.

"The shale oil question is different, psychologically, for the country," she told us. "The mythology around 'energy security' is the product of a discourse over decades. Now that things have gotten more complicated [with North America leading energy production], our political rhetoric really isn't adjusting fast enough to understand the new position the United States is in."

The notion of the U.S. being a net exporter was never part of the conversation, so it's hard to reconcile with our current situation. After pushing the agenda that energy security equals holding onto it for so long publicly, Casey concedes that it's hard to reverse directions and say, "Oh, but we should export now."

Yet crude isn't the only energy we have to export, nor the only energy source where export is curtailed by the U.S. government. The shale energy source we really need to export—the prices of which have fallen just as drastically as oil and the clean-burning fossil fuel that shale is best known for—is natural gas.

CHAPTER 16

LNG: WHAT IS IT— AND WHY CAN'T IT GO TO JAPAN OR UKRAINE?

It might not have the old-school swagger of a James Dean or the modern-day cachet of a hipster's nose ring, but liquefied natural gas is definitely cool.

As in minus-260-degrees-Fahrenheit cool.

That's the temperature to which methane, the key component of natural gas, is chilled to become clear, colorless liquefied natural gas, more commonly called LNG. At that frosty point—only slightly warmer than the surface of the moon—not only has the gas been converted to liquid, its volume has been reduced about 600 times. As the Center for Liquefied Natural Gas explains, that's like "reducing the volume of a beach ball to the volume of a Ping-Pong ball."[1]

As a condensed liquid, LNG can be transported around the world to a receiving hub. Then, through a warming process rather ignominiously known as regasification, it's changed into a vapor and marketed as fuel.

Although the super-chilled science of methane conversion is pretty nifty in its own right, that's not what was on the minds of hundreds of LNG experts who converged upon downtown Houston in the fall of 2014. Instead, they convened to discuss how North American LNG producers, rich with a flood of shale-sourced natural gas, might be able to meet the world's red-hot demand—particularly in places like Asia, which comprises two-thirds of the global LNG market.

Behind the LNG Eight Ball

Since 2000, the blue flame of natural gas has been burning brighter than ever, with global LNG demand up an estimated 7.6 percent per year. Like a Ping-Pong ball magically swelling into a beach ball, that trend is expected only to grow over the next few years: By 2030, Ernst & Young LLP expects global demand to reach 500 million metric tons, which is about double the 2012 level. Most of that spring-loaded demand is coming from Japan, Korea, India, China, and Taiwan, although there are also opportunities in Europe, as the continent tries to diversify its energy sources.

Traditionally, much of the world's LNG has come from countries like Qatar, Australia, Malaysia, and Indonesia, but it's no secret that other LNG-producing nations are trying to strike while the iron is hot. In fact, analysts suggest that approximately 80 percent of future capacity will be sourced from Australia, Canada, East Africa, Russia, and the U.S. (which recently ascended to the lofty position of world's largest natural gas producer because of—you guessed it—surging supplies from shale).

Despite America's production primacy, we're still well behind the competition when it comes to exporting LNG.

Australia is currently poised to overtake Qatar for the top spot, a feat it should achieve by 2018. Australian LNG trade grew 74 percent between 2005 and 2012, reaching 327.9 billion cubic meters per year. In 2013 alone, Australia exported 47 percent of what it produced.

Compare that to U.S. LNG stats: We re-export approximately 1.5 billion cubic meters of LNG to Canada and Mexico, but we haven't shipped domestic LNG abroad since 2011.

If all projections hold and all thirty of the proposed U.S. export facilities come online within fifteen years, the U.S. should be exporting 23 billion cubic feet of LNG by the end of 2028.[2] Not only would that be good for global energy-seekers and U.S. LNG producers, it would create an American economic bonanza: A study by ICF International projects that LNG exports will contribute up to 665,000 net jobs nationwide and add as much as $115 billion to U.S. gross domestic product (GDP) by 2035.

As is often the case, however, not everyone sees eye to eye on this issue. As Garten Rothkopf's Claire Casey pointed out when our team spoke with her in April 2014, one segment—namely the petrochemical industry—put up quite a fight. Petrochemicals led a charge against LNG exports, Casey said, for very good reason: "Having natural gas at home—and having it be cheap—gives them a competitive advantage in a very competitive international industry."

But Casey noted that the fight ultimately failed: "The key decision was getting the LNG export terminals approved. Now that those processes are in line, studies have come out that it does not have a negative impact on the U.S. economy."

And that's why the LNG pros had gathered in Houston: to figure out how to use the momentum to overcome a regulatory process that's hamstringing their efforts to get exports off the ground to begin with.

The Geopolitics of Freezing Imports

The fact is that exporting LNG would signal a reversal of sorts in the U.S. energy trade.

In order to meet our escalating energy needs, for years we relied on a rising tide of LNG *imports*. Even as recently as a decade ago, our need for LNG imports seemed unassailable. In 2005, no less an authority than the Department of Energy (DOE) estimated that net imports of natural gas would grow from 19 percent of total U.S. consumption in 2010 to 28 percent in 2025.[3]

Of course, the DOE hadn't anticipated how the impact of U.S. shale might change the calculus.

Since 2005, U.S. natural gas production has increased 41 percent. By harnessing our homegrown LNG supplies, in the six years between the 2007 start of the shale revolution and 2013, the amount of LNG imported into the U.S. plunged some 80 percent. Even more remarkable is the fact that, in November 2014, *the U.S. didn't import any LNG at all*. That was the first time since 1996 we could make that claim.[4]

With the Energy Information Administration (EIA) projecting a further 48 percent increase in production from 2010 to 2035, we've got enough natural gas to satisfy our own needs *and* supply the world. In fact, the total volume of U.S. natural gas recoverable with existing technology is more than 100 times greater than current domestic consumption.

This illustrates that being an expert isn't the same as being clairvoyant. But today, forward-thinkers say that, with imports down and production soaring, we should be exporting our domestically produced natural gas as LNG. As America's Natural Gas Alliance suggested, the U.S. could reap economic, environmental, and geopolitical benefits by building terminals to "give abundant domestic supplies of the fuel full access to world markets."[5] Exporting inexpensive natural gas will help the U.S. trade balance, promote the cause of clean-burning fuels worldwide, and give our allies a reliable, trusted energy source.

Senator Cory Gardner (R-CO) supports a U.S. commitment to export LNG—and even introduced legislation in Congress to this effect with the Domestic Prosperity and Global Freedom Act during the 113th Congress of 2013–2014—because it would provide additional tools for our global partners in their energy negotiations with aggressive nations. "Even in addition to the energy we may be sending them, we give them an additional bargaining tool when it comes to their long-term agreements for their energy supplies," Gardner told us in April 2014.

"This means a great deal for the cavalry riding over the hill, so to speak—the fact that you do have the promise of future supply, a policy put in place that will mean the eventual delivery of LNG and a supply that can and will impact world markets," Gardner continued. "If you know that the U.S. is coming online, maybe you don't enter into a twenty-year agreement. Maybe you enter into a shorter-term agreement, which allows you greater bargaining power and leverage."

Logical, sure. But not nearly so easy as it sounds. Especially when the rest of the world is watching.

"The geopolitics will drive a great deal of this as those permits are approved and as the White House and the administration—whoever it is—looks toward the U.S. energy response in terms of helping our allies," said Gardner, "so I do think that energy security considerations will remain a large focus of LNG exports."

Building Momentum Toward Export

Gardner's bill, among several circulating in the House and Senate, modifies the standard of review for future LNG export applications, shifting the benchmark from Free Trade Agreement (FTA) countries to World Trade Organization (WTO) members. Under current law, LNG export facilities shipping gas to countries without free-trade agreements with the U.S. require additional DOE approvals, a process marked by extensive delays. A further environmental and safety review is required for non-FTA export facilities by the Federal Regulatory and Energy Commission (FERC). Both agencies must give their blessings to any export facility construction project. Because neither agency has to follow any set timetable, the review—extensive, intensive, and expensive for the proposing company—can drag on for years. Case in point: To date, only seven export applications have been approved (one final, six conditional), while twenty-four applications are still awaiting action.

For now, the U.S. LNG situation is muddied by the regulatory complex. American LNG can be sold to our twenty free-trade partners—think Australia (which certainly doesn't need our LNG), Canada, Honduras, Israel, Oman—but there's a prickly little statute in the law requiring a public interest determination for export of LNG to non-free-trade countries.

Right now, there's only one U.S. LNG export facility in operation: the ConocoPhillips Kenai LNG Terminal near Anchorage, Alaska, which ships fuel mainly to Japan. (Although Kenai is the only fully functional American LNG *export* facility, there are actually more than 110 LNG operations in the U.S., according to FERC. Some re-export natural gas, some provide natural gas supply to the interstate pipeline system or local distribution companies, and others are used to store natural gas for periods of peak demand. Still other facilities produce LNG for vehicle fuel or for industrial use.)

One of the lucky few that has been approved is Dominion Resources' Cove Point, located on the western shore of Maryland's Chesapeake Bay.

Following a two-year regulatory review that included more than sixty approvals and permits, Cove Point finally received FERC approval in 2014 for the $3.8 billion project—although it still had to meet seventy-nine environmental conditions before construction could begin. With all approvals now in hand, Cove Point is expected to begin exporting LNG to Japan in 2017.

Michael D. Frederick, Dominion Resources vice president of LNG operations, was the keynote speaker at the 2014 Houston LNG conference. Not only did he express relief at the long regulatory journey being behind him, he recounted the years of wrangling the company went through with those opposed to the project—chiefly environmentalists and anti-frackers who believed, Frederick said, that by "stopping Cove Point, they could stop fracking."

After a pitched PR battle—which Frederick considered a "grassroots mission to correct misinformation" that included fact books, phone calls, open houses, and ads refuting "the seven main myths" surrounding the project—public opposition to Cove Point finally abated. It didn't hurt that Dominion has, in Frederick's words, "moved beyond what we were expected to do environmentally, including creating a nature preserve around the plant." The company was also able to convince its neighbors that any greenhouse gases it produces will be offset by the fact that the LNG is going to Japan, where replacing other fuels with natural gas should help that nation lower its own CO_2 emissions.

Justifying the Holding Pattern

Cove Point is just the fourth LNG export project to receive final approval. The others are Houston-based Cheniere Energy's Sabine Pass LNG Terminal in Cameron, Louisiana; San Diego–based Sempra Energy's Cameron LNG project in Hackberry, Louisiana; and Houston-based Freeport LNG's project on Quintana Island in Texas.

As Frederick noted, it took years to get the approvals necessary to move Cove Point ahead. That experience was hardly the exception. According to the American Natural Gas Alliance, Cheniere Energy waited nearly two years from the time it applied to the DOE until it was granted final approval. For Cameron LNG and Freeport LNG, the delay was even longer—three and four years, respectively.

Jon B. Wellinghoff, FERC chairman (2009–2013), followed Frederick on the Houston stage later in the day. Unsurprisingly, he defended FERC's delays in granting LNG approvals.

Wellinghoff, who speaks in the careful, measured tones of a government official, said that one issue is simply a lack of manpower in the midst of a blizzard of applications. But more important, he suggested, is that FERC has to take considerable care in assessing the long-term economic viability of each proposed facility. FERC has had to weigh whether natural gas supply will continue to outpace demand. He asserted the agency's conviction that it will, after 2015—although excess capacity still remains a concern. In light of the possibility of excess capacity, Wellinghoff said, "being first matters."

Which may not be such good news for projects that are still in a holding pattern. Like Golden Pass LNG.

Renewed Hope?

On the Texas Gulf Coast—less than a hundred miles southeast of the LNG pros' gathering in Houston—Golden Pass LNG is a monument of sorts to the capricious fortunes of American energy.

Originally built to receive and distribute LNG from Qatar, the terminal was completed in 2010 at a cost of more than $1 billion. It's been nearly idle ever since, a testament to America's dried-up need for Qatari gas.

If ExxonMobil and the government of Qatar can at last work their way through the regulatory process, the facility will undergo a $10 billion overhaul and be reborn as an export terminal. But forward-thinking Golden Pass will retain its import capabilities, should the winds of change shift again in the future and new market conditions emerge.

Studying Golden Pass's online newsroom is like looking at a calendar flip in slow motion:

- October 26, 2012: Golden Pass Products Files Application with U.S. Department of Energy to Export Liquefied Natural Gas to Non-FTA Countries
- May 16, 2013: Golden Pass Products Starts FERC Pre-filing Process
- July 7, 2014: Golden Pass Products Files Formal FERC Application

Since then, no other updates have been posted. Nearly two-and-a-half years have passed, and still no progress. Although the DOE has made improvements to its permitting procedures, the process remains redundant and unpredictable. And FERC's foot-dragging continues to hold things up—and hold U.S. LNG potential back.

But there's new hope for companies whose applications have been languishing at the federal level: In January 2015, the U.S. House of Representatives passed legislation that would help such companies. The bill, H.R. 351 LNG Permitting Certainty and Transparency Act, sponsored by Gardner's Ohio House of Representatives colleague Bill Johnson, calls for an expedited federal approval process for LNG exports. It's currently sitting in the Senate Committee on Energy and Natural Resources.

"The window of opportunity for LNG exports will not remain open indefinitely, so it's important that Congress act immediately," Johnson said.[6]

And he's right.

Removing the barriers to exporting LNG will contribute significantly to the financial health of the U.S. But remember what former FERC chair Wellinghoff said about being first. Right now, in a race that's heating up day by day, we're struggling to catch up to more agile global competition with a strong lead. Here's hoping that Congress will keep us from being frozen out altogether.

And here's hoping that Casey's prognosis is accurate: "We should expect to see the U.S. become an LNG exporter in the next decade. I would be shocked if they were not."

Once again, the shifting "mix" of energy imports and exports changes the political calculus of the world.

CHAPTER 17

YET ANOTHER VETO

February 10, 2011, was a grim day in Allentown, Pennsylvania. Sirens still roared as emergency responders rushed to a residential neighborhood, where several buildings had been burning all night. The city street was a pile of rubble—and so were some of the houses.

One resident said that he thought a bomb had gone off. But it wasn't a bomb. The explosion was caused by a ruptured pipeline carrying natural gas below the city street. The ensuing chaos damaged fifty buildings. And even worse, it killed five people.

The Allentown tragedy occurred just five months after a similar explosion in San Bruno, California, which damaged more than forty homes, killed eight people, and injured dozens more.

Unfortunately, these are two of many instances. Since 1986, U.S. pipeline accidents have killed more than 500 people, injured more than 4,000 more, and cost nearly $7 billion in property damage.

It's horrifying to know that at any given time, the ground below your street could explode, or that a pipeline could spill thousands of barrels of crude oil onto your property. So what on earth is going on with U.S. pipelines? And how do we fix it?

To answer that first question: U.S. pipelines are just getting too old. The fact that the United States has a pipeline infrastructure in place has certainly been touted as a benefit of our oil and gas industry, but the fact is that more than half of the nation's pipelines were constructed during the 1950s and 1960s, and about 15 percent of American oil pipelines are even older. Plus, approximately 3 percent of the gas distribution mains in service today are made of troublesome cast iron or wrought iron and were constructed during the first half of the twentieth century.[1]

That Allentown pipeline that exploded and killed five people? It was eighty-three years old at the time. And the one in San Bruno? Forty-four years old.

Fast-forward to today. Not only are these "mature" pipelines still in use, they're being taxed more than ever because of the growth in shale drilling. And obviously, they can no longer handle the pressure.

But building new pipelines has its own set of problems—political ones. The accidents caused by old pipelines—in addition to some other environmental issues—have given a bad rap to building Keystone XL. But is Keystone's bad rap warranted—or is Keystone in the national interest after all?

From the Frying Pan into the Fire

Before getting into the political red tape behind building Keystone, it's helpful to understand what's causing most of the current pipeline accidents in the old pipelines. The problem with these aging pipelines is in the material. They're mostly made of cast iron, and unfortunately, cast iron is less durable than we realized at the time. True, Grandma might have a cast-iron skillet that she's used since 1935, but it turns out that cast iron is a crankier material for oil and gas transportation. It's nonmalleable: It can't be bent, stretched, or hammered into shape. Because it's brittle, cast iron can crack or break easily, sometimes as a result of ground movement in proximity to buried pipe.

We can't really blame the pipeline designers for employing the best material available at the time, and it's doubtful that they anticipated their products would be expected to have an eighty-plus-year life span. Even though experts say that pipeline age isn't necessarily a threat on its own, inadequate materials plus outdated engineering can be a formula for increased danger to people and property. In short, old pipelines of cast iron and other inadequate materials might be sending us from the frying pan quite literally into the fire.

When midcentury pipeline designers started working with bare steel instead of cast iron, they probably felt like prospectors who had hit pay dirt. Finally, they had access to a material that offered even greater strength, flexibility, and high-pressure operating capacity. But as a transportation corridor for oil and gas, bare steel's record hasn't been perfect, either. When it comes in contact with moisture—either from inside the pipes or from the ground—bare steel can corrode. And corrosion in welds and couplings can lead to failures: leaks, ruptures, even explosions. In fact, corrosion has caused between 15 percent and 20 percent of the 1,400 reported pipeline incidents since 1986 that resulted in death, injury, or extensive property damage. And distribution mains made of cast iron or bare steel leak eighteen times more natural gas than plastic pipes, and fifty-seven times more gas than protected steel.[2]

"Newer" steel pipelines are coated to prevent corrosion and its damage. But that's not a foolproof solution, either: Some coatings are more effective than others, and the older the pipeline, the more likely it is to have been coated with something like polyethylene, a plastic that degrades over time. Since the 1970s, most pipelines have been made from medium- and high-density polyethylene. The National Transportation Safety Board has reported that plastic pipe installed in natural gas distribution systems from the 1960s through the early 1980s may be vulnerable to brittle-like cracking, resulting in gas leakage and potential hazards to the public.

Further complicating the issue is that many of today's pipelines no longer transport the product that was part of their original job descriptions. The shale boom has changed the game for existing pipelines: The products are different and might require higher pressures; plus some pipelines are being reversed to flow in the opposite direction. These changes mean that cracks and other anomalies that weren't necessarily a problem before can result in a catastrophe when a pipeline begins operating outside of its design limits. For example, there's the 2010 Kalamazoo River spill in Michigan—the largest, costliest inland spill in U.S. history. This accident occurred along a forty-year-old reversed pipeline that was carrying diluted bitumen from the Alberta, Canada, tar sands. Because the product was so different than the crude oil the line was originally intended to move, pressure-cycle-induced fatigue activated defects and cracks to the point they ruptured.[3]

Potentially dangerous pipelines will continue to grow older, aging beyond what could reasonably be expected to be a useful life. And with each new candle on the cake, the chances that it will spark a disaster only increase.

Easing the Glut—for Good

Obviously, the U.S. has a problem here: We need pipelines to move oil and natural gas, but we need to maintain them. Plus, we need to build more. For a while, U.S. pipeline capacity couldn't keep up with recent production hikes from shale fields. The glut created gridlock, which sent crude prices spiraling downward. This was a good situation for refiners with access to Texas and North Dakota stock, sure, but discouraging to producers.

The industry is off to a decent start with expansion of the pipeline system. It's estimated that 16,500 miles of new gathering lines (the pipelines closest to the wellhead that transport oil or gas to a storage facility or larger main pipeline) will be constructed annually in North America through 2035, for a total of 400,000 miles of new gathering lines in slightly more than two decades.

Although the glut has been eased somewhat, if the U.S. is to truly capitalize on the recent production gains in the wake of the shale gale, there must be alternative routes. The oil and gas industry can either continue to expand its use of other forms of transportation, or more pipelines have to come online.

The biggest project for easing the shale gale glut is the Keystone XL Pipeline, a proposed stretch of 1,179 miles from Hardisty, Alberta, to Steele City, Nebraska, shown on the map (Figure 17.1). This extension—first proposed back in 2008—would move Canadian oil and support U.S. production growth from the Bakken. Along with transporting 700,000 barrels of Canadian crude oil per day to refineries around Houston and the Gulf of Mexico, the $7 billion pipeline would also support the significant growth of domestic production from the Bakken by adding pipeline capacity.

When folks talk about "The Keystone," there's likely some misunderstanding. The Keystone Pipeline System is actually a phased network connecting Alberta to the Gulf of Mexico. Three phases are already fully operational, and an extension of the last of these phases is going online this year. But the squeaky wheel is the controversial fourth phase, Keystone XL.

Because of the fairly recent fatal accidents and environmental disasters caused by malfunctioning pipelines, debate rages over whether building the Keystone XL is in the national interest. Do the pros outweigh the cons? Answering that for the Keystone XL has been difficult, to say the least.

Because the Keystone XL pipeline would cross the border between Canada and the U.S., it needs to be approved by the U.S. Department of State, which means President Obama could veto the project outright if he wanted to. And in 2012, Obama did reject the proposal. At the time, many observers said the president's response was pushback against Republicans who were trying to force the issue. Of course, there was also considerable concern about the route the proposed pipeline would take through the environmentally sensitive Sand Hills region of Nebraska—a path that even the state's Republican governor opposed. But after TransCanada rerouted the pipeline to avoid Nebraska's Sand Hills, officials signed off on the new proposal, which was sent back to the State Department for further study.

In February 2014, the State Department released the next report on the Keystone XL—an extremely thorough examination that concluded that building Keystone won't have a large environmental impact.[4] Stopping the Keystone won't do anything about climate change (the environmentalists' hot-button issue), but building it will create jobs (the pro-Keystone faction's chief key contention). That study certainly helped get the proposal through Congress—and even earned support across party lines.

One of the most strident voices has been former senator Mary Landrieu, a Democrat from Louisiana. In 2014, Landrieu, then-chair of

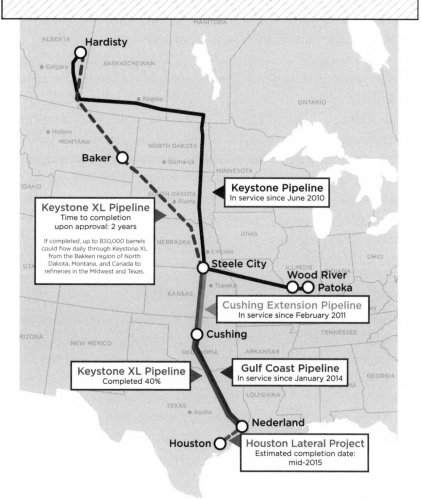

LITTLE-KNOWN FACT ABOUT THE KEYSTONE XL PIPELINE:
40% has already been built and is in use—from
Steele City, Nebraska, to Nederland, Texas. Only 1,169
miles of additional pipe is needed to complete
Keystone XL's northern segment.

Hardisty

Baker

Keystone Pipeline
In service since June 2010

Keystone XL Pipeline
Time to completion
upon approval: 2 years

If completed, up to 830,000 barrels
could flow daily through Keystone XL
from the Bakken region of North
Dakota, Montana, and Canada to
refineries in the Midwest and Texas.

Steele City

Wood River
Patoka

Cushing Extension Pipeline
In service since February 2011

Cushing

Keystone XL Pipeline
Completed 40%

Gulf Coast Pipeline
In service since January 2014

Nederland

Houston

Houston Lateral Project
Estimated completion date:
mid-2015

the Senate Energy and Natural Resources Committee, called the delay to approve the pipeline "irresponsible, unnecessary, and unacceptable."[5]

Fellow former Democratic senator Mark Pryor of Arkansas has been widely quoted as saying, "When it comes to the Keystone XL pipeline, there's no excuse for another delay. The president needs to approve this project now to ensure our future energy security and create jobs here at home."[6]

In May 2014, Pryor took it a step further: He and his re-election opponent, Republican representative Tom Cotton, made a joint appearance at a Little Rock pipe manufacturer to call for an end to the impasse.

Alaska's Democratic senator Mark Begich has also chimed in: "I am frankly appalled at the continued foot-dragging by this administration on the Keystone project."[7]

In February 2015, the proposal finally met bipartisan approval in Congress—passing with strong Democratic support in both the House and Senate. But the action was quickly tempered just a few days later by President Obama's use of his executive veto power—for only the third time in his presidency. The Senate's early March vote failed to reach the two-thirds majority required to override a presidential veto. Which means we're practically back to square one on the XL debate.

The Granddaddy of Stalled Projects

So what's the big deal with Keystone XL? How does one pipeline extension take so long to be approved?

The reason that Keystone XL is the granddaddy of all stalled projects is that people can't agree about whether or not the pipeline's advantages outweigh the costs. As Michael A. Levi, energy fellow at the Council on Foreign Relations said, "This is a tricky political challenge for the president—the reality is everyone has defined the stakes on Keystone in such absolute terms that it is borderline impossible to see a compromise that will satisfy all the players."[8]

After the State Department's report, Americans (except for our legislators) seemed to shift toward building the pipeline. A Pew Research survey said that 61 percent of Americans supported construction of the pipeline, while only 27 percent opposed it. But those 27 percent are very vocal and persuasive in their opposition.[9]

For Keystone XL opponents, the two biggest issues are environmental impact and safety. Environmentalists are worried that the pipeline will carry oil derived from tar sands, which involves a process that is dirtier than other forms of oil production and that releases more carbon dioxide. Their fear is that increased carbon dioxide will contribute to global warming. Then, of course, there's the issue of safety: People who live in proximity to the proposed route are concerned about a potential pipeline rupture. After all, they saw the news after the San Bruno accident.

As far as the environmental issues go: Two government bureaus—the Environmental Protection Agency and the Pipeline and Hazardous Material Safety Administration—reviewed the proposal and voiced no public opposition. The State Department's 2,000-page impact statement also provided no environmental rationale against the pipeline.

As noted earlier in the chapter, pipelines can rupture, and that's an inherent risk. But remember, we're talking about a brand-new pipeline here—not an octogenarian like the one that caused the Allentown explosion. Consider this: The Manhattan Institute for Policy Research, which has researched and influenced U.S. economic thought and policy for more than thirty years, went all the way back to 1992 to investigate the U.S. pipeline safety record. It thoroughly examined safety and accident statistics provided by the U.S. Department of Transportation for the extensive network of existing U.S. pipelines, including many linked to Canada. In addition to enjoying a substantial cost advantage, it found, pipelines result in fewer spillage incidents than road and rail.[10]

As for personal injuries and fatalities, the group said that the average American is more likely to get struck by lightning than to be killed in a pipeline accident.

In fact, pipelines are considered to not only be the fastest way to transport crude, but also one of the safest and cleanest. The alternative to pipelines? Mostly trucks and railroads—neither being super efficient, clean, or safe.

WHAT'S THE BEST METHOD OF CRUDE OIL TRANSPORT: TRUCK, RAIL, OR PIPELINE?

THE ANSWER IS IN THE HARD FACTS.[11-20]

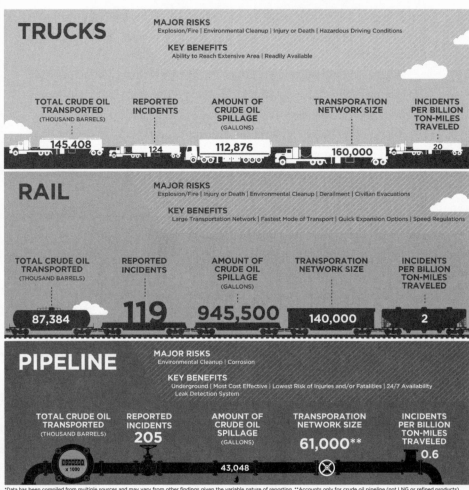

TRUCKS

MAJOR RISKS
Explosion/Fire | Environmental Cleanup | Injury or Death | Hazardous Driving Conditions

KEY BENEFITS
Ability to Reach Extensive Area | Readily Available

TOTAL CRUDE OIL TRANSPORTED (THOUSAND BARRELS)	REPORTED INCIDENTS	AMOUNT OF CRUDE OIL SPILLAGE (GALLONS)	TRANSPORATION NETWORK SIZE	INCIDENTS PER BILLION TON-MILES TRAVELED
145,408	124	112,876	160,000	20

RAIL

MAJOR RISKS
Explosion/Fire | Injury or Death | Environmental Cleanup | Derailment | Civilian Evacuations

KEY BENEFITS
Large Transportation Network | Fastest Mode of Transport | Quick Expansion Options | Speed Regulations

TOTAL CRUDE OIL TRANSPORTED (THOUSAND BARRELS)	REPORTED INCIDENTS	AMOUNT OF CRUDE OIL SPILLAGE (GALLONS)	TRANSPORATION NETWORK SIZE	INCIDENTS PER BILLION TON-MILES TRAVELED
87,384	119	945,500	140,000	2

PIPELINE

MAJOR RISKS
Environmental Cleanup | Corrosion

KEY BENEFITS
Underground | Most Cost Effective | Lowest Risk of Injuries and/or Fatalities | 24/7 Availability
Leak Detection System

TOTAL CRUDE OIL TRANSPORTED (THOUSAND BARRELS)	REPORTED INCIDENTS	AMOUNT OF CRUDE OIL SPILLAGE (GALLONS)	TRANSPORATION NETWORK SIZE	INCIDENTS PER BILLION TON-MILES TRAVELED
x 1000	205	43,048	61,000**	0.6

*Data has been compiled from multiple sources and may vary from other findings given the variable nature of reporting. **Accounts only for crude oil pipeline (not LNG or refined products)

Trucks and Trains Can't Always Keep Oil Rolling

Although Keystone XL has endured nearly seven years of pushback, the U.S. pipeline system remains America's most used petroleum supply line. The domestic network—all 2.3 million miles of it—transports more than 11.3 barrels per year, about 52 percent crude oil and the rest refined petroleum products.[21] Oversight of construction, safety, environmental impacts, and other operational aspects help maintain safety and efficiency of transporting crude in large amounts.

When an area can't depend on pipelines, operators must resort to truck and rail. North Dakota, where so much of the nation's new oil originates, is a good example. The Plains States are woefully lacking in pipeline infrastructure, so as a result, about 75 percent of North Dakota's enormous crude oil production is transported by truck to railcars for the journey to Gulf Coast refineries. But in a state associated with treacherous weather, relying on truck travel can be hazardous. If trucks can't move oil because of heavy snow or icy conditions, price-preserving production declines can occur. And once on-site storage tanks at production sites are full, production stops until the trucks are rolling again.

Shipping oil by rail isn't new. Railcars were the most efficient option when the first American oil boom began in the late 1800s. As pipelines were developed, trains generally couldn't compete on price, but as it turns out, rail transportation has become somewhat of a savior for today's energy industry. Because drillers are extracting more oil than current pipelines can carry, production companies have returned, out of necessity, to rail. During 2012, more than 230,000 carloads of crude traveled by train—that's twenty-three times more than the 9,500 carloads moved just four years earlier, in 2008.[22]

The U.S. Federal Railroad Administration is a strict regulator of all things related to train transportation, and the domestic railroad industry has imposed its own stringent standards on tank cars that exceed federal guidelines. But it takes just one event, like the deadly 2013 tank car explosion in Quebec, Canada, that killed forty-seven people, to bring to the forefront the risks of moving oil by train.

The State Department's 2014 report found that blocking the Keystone XL won't have much of an environmental impact because the oil and gas will be produced and transported anyway—and if it's transported by truck and rail, the carbon dioxide impact will be the same or worse. Plus, truck and rail pose more of a threat to human life.[23]

So what will happen if opponents get their way and successfully block TransCanada's plans? Just because the pipeline isn't there doesn't mean oil and gas will go away. Instead, there will be more potentially dangerous trucks and trains hauling it, with increased demand for infrastructure and maintenance certainly close behind—development that has its own environmental perils.

What We Stand to Gain

While the arguments against the pipeline are mostly about safety and the environment, the arguments for the pipeline are mostly economic. If approved, the biggest gain will be in jobs that are created without a dime of support from the government.

The State Department's report estimates that the pipeline's construction would result in almost 4,000 jobs over two years, eventually supporting as many as 42,000 related jobs.[24] According to the Canadian Energy Research Institute, total Canadian employment related to oil sands development, both new and existing projects, is expected to continue growing from the current level (2014) of 514,000 jobs to a peak of 802,000 jobs in 2028.[25]

Other benefits that the State Department expects out of the Keystone XL project:[26]

- The project would contribute $3.4 billion to U.S. gross domestic product (GDP). This figure includes not only earnings by workers, but all other income earned by businesses and individuals engaged in the production of goods and services demanded by the proposed project, such as profits, rent, interest, and dividends. When compared with the

GDP in 2010, the proposed project's contribution represents approximately 0.02 percent of annual economic activity across the nation.

- It would generate approximately $3.1 billion in construction contracts, materials, and support purchased in the U.S., with another $233 million spent on construction camps. During construction, this spending would support a combined total of approximately 42,100 average annual jobs and approximately $2 billion in earnings throughout the U.S.

- Approximately 16,100 jobs would be direct jobs at firms that are awarded contracts for goods and services—including construction—directly by Keystone. The other 26,000-some jobs would result from indirect and induced spending. This would consist of goods and services purchased by the construction contractors and spending by employees working for either the construction contractor or for any supplier of goods and services required in the construction process.

- The proposed project would temporarily increase the population in the proposed project area as workers relocate to build the pipeline. Approximately 10,400 construction workers engaged for four- to eight-month seasonal construction periods would be needed, equating to approximately 3,900 jobs (or 1,950 per year if construction took two years). Because of the specialized nature of the work, Keystone estimates that only approximately 10 percent of the construction workforce would be hired from the four proposed project area states. (The proposed project pipeline would go through Montana, South Dakota, and Nebraska, with two additional pump stations in Kansas. There would also be a pipe yard and rail siding located in North Dakota.)

Between the boost to the U.S. economy, job gains by American workers, and the State Department's admission that the Keystone won't harm the environment, the pipeline project appears to be a good deal—even to a rare bipartisan crowd in Congress—and that's why they passed the proposal in February 2015.

Downside of U.S. Indecision in Canada

The U.S. gets along very well with our friendly neighbors to the north. And Canada has spent a lot of money in the hopes that Keystone XL will come to fruition. Canada has invested more than $100 billion in the oil sands over the last decade, and production is already tied to 75,000 jobs nationwide. If the Keystone is not completed, future Canadian oil sands projects may be jeopardized, which will slow that country's economy.

Experts say that the domestic shortage of pipeline capacity that glutted North Dakota forced down the price of Canadian crude to a point well below American and international benchmarks. As a result, it became considerably less profitable for Canada to export the 2.4 million barrels it sends to the U.S. each day.

To counter the slowdown, Canada may have to look to other markets. China has already replaced the U.S. as the largest energy consumer on the planet; a planned Canadian pipeline to Vancouver will make satisfying Chinese demand easier.[27] Although the U.S. is on its way to energy independence—we could actually become a net exporter by 2035—postponing the Keystone XL pipeline is simply decelerating our drive.

So will Keystone XL get a chance to ease the glut, or not? That remains to be seen.

PART V

WHAT'S NEXT?

CHAPTER 18

CAPTAIN AMERICA—THE AMERICAN IDEAL RETURNS

"He who has oil has empire."

—Advisor of French Prime Minister Georges Clemenceau, December 1919

In the 1940s, while America was waging the "Good War" against the Axis powers, cartoonists Joe Simon and Jack Kirby dreamed up a big-muscled cartoon character, Captain America, a superhero who epitomized American patriotism and willingness to fight evil wherever it loomed.

Captain America was cool, so cool he became America's most popular cartoon character during World War II. He fought for truth and justice, crossing enemy lines, tackling Nazi and Japanese spies and mad scientists, even punching Adolph Hitler in the jaw on the cover of the 1941 *Captain America* comic book debut. Americans bought a million copies of that first issue. Captain America was a 2D stand-in for all the heroes—men and women—who would lay down their lives against dictatorship.

Fast-forward three decades. Americans faced Vietnam, oil shortages, stagflation, pollution, and the political assassinations of President John Kennedy, his brother Robert Kennedy, and Martin Luther King Jr. Confusion reigned. On April 22, 1970, Pogo Possum would appear on a poster publicizing the first Earth Day. The tag line: "We have met the enemy and he is us."

Oil and Fear

Sometime between World War II and the 1970s, Americans began to question our fundamental ideals and assumptions about right and wrong. As a nation, we confronted Cold War tensions and the Red Scare, bloody battles over civil rights, and the bully pulpit of Senator Joseph McCarthy, a man whose frequently unsubstantiated public attacks on the character and patriotism of political opponents, homosexuals, and artists left thousands of American careers and families in ruin.

There was also Korea and Vietnam. Although fighting against dictatorship and direct aggression was something Americans could support, going to war for darker motives, whether political, ideological, or economic, didn't seem right. And most Americans were completely unaware of the impact that growing oil dependency might have on foreign policy. But for the sixty years after World War II, conflicts and alliances to secure foreign oil became a dominant factor shaping American policy and military presence worldwide.

What choices did we have?

Just after World War II, government officials began to fear the consequences of energy shortages and supply shocks. And U.S. foreign policy and oil interests became intertwined.

"It became clear that oil was more than merely a coveted industrial commodity. The most visible and celebrated event in that history occurred when Franklin D. Roosevelt hosted King Abdul Aziz ibn Saud, the founding monarch of Saudi Arabia, aboard the USS *Quincy* on Egypt's Great Bitter Lake in February 1945. The meeting permanently linked Middle Eastern oil with American national security. It also helped forge one of the twentieth century's most important strategic relationships, in which the Saudis would supply cheap oil to global markets in exchange for American protection. A bargain was made. And so too was a future tinderbox."[1]

—Toby Craig Jones in *The Journal of American History*

Captain America seemingly faded from view. Oil, as it were, replaced the currency of right and wrong with a politics of self-interest and expediency. OPEC, centered in the Middle East, would rule the world energy market for half a century. Meanwhile, America agreed to police the sea-lanes, protecting kingships and regimes of dubious intentions just to ensure that oil would flow to our shores uninterrupted.

Oil and War Power

Fast-forward to today. Oil has become the lifeblood of the global economy. Whoever controls more energy resources has—pardon the pun—more power.

Now the global energy flows are shifting, and the U.S. has once again become a world leader in shale oil and natural gas production. Can Captain America return? Will the country rethink its foreign policies, acting less as a military policeman and more as a force for fairness and good— the same qualities that Captain America once stood for? Can America help create an *alternative* to the harsh realities of existing oil and gas cartels, and form a "Western Bloc" of energy? In other words, a bloc of energy-*interdependent* nations that remain substantially free from the economic and political grumpiness of traditional petrostates?

Let's review the situation.

As worldwide oil consumption accelerated during the past decades— from almost 60 million barrels per day in 1980 to nearly 91 million barrels per day in 2013[2]—oil-rich countries that export have experienced strong economic gains. Think Russia and OPEC, especially. Oil profits are often linked to an increase in defense spending, with oil-exporting countries better able to acquire advanced weapons systems or build their internal security capabilities.

Do improvements in military preparedness necessarily equate to saber rattling and even outright aggression? In many instances history has said yes. The U.S. has become something of a neighborhood watch—but on a global scale—while other petrostates have leveraged sky-high oil prices in recent years to build their armies and navies, missile defense systems, covert operations, and even support for paramilitary and terrorist groups.

Russia Flexes "Petroconfident" Muscles

A case in point: Russia. Russian President Vladimir Putin likes to peel off his shirt to show off his pumped-up pecs, apparently to prove he's been hitting the gym. But what's behind his military muscle flexing?

Russia's modern economy largely depends on energy exports. With oil prices rising from $17.37 a barrel in December 2001 to $73.88 a barrel in September 2007, the nation's wealth soared. And so did its military budget, increasing during that same period by 400 percent, from $7.3 billion to $31 billion.[3]

Between 2005 and 2006, Russia went on a homeland security spending spree, purchasing more than a dozen intercontinental ballistic missiles, two strategic bombers, 15 fighters, 15 satellites, 48 T-90 tanks, more than 250 armored personnel carriers, and 7,500 military vehicles.[4]

Oil and gas revenue fueled the arsenal. Russia's government was riding high on its oil and gas revenues until late 2014—when the ruble went into free fall along with global oil prices and the effects of Western economic sanctions against Russian aggression in eastern Ukraine.

In order to prove their theory that higher oil revenues bankrolled Putin's drive for greater domestic power, analysts at the American Enterprise Institute (AEI) created an "aggression index" that looked for a correlation between rising oil prices and more aggressive foreign policy.[5] The AEI assigned values to eighty-six Russian foreign policy events that occurred between January 2000 and September 2007, roughly the same period when oil prices took off. Acts such as import bans and diplomatic expulsions earned a relatively low value of 1 or 2. Acts that were clearly more threatening in nature—think arms sales to terror-sponsoring states and interrupting energy supplies to neighbors—received higher values. In order to eliminate bias, aggression ratings were assigned before oil price data were examined.

RELATIONSHIP BETWEEN OIL[6] PRICE AND RUSSIAN AGGRESSION

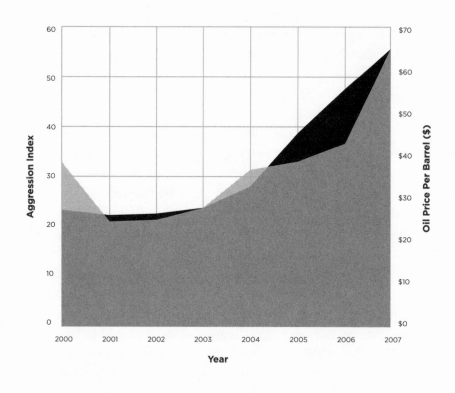

Aggression Index

Oil Prices

Source http://www.american.com/archive/2008/february-02-08/liquid-courage

The result: Oil prices and military expenditures do, indeed, go hand-in-hand. The AEI analysts found that, during the years when oil fortunes increased, Russia's aggression index rose from 17 to 55.

Oil revenues had both indirect and direct effects on Russia's defense and foreign policy activities. Because the nation was able to erase its $16.9 billion debt to the International Monetary Fund (IMF), the country no longer relied on Western cash (or Western friendships) to keep its economy going. And because Russia was also less dependent on neighboring trading partners, it could reject countries that had offended the Kremlin by their own pro-Western leanings.

During a two-year time frame in the mid-2000s, for instance, Russia banned imports of Polish meat, cut off imports of Ukrainian meat and dairy, and blockaded Georgia's economy almost entirely. In 2006, 2009, and 2014, as we've noted, Russia even stopped the flow of gas to Ukraine, a pipeline hub through which more than 50 percent of all Russian gas flows to Eastern and Western Europe.

Granted, boycotts of milk or meat are not as deadly as armed confrontation or, for that matter, long-term gas boycotts. But no matter what the tactic, Russia's ambitious military buildup through 2015—a program that includes 60 Iskander missiles, more than 1,000 new and modernized aircraft, five nuclear-powered submarines, and 69 SS-27 strategic nuclear missiles, along with Russia's aggression in Crimea and Ukraine—has alarmed close neighbors and caused NATO to rethink defensive policy in the area.[7] Even today, with falling oil prices and Russia's current economic troubles, there is no evidence that military plans are being scuttled; in fact, Russia seems to be increasing aggression in Europe, possibly as a distraction from domestic economic woes.

Some analysts believe that oil pricing instability and currency hardships will only make Putin more pugnacious, as he "may again resort to the dual levers of nationalism and foreign adventurism to shore up his popularity at home," at least for the short term, according to Rand analysts Hans Binnendijk, Christopher Chivvis, and Olga Oliker, writing in *The*

New York Times.[8] Russian separatist aggression in Ukraine continues and has actually intensified, according to Oleksander Turchynov, secretary of the Ukrainian National Defense Council. He noted that 8,500 Russian regular servicemen were now deployed in eastern Ukraine.

Iraqi Oil Infrastructure

Russia didn't make the list of countries named by James A. Paul, executive director of the Global Policy Forum (a policy watchdog that follows the United Nations), when he described the relationship between petroleum and war as "close." But nearly a dozen more came to mind, suggesting that "almost all of the world's oil-producing countries have suffered abusive, corrupt and undemocratic governments and an absence of durable development."[9] In many cases, the U.S. has continued to support or ally with such governments because it is in our national—and energy security—interests to do so. Paul decried these governments' "sad record, which includes dictatorships . . ., bloody coups . . ., militarization of government and intolerant right-wing nationalism." Key offenders? Libya, Angola, Algeria, Colombia, Venezuela, Mexico, Indonesia, Saudi Arabia, Kuwait, Iran, and Iraq.

So let's consider Iraq.

Oil is Iraq's most important asset, accounting for 90 percent of the government's revenue and 58 percent of the country's GDP. Iraq has the third-largest oil reserves in the Middle East, surpassed only by Saudi Arabia and Iran. Not only is the Middle East resource-rich, these countries are big spenders on war matériel—ostensibly to protect their oil assets. In fact, defense spending in the countries of the Middle East generally represents between 10 percent and 20 percent of total state expenditure annually:

War motivated by the quest for oil has been part of Iraq's modern history all the way back to World War I, when Britain conquered the area known historically as Mesopotamia. Although Britain granted nominal independence to Iraq in 1932, it kept a large military force in the country. In 1941, when it seemed likely that Germany would try to capture the Iraqi oil fields, the British again seized direct political power through military force.

During the protracted Iran-Iraq war during the 1980s, Iran's oil storage and exports capacity were an early target of Iraqi aggression. In 1990, in a move that would draw the U.S. to the battlefield, Iraq invaded Kuwait in an effort to control more of the region's oil. It's interesting to note that, when Kuwait began providing economic assistance to then-Iraqi leader Saddam Hussein during his country's earlier battles with Iran, Iran responded by attacking Kuwait's oil tankers.

When the U.S. became embroiled in the Iraq War in 2003, the first combat operation included Navy commandos storming an offshore oil-loading platform.

Iraq waged a two-front war: The battles for control over its cities and the constant struggle to protect its far-flung petroleum infrastructure against sabotage and attack. Oil, according to U.S. and Iraqi policy makers, was the lynchpin for a "stable" Iraqi future; and a decade after the war began, the once closed, nationalized oil fields in Iraq were productive and largely privatized, with such firms as ExxonMobil, Chevron, BP, Halliburton, and Shell holding stakes in the region, especially in Kurdistan.

Most recently, oil has played a significant role in the U.S. decision to launch airstrikes on militant ISIS strongholds in Kurdistan, where American oil companies such as ExxonMobil and Chevron are concentrated. Of course, the U.S. is also attempting to stop ISIS from continuing its slaughter of Kurds and Iraqi Yazidis who have fled to the north. But the Obama administration authorized airstrikes only when ISIS began encroaching on Erbil, an oil boomtown where Chevron and ExxonMobil are headquartered. Since Iraq is now the seventh-largest oil producer worldwide, with Kurdistan producing roughly 10 percent of the total, it's no wonder that a significant U.S. military presence in the area continues right along with disputes about how to protect and divvy up oil revenue. As a U.S. senior officer told *The New York Times*, "There may be no other place where our armed forces are deployed that has a greater strategic importance."[10]

The China Syndrome

Ironically, though, China has become the major beneficiary of the U.S. military presence in Iraq. China buys fully half of Iraq's oil, roughly 1.5 million barrels a day, and has poured more than $2 billion into the region, agreeing to abide by the Iraqi government's stringent rules and winning contracts by being willing to accept lower profits in exchange for reliable energy supplies.

U.S. oil companies, by contrast, have focused on short-term profits—often losing valuable bids for new contracts. "We lost out," said Michael Makovsky, a former Defense Department official in the Bush administration who worked on Iraq oil policy. "The Chinese had nothing to do with the war, but from an economic standpoint they are benefiting from it, and our Fifth Fleet and air forces are helping to assure their supply."[11]

In the Persian Gulf region, providing oil security has been a staple of U.S. foreign policy agenda since 1936, when Standard Oil discovered massive oil deposits in Saudi Arabia. The U.S. spent $7.3 trillion defending the Persian Gulf from 1976 to 2007 and now spends $50 billion a year securing access to Middle Eastern oil.[12] The 1973–1974 OPEC oil embargo and the 1990 invasion of Kuwait are both dramatic examples of how regional forces have challenged U.S. access to fuel. The U.S. military seeks to provide a counterbalance to the multiple (and often conflicting) oil interests that compete for Middle East energy resources.

Although the Middle East accounts for about 30 percent of the world's oil supply, the bulk of its production today goes to Europe and the Far East, not the U.S. Our need for Saudi oil has declined drastically in recent years, and now makes up only 13 percent of our oil imports. However, our role as a global superpower roughly equates to the responsibility of policing the sea-lanes. We continue to patrol many of the world's oil "choke points," including the Strait of Hormuz, probably the most strategic strait on the planet.

Through the strait's waters, oil tankers pass from Bahrain, Iran, Iraq, Kuwait, Qatar, Saudi Arabia, and the United Arab Emirates. Iran borders the strait to the north while Oman's Musandam Peninsula and the United Arab Emirates share the southern border. Boats from many countries patrol these waters, but Americans have dominated Persian Gulf security since the 1970s, when Britain withdrew its resident military from the region.

About 17 percent of the Middle Eastern oil supply passes through the strait for delivery to India, Japan, China, and South Korea. Even though these countries import anywhere from 40 percent to nearly 80 percent of their total oil supply through this route, they pay exactly nothing to secure the flow. At the same time, the U.S. spends billions of dollars each year to police these choke points.

A Thankless Job

Is this fair? Are we playing Captain America after all, but without the "feel-good" benefit of approbation from our neighbors? The verdict is mixed. Although the physical oil needs of the U.S. economy can be met closer to home—from Canada, Mexico, South America, the North Sea, and, increasingly, from domestic shale development—we recognize that a massive shortfall of oil in the Middle East not only affects the price of oil everywhere but also can have stunning ramifications on the worldwide economic system.

For example, the U.S. has assumed significant responsibility for protecting the 1,099-mile Baku-Tbilisi-Ceyhan pipeline running a perilous route from Baku, Azerbaijan, to the Mediterranean port city of Ceyhan, Turkey. Owned by a consortium of eleven energy companies from the U.S., Europe, and Asia, this pipeline first pumped oil in 2005.

In Colombia, where guerrillas have repeatedly tried to sabotage that country's vulnerable oil pipelines that run from fields in the interior to ports on the Caribbean coast, Washington has spent hundreds of millions of dollars to enhance oil infrastructure security. U.S. Army Special Forces personnel trained and equipped Colombian forces to guard the 480-mile pipeline.

Although African oil imports to the U.S. have fallen off since the rise of domestic shale, U.S. military involvement in that region increased during the period from the late 1990s to the mid-2000s, when we were more dependent upon Nigerian sweet, light crude in particular. The Africa Crisis Response Initiative, established by President Bill Clinton in 1997, was designed to increase the amount of U.S. security assistance to African regimes. The effort was expanded and renamed the African Contingency Operations Training and Assistance program in 2004. Its goal: to protect

U.S. access to oil resources because "disruption of supply from Nigeria would represent a major blow to the oil security strategy of the U.S."[13]

Do other countries endorse our policing presence? Not always. China, in particular, has voiced criticism of the United States. Responding to the Obama administration's claim that China has enjoyed a "free ride" in the Strait of Hormuz, refusing to contribute to sea patrols, Dr. Jin Liangxiang of the Shanghai Institute for International Studies retorted: "China's stable oil imports helped prevent Gulf countries from being plunged into deeper economic difficulties during the global economic crisis since 2008. China's investment in Iraq has eased economic difficulties of the country." He also said that the U.S. invests billions to "protect" the Hormuz—but not necessarily to provide security for the public good.[14]

Bottom line: America's position as Middle East oil policeman has become difficult and, essentially, thankless. Further, our transformation into a major oil and gas *producer* begs the question of whether we should maintain or diminish our current policing agenda and encourage other oil powers to take on the role. Meanwhile, much discussion has ensued about creating a breakaway Western Bloc of energy producers located in our hemisphere, which would include Canada, the U.S., Mexico, and parts of South America, most notably Brazil. Such an alliance could, in theory, actively compete against the Middle East and Russia, helping further stabilize world energy prices. But roadblocks exist—in particular, the structure of global petroleum pricing. (See the sidebar "A Western Cartel.") Energy remains an extremely interconnected commodity; so the possibility of "walling" a hemisphere off from the tensions and political mayhem of the Middle East seems more a pipe dream than reality at this time.

Less Force, More Excitement

Today, China has overtaken us in terms of OPEC oil imports.

This change could be a challenge for both China and the U.S. The Chinese economy depends in part on oil from a region dominated by the U.S. military. After all, when tankers leave Persian Gulf terminals headed for China, it's the U.S. that's securing the area.

At the same time, the U.S. is spending military dollars to help a country that has formed partnerships with Iran—historically a U.S. adversary. Over the past several years, China has become Iran's biggest oil customer. And in addition to purchasing Iranian oil and natural gas, in 2011 China signed a $20 billion agreement to boost bilateral cooperation in Iran's industrial and mining sectors. Both moves could ultimately offset some of the U.S. power in the Middle East.

But even without China as a factor, the U.S. shale revolution could alter our global policing options. As we become more self-reliant in energy, we may see "a more balanced look at our foreign policy," said retired U.S. Marine Corps Major General Anthony L. Jackson.[15] U.S. influence there might shift in the Middle East as we form a stronger "energy block" in the Western Hemisphere. Some scenarios:

- The U.S. could reevaluate its military presence around the world, leading to lower military spending reinvested domestically.

- The U.S. government could engage in more "soft" diplomacy—or at least enable a clearer distinction between economic and humanitarian interests.

- Armed U.S. interventions could become less likely in the Middle East, as shale empowers a scaled-back reliance on unstable regimes.

Many of our greatest energy and foreign policy experts have expressed optimism about needed policy changes. According to Anders Aslund, senior fellow at the Peterson Institute for International Economics, U.S. energy self-sufficiency means America could be less tied to the global market and, therefore, less likely to intervene in Middle East affairs. "The United States is already self-sufficient in natural gas, and its dependence on oil imports is set to fall. This change will have a huge impact on U.S. foreign policy," he told us in December 2013.

While it's inconceivable that America would return to isolationism—there is so much energy and durable goods trade interdependency worldwide that no country or countries can thrive by standing alone—greater energy self-sufficiency gives our government more foreign policy options.

"We don't need to be independent from our friends, but there's a whole range of countries that I'd like to be clearly independent from in terms of relying on them for energy," noted former Secretary Tom Ridge during a July 2014 conversation with my team.

Further, the U.S. has the option of "weaning" countries away from hostile energy suppliers by providing them with affordable alternatives (think: oil and gas exports). Abundant energy at home means a "foreign policy dividend" abroad, according to energy and environmental policy experts Don Smith and Rebecca Watson, writing in *The Denver Post*.[16] Or as Tom Donilon, National Security Advisor to the President, remarked at the launch of Columbia University's Center on Global Energy Policy in April 2013, "America's new energy posture allows us to engage from a position of greater strength . . . It also affords us a stronger hand in pursuing and implementing our international security goals."[17]

A Western Cartel

Can North America form an "energy cartel" or "Western Bloc" of energy? Perhaps, but with significant caveats.

Such a cartel would depend on the intentions of the three nations— and Mexico would be the reluctant partner. "It's highly unlikely that Mexico would want to join into a formal cartel," said Jorge Piñon of the University of Texas at Austin when my team interviewed him in September 2014.

When considering all the realities of the twenty-first-century oil marketplace, it's critical to remember that OPEC has tried unsuccessfully to bring Mexico into its fold for more than twenty years. Mexico did not want to become entangled in the "geopolitics" of the Middle East, Piñon said, choosing instead to retain its autonomy.

Peter Cook, president of the U.S.-based Petroleum Connection, recently organized a symposium on the topic of Mexican Petroleum Infrastructure. He has a different take on it: Petróleos Mexicanos, the state-run energy monopoly more affectionately known as Pemex, provides an enormous amount of the Mexican budget. "Maybe that keeps taxes low and that type of thing, but the fact is, because they don't retain any of their earnings, they're unable to reinvest, and now they're way behind," Cook told my team in a September 2014 interview. "They could have been leaders in the shale gas and hydraulic fracturing world, but instead they have almost no one in the country with expertise in the field."

So without the inclusion of Mexico, what about the United States and Canada? "I don't believe that the U.S. and Canada would agree to a formal cartel," Piñon said. Questions of leadership, restrictions on trade policy, and unfinished infrastructure business (think: Keystone Pipeline) will hinder an agreement.

But just because an outright Western Bloc remains an elusive concept, don't mistake this to mean that North American cooperation is missing. Rather, we should consider a future Western Bloc relationship as "symbiotic," said Thomas Edgar, director of the University of Texas at Austin's Energy Institute. During a September 2014 conversation with my team, Edgar explained that he's looking for an alliance that provides mutual benefits from energy *interdependence,* a situation in which cooperative parties offer each other complementary (but not identical) energy resources, products, technologies, and infrastructure to facilitate growth and social stability. Interdependence does not necessarily mean "energy independence," as in complete self-sufficiency, but it does means robust trade and exchange of assets and resources.

As for a positive and mutually beneficial relationship, it's already happening, Edgar insisted.

"Canada is closer to energy self-sufficiency and is already exporting oil and gas to the U.S.," Edgar said. "The U.S. is currently exporting oil and gas to Mexico, especially because of the cheap natural gas available. In the symbiotic relationship, the U.S. will benefit from the privatization of the oil industry in Mexico, especially for deep oil. Over time, the U.S. will move more towards self-sufficiency before Mexico, and it will become an oil and gas exporter in the next five years, probably to countries in Asia and Europe."

> Edgar believes that with all that is going on in North America, the U.S. could achieve energy *self-sufficiency by around 2020*. Energy cooperation among the three neighboring Western Hemisphere nations can lead to greater influence in the global energy marketplace and, ultimately, stronger national energy security.

No Guarantees

There is certainly no guarantee that the world will become a more stable place now that the U.S. is enjoying an energy revolution. But it looks that way. We do know that more energy at home means (1) a cushion against global supply and price shocks and (2) greater leverage to negotiate robust trade and energy agreements with friends and allies.

However, any scenario that predicts the speed of U.S. military disengagement abroad will depend on our political orientation at home, and on whether we see a vacuum at "choke points" abroad. For example, a variety of religious and ethnic forces will continue to vie for power in the Persian Gulf kingdoms, while Iran, an economy largely dependent on oil sales and facing severe budget shortfalls from sanctions, will also face critical foreign policy choices. Iran will have to decide whether it can truly join the international community, or whether it will continue to fund proxy wars and nuclear weapons development as a key part of its long-term survival strategy.

For Americans who care about energy, though, Captain America is back. Our domestic shale revolution has given our government the option to decide whether to engage the world with new tools, renewed values, and hopefully, wiser perspectives. No longer must we maintain military ties with dictators and oligarchs while continuing to ship hundreds of billions of dollars each year to hostile countries just out of fear of disrupting our energy supply. New alignments of trade, politics, and energy abundance could very well upend the traditional global axes of power.

In fact, energy author Daniel Yergin contends that the increase in U.S. oil production has already had a significant impact. Even with global supply disruptions and the current worldwide oil glut, "what is unfolding in the U.S. will continue to change its economy and affect both international relations and the global energy outlook," Yergin wrote in the 2012 *Financial Times*.[18]

It's a remarkable transformation. Energy abundance has given Captain America new powers. He's grown in confidence and sophistication, and he can see more readily how the Chinese, Russians, and Saudis play the game.

Lessening Imports,
Growing Exports

STRENGTHENING NATIONAL SECURITY

U.S. CRUDE

U.S. NATURAL GAS

2004

U.S. Imports 376 Times
as Much Crude Oil as it Exports

Exports = 9,783
Thousand Barrels

Imports = 3,692,063
Thousand Barrels

Nearly 52% from volatile nations, including OPEC member countries and Russia

U.S. Imports 5 Times
as Much Natural Gas as it Exports

Exports = 854,138
Million Cubic Feet

Imports = 4,258,558
Million Cubic Feet

2008

Imports Rise
57%
from Volatile Nations

Imports Marginally Decline by
6%

2009

SHALE BOOM BEGINS CREATING LARGER DOMESTIC SOURCE OF NATURAL GAS AND CRUDE OIL

2010

Oil Production Increases by
19%

Natural Gas Production Increases by
13%

2013

Imports Drop by
24%

Exports Rise by
400%

Imports Drop by
32%

Exports Rise by
84%

30% less from OPEC / 73% less from Russia

Total Reliance on Volatile Nations Decreases by 32%

2014

National Security Strengthened as Imports Continue to Decline

228

CHAPTER 19

2035

What will the energy world look like in 2035?

We can predict with certainty that new energy technologies—even new energy forms—will emerge unexpectedly.

For example, the world may see controlled nuclear fusion harnessed to power the electric grid or propel spaceships to distant galaxies. We could have car batteries operating on air, carbon nanotubes sopping up toxic waste from superfund sites, even hybrid automobiles that use combinations of energy-sipping gasoline-solar power (minimum seventy-five miles to a gallon) or natural gas–solar, especially in sunny parts of the world.

The U.S., very likely, could become oil independent by 2035. Natural gas independent even sooner. Alternately, our oil production could peak from lack of interest or investment, falling prices, government mandates for alternative fuels, or bad planning (really bad planning).

The choice is ours.

Let's look at what experts project for the next twenty years:

Worldwide, the energy mix of the next two-and-half decades may look very different. Here are the estimates of the International Energy Agency (IEA), which shows that global energy demand will increase by at least a third by 2035, possibly 37 percent by 2040. Moreover, the share of fossil fuels will drop slightly from 82 percent to 76 percent, and low-carbon energy sources (renewables and nuclear) will meet around 40 percent of the *growth* in primary energy demand. Nearly half of the *net increase in electricity generation* worldwide will come from renewables.[1]

While dependence on imported oil and gas will rise in many countries—for example, India will continue to import huge amounts of coal as part of its development programs, and China will become the world's largest importer of oil and gas—the IEA anticipates that the United States will ultimately begin exporting natural gas (in the form of liquefied natural gas, or LNG) throughout the world. The U.S. may also export oil, if antiquated crude export bans are lifted. In any event, the U.S. is expected to become a minimal importer of foreign oil, most of it coming from Western hemisphere trading partners such as Canada or Mexico. (The latter is also our largest oil trade partner now.)

The U.S. oil and gas bonanza will have a stunning impact on world energy markets over the coming twenty-five years. North American oil sands and light, tight oil from shale will provide 40 percent of the world oil-supply capacity growth. By 2035, almost 90 percent of Middle Eastern oil exports will shift to Asia; and North America's emergence as an energy-independent state and net exporter will accelerate the eastward shift in energy trade toward developing nations. The outward flow of unconventional gas and LNG from the U.S. and competitive suppliers (including Russia, Australia, Africa, Indonesia, even the Middle East) will increase the flow of natural gas to Asia.

The IEA is not the only prognosticator of our energy future. BP recently published its highly touted *World Energy Outlook,* and its view is that oil, gas, and coal will, for the first time in history, roughly "converge" in equal proportions on or around 2035.[2] This means that each fossil fuel could claim roughly 27 percent of world energy market share. As a result, we should expect a significant reduction in polluting coal usage, higher amounts of natural gas produced and consumed, and oil continuing to play a major role in world transportation and industries.

While demand for oil is rising, we're learning that prices won't necessarily follow the same trend; they will, most likely, gyrate. Production capacity has increased at such an unprecedented clip that supplies now outstrip demand. But as of this writing in mid-2015, wholesale gasoline

GLOBAL IMPACT OF UNITED STATES SHALE

The surge in unconventional oil and gas production has implications well beyond the United States.

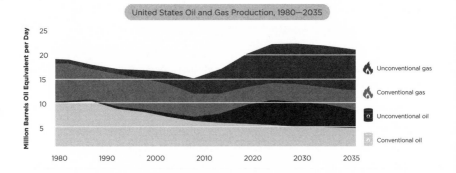

United States Oil and Gas Production, 1980–2035

- Unconventional gas
- Conventional gas
- Unconventional oil
- Conventional oil

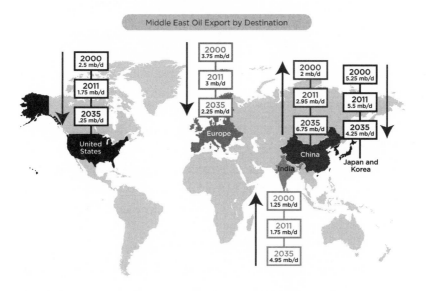

Middle East Oil Export by Destination

United States
2000	2.5 mb/d
2011	1.75 mb/d
2035	.25 mb/d

Europe
2000	3.75 mb/d
2011	3 mb/d
2035	2.25 mb/d

China
2000	2 mb/d
2011	2.95 mb/d
2035	6.75 mb/d

Japan and Korea
2000	5.25 mb/d
2011	5.5 mb/d
2035	4.25 mb/d

India
2000	1.25 mb/d
2011	1.75 mb/d
2035	4.95 mb/d

Source https://www.iea.org/newsroomandevents/speeches/APR4OilSummitEDslidepresentation.pdf

prices are inching up again as U.S. oil refineries cut production. What will happen when the pendulum swings the other way? Consumers will continue to buy products and services made from cheap fuel (even airlines are buying cheaper fuel and passing savings along to consumers) until the glut is done and supplies tighten. Alternately, the Saudis will change their minds and cut OPEC production, and prices will rise again. Oil- and gas-dependent economies—Russia and Venezuela, for example, which were hammered by the late 2014 pricing freefall—will start to see a turnaround.

And what of America? The U.S. shale renaissance, which proved resilient to sliding prices late in 2014, has reportedly shown signs of the strain, with oil producers pulling drilling rigs out of fields in Texas and North Dakota. Ditto the Marcellus Shale: gas explorers pared down the numbers of rigs in the past two years, thanks to a plateau in gas prices.

But over the next twenty years, to the year 2035, we're likely to see an energy metamorphosis. Big, big changes, in other words, and not just to the energy mix.

Will OPEC Survive?

In October 2012, OPEC production fell to 31.32 million barrels per day; by January 2013, daily production had slipped to 30.34 million barrels. By the next month, a record surge in U.S. shale energy production in the first ten months of 2012 meant that the U.S. had met 84 percent of the country's domestic energy needs. Indeed, U.S. shale "now threatens the very existence of OPEC," according to Peter C. Glover and Michael J. Economides, coauthors of *Energy & Climate Wars*.[3]

That prediction may be hyperbole. And it may not be.

Woodrow Wilson Center energy scholars Amy Myers Jaffe and Edward L. Morse also document OPEC's challenges as it moves into the next several decades. Their *Energy Security* essay "OPEC: Can the Cartel Survive Another 50 Years?" states the world's dominant crude oil cartel faces five major issues as it attempts to hold onto its market hegemony:[4]

1. **Rising internal demand and falling capacity.** "OPEC's exportable surplus had a recent peak of 24.2 [million barrels per day] in 2007, when the organization's market share was 60.1 percent." Rising demand through 2020 could mean that OPEC must exceed current daily production by at least 3 million barrels, thus eroding exportable surplus of almost every OPEC country with Iraq excepted.

2. **Governance issues.** The emergence of more vocal OPEC member nations is making it harder to forge single cartel agreements that mean sacrificing revenue to preserve market share. Up until now, Saudi Arabia has been able to keep OPEC members on a budgetary and pricing line; that discipline may be challenged by renegade members like Nigeria and Venezuela, which have suffered from oil supply shocks in recent years.

3. **Iraq's reintegration as global oil provider.** Iraq's rebounding oil production could turn out to be a "serious challenge to OPEC unit and overall OPEC output controls."

4. **Saudi Arabia's changing OPEC role.** Once the enforcer of OPEC pricing and production discipline, Saudi Arabia is now challenged from within by decreasing spare production capacity and also by competing priorities requiring higher production for domestic consumption. "The pressure for higher defense and social spending makes it harder for the government to justify a massive campaign to expand its oil sector. In sum, it will not be easy for Saudi Arabia to mobilize a major price war as time goes on, thereby reducing its ability to police OPEC by threatening to drive prices lower to punish members who cheat on quotas."

5. **Emergence of unconventional oil and gas.** The North American unconventionals revolution is challenging OPEC as never before. Once the major destination for OPEC surplus crude, "North America could become a potential export competitor." High prices have made it more economical to develop the more expensive technologies needed to extract oil and gas from shale reserves. Moreover, tight

oil is among several new supply streams—among them biofuels, oil sands, and deepwater deposits—that have not only given North America an energy edge, but also eroded OPEC's ability to preserve market share and balance the market.

Commentators worldwide agree that shale is a force for global change. "If shale does deliver on its promise and keeps prices low for decades, it will be a mortal threat to OPEC states that rely on oil revenue to cover social spending and placate fast-growing populations," wrote energy commentator Ambrose Evans-Pritchard in the UK newspaper *The Daily Telegraph.*[5]

OPEC itself, which has been dominant since forming in 1960, at first dismissed North American shale as a transient phenomenon that was no threat to the cartel. But in July 2013, OPEC acknowledged that growing U.S. oil production could displace imports from member states, and both IEA and IHS supported this conclusion in separate reports. Further, Saudi Arabia's most prominent businessman, Prince Alwaleed bin Talal, wrote an open letter in summer 2013 to the oil minister and his own uncle, King Abdullah, urging them to be more aware of the "continuous threat" the kingdom faces because of its financial dependence on exporting oil. "The world is increasingly less dependent on oil from OPEC countries including the kingdom," he wrote.[6]

Will NATO Weaken?

Another alliance, the North Atlantic Treaty Organization (NATO), is likely to face major challenges as conflicts between Russia, the Baltic States, and the Middle East continue to simmer. According to Jeppe Kofod, a Danish lawmaker who wrote a report on the oil and gas revolution for NATO's Parliamentary Assembly, growing U.S. energy independence could mean a weakening of the alliance and less involvement of the U.S. in European, Middle Eastern, and African affairs.

"This is something that is going to change not only the energy market in the world, but everything else," Kofod said.[7]

"The alliance is premised on the notion of shared security interests . . . a significant divergence in energy security perspectives could begin to erode this foundation," Kofod's report stated.

U.S. energy self-sufficiency may mean that the U.S. will not police the supply flows out of the Persian Gulf region; European nations will need to develop their own energy security measures.

For the Europeans, though, the shale revolution is also largely positive. A greater variety of gas supplies from LNG originally destined for the United States are becoming available to European markets; by 2020, LNG is likely to begin arriving in Europe in significant quantities, enabling Central and Eastern Europe to buy gas in a truly competitive marketplace rather than being subject to the inflated prices fixed by Gazprom, the Russian monopoly. Further, there is also the prospect of some domestic shale gas becoming available. Europe will also benefit from the second stage of the shale revolution as oil prices come under pressure. However, American self-sufficiency in oil is of greatest concern to the European Union. The danger is that the United States will no longer have any direct interest in ensuring supply flows out of Persian Gulf. Washington may likely demand that Europe take greater responsibility for its own energy security.

Who Will Frack Next?

The flip side of challenges to existing energy security alliances is the emergence of new energy players. Shale energy, particularly natural gas trapped in coal and shale seams, has been identified in Eastern and Western Europe, Canada, Australia, China, South Africa, and the cone of South America. It's now a race to see who invests wisely and can emulate North American successes while adapting shale fracking and drilling technologies to unique (and often quite different) geological formations.

"Everybody around the world has taken notice [of shale in] the past few years. They're taking notice and starting to wonder if they can get a part of the same energy revolution that we have here," said Daniel Simmons, an energy scholar with the Institute of Energy Research.[8] Tempted by the fracking and horizontal drilling successes in the U.S., several countries are beginning similar projects to extract energy from shale—and with varying results. Following are highlights of the most promising initiatives.

China's Billion-Dollar Shale Question

Simply put, China's shale reserves are massive. The country may have more recoverable shale gas than any nation in the world, with preliminary measurements in the range of 1,115 trillion to 1,275 trillion cubic feet. Bolstered by such estimates, the country's chief administrative authority in October 2013 called for the energy industry to produce 229.5 billion cubic feet of natural gas from underground shale formations by 2015.[9] Excavation is already underway in Sichuan Province, where Chinese energy company Sinopec drilled the first shale well in Jiaoshizhen and has plans to drill at least 100 more in the area (despite a deadly explosion in April 2013).

The billion-dollar question remains whether the country can overcome substantial barriers to achieve rapid shale development. These include not only the basics like a dearth of existing pipeline infrastructure, water scarcity in shale-rich areas, and the absence of regulatory frameworks to guide upstream activities—but also the lack of a homegrown knowledgeable workforce with the experience to support the shale industry.

"Oil companies and foreign interests—China and the rest—are [currently] gaining both the technical understanding and trying to figure out how to apply these techniques to reserves in their lands," Paul Hagemeier, senior advisor and vice president of Tulsa's ALL Consulting, told my team in a September 2014 phone conversation. "That is a much more difficult task in a foreign country than it is in the United States—and there are an awful lot of drivers."

That said, Hagemeier definitely sees China developing its capabilities, solving the conundrum of domestic expertise through imports: "They have been very keen on making U.S. deals so they can participate here and learn the technology. In some cases, they're taking people with them." (Consider Sinopec's move in 2012, paying $2.2 billion for a 30 percent stake in Devon Energy's U.S. shale gas and petroleum operations.) "Finding experienced geologists and petroleum engineers and environmental engineers that have experience with this—building a workforce that's needed to take it on—I think they're going to have to import an awful lot of that," Hagemeier noted.

But even myriad U.S. experts might not help. Also marring the development of shale recovery is China's unique "buckled" geology: Folded, twisted faults require wells dug two to three times deeper than those in the United States. The fracking and horizontal drilling technology developed in the U.S. needs further adaptation to work in a geology as complex as Sichuan's. As Tao Wang of Beijing's Carnegie-Tsinghua Center for Global Policy put it, "There is no guarantee that the technology will be suitable for China."[10]

Argentina's Not Crying Over Spilled Shale

Argentina sits on top of the second-largest reserves of shale gas and the fourth-largest reserves of shale oil in the world. Vast oil deposits, amounting to 927 million barrels of total proven reserves, were discovered in the Vaca Muerta formation in 2010. The U.S. Energy Information Agency (EIA) estimates total recoverable hydrocarbons are 16.2 billion barrels of oil and 308 trillion cubic feet of natural gas. At a depth of about 9,500 feet, the formation covers a total area of 12,000 square miles—almost twice the size of Texas's Eagle Ford shale.

With all these reserves, Argentina has been one of the first countries to commercially develop shale after the U.S. And foreign investors are already targeting the Vaca Muerta. For example, multinational Royal

Dutch Shell PLC and French supermajor Total SA are partnering with Gas and Oil Neuquen, an energy company owned by the Argentine province of Neuquen (home of the Vaca Muerta), to develop two shale oil and gas projects. Argentina's state-run oil company, YPF SA, has entered into an agreement with Malaysia's Petronas to look for oil in the Vaca Muerta shale formation. And U.S. major ExxonMobil reported success in December with its second shale oil and gas well there: Its first test produced daily flow rates of 448 barrels per day of oil and 1 million cubic feet of gas.[11]

Unfortunately, Argentina's shale energy industry is struggling to fulfill its true potential because of long-standing price controls on natural gas. Indeed, government energy subsidies have made natural gas and electricity 70 percent cheaper than in neighboring nations. The result has produced spikes in demand leading to winter energy rationing. Argentina saw a precipitous drop in oil production output (–27 percent from 1998 to 2010) as well as gas output (–10 percent since 2004). The country needs energy investment but has been excluded from international debt markets since its economic crisis of 2001.[12]

The situation could be changing, however. New legislation approved in October 2014 should promote foreign investment in exploration and production, particularly in shale oil and gas. The bill lowers the minimum amount that foreign companies must invest to avoid import and foreign-exchange controls. The new law also standardizes the regulatory framework, which in the past was dictated by the individual oil-producing provinces that, under Argentina's constitution, own the nation's oil and gas reserves. It also lengthens the terms of production concessions to twenty-five years for conventional deposits and thirty-five years for shale deposits—leaving YPF Argentine energy company CEO Miguel Galuccio to hope it's "probably reasonable" that his country will become a net exporter within ten years.[13]

Recovering South Africa's Game Changer

The EIA estimates that some 485 trillion cubic feet of shale gas lies beneath South Africa's Karoo Desert between Cape Town and Johannesburg, while the Petroleum Agency of South Africa estimates a more modest 40 trillion cubic feet. In either case, these resources represent a real opportunity to give South Africa the reliable energy system it needs.

A number of companies, and the government itself, see the potential in South African shale gas production. Shell Oil, for one, has received the go-ahead to begin exploratory operations for shale gas production in the Karoo, committing $200 million in gas exploration in the area. Shell is projecting that extracting 50 trillion cubic feet of gas would add $20 billion (or 0.5 percent of GDP) annually for twenty-five years to South Africa's economy and create 700,000 jobs—a dramatic number for a country facing staggering 25 percent unemployment. Such economic benefits of shale gas production could help transform the country, as President Jacob Zuma told Parliament last year: "The development of petroleum, especially shale gas, will be a game changer for the Karoo region and the South African economy."[14]

Despite such optimism, South Africa's leaders are moving forward with extreme caution, entertaining moratoria on shale gas exploration and deferring decisions on fracking regulations. In October 2014, though, the government agreed to start processing exploration permits—but only those applications received before February 2011. New applications will not be accepted until mineral resources minister Ngoako Ramatlhodi announces otherwise. While there's no word on how long such decisions will take, analysts predict that South Africa will ultimately swing toward fracking to make up for underinvesting in energy for the past several decades, which has created an abysmal energy situation, leaving the country with less than 6 percent reserve capacity.[15] As Darren Spalding, a London-based energy attorney with Bracewell & Giuliani, noted in an interview with my team in October 2014, "It is too early to tell whether South African geology can match expectations. Secondly, the regulatory environment needs to be sufficiently certain for explorers to take comfort. Finally, a battle of the hearts and minds of the general population needs to be won."

There's also the possibility that a U.S.-style shale boom will lose something in translation if attempted in South Africa, due to the lack of key considerations like a skilled workforce, any real natural gas infrastructure to speak of, and "geographic hospitality": productive shale wells are generally found in easy terrains that have plenty of water, at depths that are quick to drill—the Karoo Desert displays none of these qualities. While South Africa's energy infrastructure is far from comparable to the U.S., Spalding did share with us his hopes that South Africa doesn't give up on the promise of shale-gas production: "These are issues worth solving, as the prize is potentially enormous and could be a game changer for South African energy policy."

Poland's Polonaise for Shale

Dreaming of energy independence from Russia, Poland has issued more than a hundred shale exploration licenses to more than twenty firms.[16] Poland's minister of the environment, Maciej Grabowski, made shale gas his priority in 2014 and paved the way for much-needed regulatory reforms to speed up exploration and open the way for more Western companies to drill in Poland. By his calculations, as of October 2014, there were fifty-eight concessions for shale gas, with sixty-six exploration wells.[17]

A few of these exploratory wells have caught the attention of Western drillers. For example, Chevron has completed four Polish wells since 2012 and is partnering with state-run Polskie Górnictwo Naftowe i Gazownictwo (PGNiG, Polish Petroleum and Gas Mining) to drill a well in the southeast. And last January, Dublin's San Leon Energy Plc drew as much as 60,000 cubic feet per day in a shale formation in the Baltic Basin in northern Poland.

Poland is thought to house Europe's largest deposits of shale gas. With an estimated 768 billion cubic meters (27,121 billion cubic feet) of natural gas, Polish shale fields could hold enough to supply its domestic energy needs for sixty-five years. But the Baltic Basin (where the majority of Poland's shale resources are found) has "challenging" geologic conditions.

Poland's shale reserves are located rather deep, at 1,000–4,500 meters below the surface, with higher clay content and widely varying layers that impede fracking and horizontal drilling.[18]

At this juncture, Poland's prospects of a commercial shale-gas industry remain elusive. Only sixty-four vertical test wells have been drilled to ascertain whether the geology can sustain a viable industry (industry recommendations call for at least 200 such test wells). These wells have so far produced only 10 to 30 percent of the gas flow needed to be commercially sustainable, and these disappointing early results are causing many investors to rethink Polish shale. Slawomir Brodzinski, the nation's deputy environment minister and chief geologist, gave the bottom line: "Without technological adjustments, there won't be shale-gas success in Europe."[19]

Mixed Emotions in Russia

One country that might have all the pieces to the shale puzzle is Russia—but that doesn't mean they'll be piecing it together imminently. Putin views shale resources in other nations with hostility, as they threaten Russia's strategically vital economic interest in natural gas exports across Europe—almost all of which is extracted from conventional drilling. But if foreign experiences seem to be teaching the country something; Russia is clearly realizing shale's value, and there are indications that it is contemplating how to bring the value back home.

Multinational oil and gas companies—in conjunction with the state-owned Gazprom—are now targeting West Siberia's 570-million-acre Bazhenov source rock. As of last summer, the EIA estimates that this shale formation could hold 1,920 trillion cubic feet of natural gas, (285 trillion cubic feet technically recoverable) and 1,243 billion barrels of oil (75 billion barrels technically recoverable). If the Bazhenov's potential can indeed be harnessed, Russia could be looking at ten times the amount of North Dakota's Bakken.[20]

But there's a catch. Or two. Or three. Drillers have just started exploratory shale wells, and while their reserves are expected to be significant, the challenges they face are unique. For one, the arctic environment is particularly harsh, and in summers the ground in Siberia softens, making it impossible to drill for much of the season. For another, the Bazenhov crude may not have been "cooked" and compressed with the same geological results as American shale deposits have.

To top it all off, the government itself stands in the way. The current tax structure geared toward conventional reservoirs and political policies encourage rancor and division from the West. Last year, the Russian government instituted tax breaks for companies working in shale, but current sanctions against the country's oil sector limit the involvement of foreign companies within Russia. And while domestic producers are continuing without their foreign partners, many recognize that Russia's shale development will be slow going—if not completely grinding to a halt—without Western expertise and equipment.

Does U.S. Experience Translate?

Tim Probert, a Halliburton strategic advisor, admitted surprise that some of these foreign shale hotbeds have yet to emerge. He and other industry insiders have been expecting international fracking advancements for some time. But currently only about 100 rigs drilling in shales and other "tight" reservoirs are scattered around the world—compared to more than 1,000 in the U.S. alone.

Probert fully anticipated a ramp-up, however: "I am very optimistic about international advancements and feel we are just in the first innings."[21]

But no matter where in the world the shale industry does expand, we can be sure that American entrepreneurship and technology will drive a good deal of those developments.

"Onshore in the United States, we have a pretty robust natural gas pipeline system. That doesn't exist in China. It doesn't exist in Saudi Arabia. [This kind of thing] takes both dollars and entrepreneurial spirit, which is not necessarily a trademark of foreign governments," Paul Hagemeier, of ALL Consulting, told us when we chatted in September 2014. "So it's not a surprise that [shale energy] originated here. Not at all. And it's not a surprise that the technical know-how is going to be exported from here and make its way from here."

The End of Our Exploring

Hagemeier is right: America will become "source rock" for other countries' shale exploration program. Our entrepreneurial culture has always been big on risk-taking and proactive, out-of-box thinking, and short on naysaying and precautionary thinking. So it may be no accident at all, as Hagmeier suggested, that shale development happened here first.

And my theory goes further: One of the reasons that other countries have yet to emulate North American shale successes has less to do with geology or investment or timing or government regulations and more to do with that cultural element that Americans seem to possess in abundance: chutzpah. You can say that there's "a culture of fracking," a "frack 'til you quack" adventurism, a longing to achieve against the odds. American companies know how to put machines, metrics, and muscle behind crazy dreams—shale being one of them. And so, again, it's no accident that this discovery—born in the USA, made in the USA, perfected in the USA—is still largely a USA phenomenon. As we move forward in this twenty-first century, shale oil and gas will be remembered as an American discovery, as distinctly American as the personal computer before it, the Broadway musical, or Apollo 11's mission to the moon and Neil Armstrong's "one small step for man."

Shale energy is a new leap of faith. It's hard to extract and it's dirty, oily, and gassy. But it's spectacularly abundant. Shale gives us more energy than we ever thought possible, and because we took the risk first, Americans can enjoy the rewards and share our abundance with others.

Truth is, we don't know what will happen by 2035. But with careful planning, we can still lead the way. Imagine a world with several reliable fuel sources providing clean and affordable energy, freedom from energy poverty, a new foundation for prosperity and economic growth, and an outreach to global communities requiring economic development, political stability, and fair prices.

I can't imagine a greater contribution than that one.

Even with our doubts and expressions of caution, even with the responsibilities we carry to manage this treasure carefully and protect the environment at the same time, shale gives back a uniquely American promise: optimism, faith in our ingenuity, belief in a better life for all. These are no longer pipe dreams. Nor are they gifts we should take for granted. They're achievable goals now that American shale energy has been added to the global mix.

ACKNOWLEDGMENTS

Writing any full-length book is an act of commitment and faith. *The Switch* is no exception. In order to assemble the vast amount of energy data, graphic materials, expert insight, and geopolitical commentary forming the backbone of this book, I reached out to a group of researchers and editorial advisors from the Houston-based company, The Writers for Hire, Inc. My deepest appreciation to TWFH team—Wintress Odom, Dr. Arielle Emmett, Barbara Belzer Adams, Erin Larson, Jessica Scheider, and the other contributors—for timely research, editing, and publishing advice. I'm thankful for the fantastic graphics developed by Rob Maharaj and his team at HMX Creative.

To Honorable Governor of Pennsylvania Tom Ridge, also the first U.S. Secretary of Homeland Security, my deepest thanks for your insights on energy and geopolitics.

I'd also like to acknowledge the wonderful contributions to this book by Latin American energy expert Thomas McClarty; former Defense Secretary Leon Panetta, who provided insights into our military budgets and requirements for energy; and Olena Tregub, an independent oil and gas scholar who generously shared insights on energy politics and corruption in the Ukraine and Russia.

Special thanks to Tom Leyden, CEO of SolarGrid Storage, for insights on the solar industry and fossil fuels; Mark Brownstein, the Environmental Defense Fund's chief counsel, for information on carbon containment and natural gas; David Spence, a University of Texas at Austin professor of law, regulation, and policy, who provided invaluable advice on the fracking debate; and Dr. Anthony Ingraffea, the Dwight C. Baum Professor of Civil and Environmental Engineering at Cornell

University, an expert on shale geology, safety issues, and an advocate for aggressive U.S. renewables development.

Issac Orr, a research analyst, and H. Sterling Burnett, PhD, the research fellow in energy and environment at The Heartland Institute, also provided excellent commentary on the need to alleviate energy poverty worldwide. I'm deeply grateful to Anders Aslund, senior fellow at the Peterson Institute for International Economics, who reviewed issues of Middle East energy policy and U.S. obligations in the Gulf.

This book would not be possible without the direct assistance of David Spigelmyer, the president of the Marcellus Shale Coalition, who not only provided timely information and safety data on Pennsylvania's natural gas "boom," but also gave our researchers a direct on-the-ground tour of several horizontal drilling wells.

My appreciation and admiration to the men and women of Canary, LLC. Their hard work and focus provided my inspiration of America's energy future.

Finally, thanks to my wife Farah for your patience and loving support during all those late nights and weekends of work.

ENDNOTES

Chapter 1

1 "Natural Gas," Data: U.S. Natural Gas Marketed Production (table), U.S. Energy Information Administration, released July 31, 2015, http://www.eia.gov/dnav/ng/hist/n9050us2a.htm.

2 Jim Efstathiou Jr., "Fracking Will Support 1.7 Million Jobs, Study Shows," *Bloomberg Businessweek*, October 23, 2012, http://www.bloomberg.com/news/articles/2012-10-23/fracking-will-support-1-7-million-jobs-study-shows.

3 Tim Bowler, "Falling Oil Prices: Who Are the Winners and Losers?" *BBC News*, January 19, 2015, http://www.bbc.com/news/business-29643612.

4 "U.S. Imports from OPEC Countries of Crude Oil," U.S. Energy Information Administration, July 31, 2015, http://www.eia.gov/dnav/pet/hist/LeafHandler.ashx?n=pet&s=mcrimxx1&f=a.

5 "U.S. Natural Gas Imports," U.S. Energy Information Administration, July 31, 2015, http://www.eia.gov/dnav/ng/hist/n9100us2a.htm.

Chapter 2

1 "Hydraulic Fracturing of Oil & Gas Wells Drilled in Shale," Geology.com, n.d., http://geology.com/articles/hydraulic-fracturing/.

Chapter 3

1 Brian Handwerk, "Pictures: World's Worst Power Outages," National Geographic, August 21, 2012, http://news.nationalgeographic.com/news/energy/2012/08/pictures/120821-world-s-worst-power-outages/#/energy-worst-power-outages-skyline-nyc_58535_600x450.jpg.

2 Joe Seeber, *Wired for Greed: The Shocking Truth about America's Electric Utilities*, (Lincoln, NE: iUniverse, 2005).

3 Email responses, Blackout History Project, n.d, http://blackout.gmu.edu/archive/submissions/summary.txt.

4 John Summers, "Forum: Interviews: Mae Rosenzweig," Blackout History Project, August 5, 1999, http://blackout.gmu.edu/forum/interviews/rosenzweig1.html.

5 "Lyndon B. Johnson: 'Memorandum Concerning the Power Failure in the Northeastern United States': November 9, 1965," The American Presidency Project (Gerhard Peters and John T. Woolley), http://www.presidency.ucsb.edu/ws/?pid=27361.

6 Martin Gottlieb and James Glanz, "The Blackout of 2003: The Past; The Blackouts of '65 and '77 Became Defining Moments in the City's History," *The New York Times*, August 15, 2003, http://www.nytimes.com/2003/08/15/us/blackout-2003-past-blackouts-65-77-became-defining-moments-city-s-history.html.

Chapter 4

1 Matt Purple, "Hagel Skewers Iraq War, Defends Greenspan's Oil Comments," CNSNews.com, July 7, 2008, http://cnsnews.com/news/article/hagel-skewers-iraq-war-defends-greenspans-oil-comments.

2 Rebecca Leung, "Bush Sought 'Way' To Invade Iraq?" *60 Minutes*, February 11, 2009, http://www.cbsnews.com/news/bush-sought-way-to-invade-iraq/.

3 "How Uninhabited Islands Soured China-Japan Ties," BBC News, November 10, 2014, http://www.bbc.com/news/world-asia-pacific-11341139.

Chapter 5

1 Pierre Noel, "European Gas Supply Security: Unfinished Business" in *Energy and Security: Strategies for a World in Transition*, ed. Jan H. Kalicki and David L. Goldwyn (Washington, DC: Woodrow Wilson Center Press, 2013), 169.

2 Jan H. Kalicki and David L. Goldwyn, *Energy Security: Strategies for a World in Transition*, (Washington, DC: Woodrow Wilson Center Press, 2013), 122.

3 Bruno Waterfield, "Germany is a Cautionary Tale of How Energy Polices Can Harm the Economy," *The Telegraph*, January 16, 2014, http://www.telegraph.co.uk/finance/newsbysector/energy/10577513/Germany-is-a-cautionary-tale-of-how-energy-polices-can-harm-the-economy.html.

Chapter 6

1   Seth Blumsack, "Are We Running Out of Oil?" Lecture notes, Penn State, College of Earth and Mineral Sciences, Department of Energy and Mineral Engineering.

2   Daniel Yergin, *The Quest: Energy, Security, and the Remaking of the Modern World* (New York: Penguin Press, 2011).

3   Charles Hall and Carlos A. Ramírez-Pascualli, *The First Half of the Age of Oil: An Exploration of the Work of Colin Campbell and Jean Laherrère* (New York: Springer Science + Business Media, 2013), 32.

4   Jimmy Carter, "Proposed Energy Policy," April 18, 1977, transcript of televisedspeech, PBS.org, Special Features: Primary Resources, http://www.pbs.org/wgbh /americanexperience/features/primary-resources/carter-energy/.

5   Yergin, Daniel. *The Quest: Energy, Security, and the Remaking of the Modern World*. (New York: Penguin 2011).

6   Grant Smith, "U.S. to Be Top Oil Producer by 2015 on Shale, IEA Says," *Bloomberg Business*, November 12, 2013, http://www.bloomberg.com/news /articles/2013-11-12/u-s-nears-energy-independence-by-2035-on-shale-boom-iea-says.

7   For a sampling of these websites, do an online search of "peak oil theory" or "are we running out of oil?" Some of the sites rightfully ask what alternative energy plans we will make when fossil fuels run low. An excellent source is the Penn State University Department of Energy and Minerals Engineer John A. Dutton e-Education Institute (www.e-education.psu.edu), which runs an entire online curriculum on the oil and gas industry and its origins.

8   U.S. Energy Information Administration, http://eia.gov.

9   Adam E. Brandt and Alex R. Farrell, "Risks of the Oil Transition," *Environmental Research Letters* 1, no. 1 (October–December 2006), doi: 10.1088/1748-9326/1/1/014004.

10 Seth Blumsack, "Potential Production of Various Petroleum Products." Lecture notes, Penn State, College of Earth and Mineral Sciences, Department of Energy and Mineral Engineering.

Chapter 7

1   *The Importance of Ethical Culture: Increasing Trust and Driving Down Risks—Supplemental Research Brief: 2009 National Business Ethics Survey* (Arlington, VA: Ethics Resource Center, 2010), http://www.ethics.org/files/u5/CultureSup4.pdf.

2   Sanne Ponsioen, "Employees More Likely to Imitate Unethical Behaviour in Subordinates than in Managers," *University of Groningen News*, April 14, 2014, http://www.rug .nl/news/2014/04/0414-ponsioen.

3   Raymond S. Nickerson, "Confirmation Bias: A Ubiquitous Phenomenon in Many Guises," *Review of General Psychology* 2, no. 2 (1998), 175–220, http://landman-psychology.com/ConfirmationBias.pdf.

Chapter 8

1   Ayoubi, Amjad, "Access to Energy as a Human Right," *Energy is a Human Right* (blog), December 4, 2014, http://www.abrosgreen.com/blog-article006.html.

2   "Sustainable Energy for All: Sector Results Profile." Results brief, The World Bank, April 9, 2014, http://www.worldbank.org/en/results/2013/04/10 /sustainable-energy-for-all-results-profile.

3   "Managing Your Energy Use: Home Heating" Consumers Energy, n.d., https://www.consumersenergy.com/content.aspx?id=1246.

4   *Transportation Energy Data Book, Edition 33*, U.S. Department of Energy, Table 2.5, July 31, 2014, http://cta.ornl.gov/data/chapter2.shtml.

5   "Inventory of U.S. Greenhouse Gas Emissions and Sinks: 1990–2012," U.S. Environmental Protection Agency (EPA), Table ES-7, 2014. http://www.epa.gov /climatechange/emissions/usinventoryreport.html.

6   "Transportation Overview: U.S. Emissions," Figures 1 and 2, Center for Climate and Energy Solutions, n.d., http://www.c2es.org/energy/use/transportation.

7   "How much oil is used to make plastic?" Frequently Asked Questions, U.S. Energy Information Administration, last updated July 10, 2015, http://www.eia.gov/tools/faqs /faq.cfm?id=34&t=6.

8   "What is U.S. electricity generation by energy source?" Frequently Asked Questions, U.S. Energy Information Administration, last updated March 31, 2015, http://www.eia. gov/tools/faqs/faq.cfm?id=427&t=3.

9   "Use of Energy in the United States Explained: Energy Use for Transportation," U.S. Energy Information Administration, last updated July 17, 2015, http://www.eia.gov /EnergyExplained/?page=us_energy_transportation.

10 "2009 RECS Survey Data: Housing Characteristics Tables," Residential Energy Consumption Survey, U.S. Energy Information Administration, n.d., http://www.eia. gov/consumption/residential/data/2009.

11 "What is U.S. electricity generation by energy source?" Frequently Asked Questions, U.S. Energy Information Administration, last updated March 31, 2015, http://www.eia. gov/tools/faqs/faq.cfm?id=427&t=3.

12 "Coal Plants Affected by EPA Data," *Governing*, n.d., http://www.governing.com/gov -data/energy-environment/coal-plants-to-shut-down-from-EPA-regulations.html.

13 "Natural Gas," Clean Energy, Environmental Protection Agency, last updated September 25, 2013, http://www.epa.gov/cleanenergy/energy-and-you/affect/natural-gas.html.

14 "Biofuels: Ethanol and Biodiesel Explained," Energy Explained: Renewable Sources, U.S. Energy Information Administration, last reviewed July 17, 2015, http://www.eia. gov/energyexplained/?page=biofuel_home.

15 Ibid.

16 "Study Released on the Potential of Plug-In Hybrid Electric Vehicles," U.S. Department of Energy Office of Electricity Delivery & Energy Reliability, January 19, 2007, http://energy.gov/oe/articles/study-released-potential-plug-hybrid -electric-vehicles.

17 "Electricity Fuel Basics," Energy.gov, August 19, 2013, http://energy.gov/eere/energybasics/articles/electricity-fuel-basics.

18 "2009 RECS Survey Data: Housing Characteristics Tables," Residential Energy Consumption Survey, U.S. Energy Information Administration, n.d., http://www.eia.gov/consumption/residential/data/2009.

19 "Heating and Cooling No Longer Majority of U.S. Home Energy Use," Today in Energy, U.S. Energy Information Administration, March 7, 2013, http://www.eia.gov/todayinenergy/detail.cfm?id=10271.

20 "2009 RECS Survey Data: Housing Characteristics Tables," Residential Energy Consumption Survey, U.S. Energy Information Administration, n.d., http://www.eia.gov/consumption/residential/data/2009.

Chapter 9

1 David Spence, "Responsible Shale Gas Production: Moral Outrage vs. Cool Analysis," Law and Econ Research Paper no. 403, University of Texas at Austin: School of Law, June 10, 2013, http://ssrn.com/abstract=2228398.

2 Stanley Cohen, *Folk Devils and Moral Panics: The Creation of the Mods and Rockers* (UK: Paladin, 1979), 9.

3 Glenn Blain, "'Fracking Kills': Yoko Ono Joins Star-Studded Cast Fighting Against Hydraulic Natural Gas Drilling in Upstate New York," *NY Daily News*, January 11, 2013, http://www.nydailynews.com/new-york/fracking-kills-yoko-fights-drilling-article-1.1238624.

4 David Spence, "Responsible Shale Gas Production: Moral Outrage vs. Cool Analysis," Law and Econ Research Paper no. 403, University of Texas at Austin: School of Law, June 10, 2013, http://ssrn.com/abstract=2228398.

5 David Biello, "Fracking Can Be Done Safely but Will It Be?" *Scientific American*, May 17, 2013, http://www.scientificamerican.com/article/can-fracking-be-done-without-impacting-water/.

6 "Dimock, Pa: 'Ground Zero' in the Fight over Fracking," *StateImpact Pennsylvania*, n.d., http://stateimpact.npr.org/pennsylvania/tag/dimock/.

7 Caulton, Dana R. "Toward a Better Understanding and Quantification of Methane Emissions from Shale Gas Development." *Proceedings of the National Academy of Sciences of the United States of America* 111, no. 17 (March 12, 2014): 6237–6242, doi: 10.1073/pnas.1316546111, http://www.pnas.org/content/111/17/6237.abstract.

8 Andrew C. Revkin, "A Deeper Look at a Study Finding High Leak Rates from Gas Drilling," *Dot Earth* (blog), *The New York Times*, April 23, 2014, http://dotearth.blogs.nytimes.com/2014/04/23/a-deeper-look-at-a-study-finding-high-leak-rates-from-gas-drilling.

9 David Biello, "Fracking Can Be Done Safely but Will It Be?" *Scientific American*, May 17, 2013, http://www.scientificamerican.com/article/can-fracking-be-done-without-impacting-water/.

10 "Earthquake Facts and Earthquake Fantasy," Earthquake Topics for Education, USGS, last modified May 28, 2015, http://earthquake.usgs.gov/learn/topics/megaqk_facts_fantasy.php.

11 Ibid.

12 Earthquakes, Megaquakes, and the Movies," Earthquake Topics for Education, USGS, last modified May 28, 2015, http://earthquake.usgs.gov/learn/topics/megaquakes.php.

13 Sarah Phelan, "Could Fracking the Monterey Shale Lead to the Next Big One?," *Bay Nature*, September 17, 2013, http://baynature.org/articles/could-fracking-the-monterey-shale-lead-to-the-next-big-one.

14 "How Americans View the Top Energy and Environmental Issues," Pew Research Center, January 15, 2015, http://www.pewresearch.org/key-data-points/environment-energy-2/.

Chapter 10

1 "Purity Concerns: German Beer Brewers Foaming over Fracking," Spiegel Online, May 23, 2013, http://www.spiegel.de/international/business/german-brewers-oppose-fracking-because-of-fear-over-clean-water-a-901474.html.

2 Mary Tiemann and Adam Vann, "Hydraulic Fracturing and Safe Drinking Water Act Regulatory Issues," Congressional Research Service, January 10, 2013, https://www.fas.org/sgp/crs/misc/R41760.pdf.

3 Abrahm Lustgarten, "Buried Secrets: Is Natural Gas Drilling Endangering U.S. Water Supplies?," *ProPublica*, November 13, 2008, http://www.propublica.org/article/buried-secrets-is-natural-gas-drilling-endangering-us-water-supplies-1113.

4 "Oil and Natural Gas Air Pollution Standards," United States Environmental Protection Agency, last updated August 5, 2015, http://www.epa.gov/airquality/oilandgas/.

5 Coral Davenport, "White House Unveils Plans to Cut Methane Emissions," *The New York Times*, March 28, 2014, http://www.nytimes.com/2014/03/29/us/politics/white-house-unveils-plans-to-to-cut-methane-emissions.html.

6 Jennifer A. Dlouhy, "Oil Industry Says Methane Plan Unneeded," *Houston Chronicle*, January 14, 2015, http://www.houstonchronicle.com/business/energy/article/Plan-to-cut-methane-emissions-brings-quick-rebuke-6016116.php.

7 "Interior Department Releases Final Rule to Support Safe, Responsible Hydraulic Fracturing Activities on Public and Tribal Lands," News release from the Bureau of Land Management, March 20, 2015, http://www.blm.gov/wo/st/en/info/newsroom/2015/march/nr_03_20_2015.html.

8 "North Dakota Joins Wyoming in Suing Feds," *OK Energy Today,* April 2, 2015, http://okenergytoday.com/2015/04/north-dakota-joins-wyoming-in-suing-feds/

9 Jody Freeman and David Spence, "Should the Federal Government Regulate Fracking?" *The Wall Street Journal,* April 14, 2013, http://www.wsj.com/articles/SB100 01424127887323495104578314302738867078.

10 Jenni Bergal, "Democratic-Dominated Cities Pass Measures That Could Conflict with State Laws," *Huffington Post,* January 15, 2015, http://www.huffingtonpost.com/2015/01/15/state-laws_n_6478964.html.

11 "Oil and Gas Drilling Advantages in U.S. Tax Code," Investments and Acquisitions, n.d., http://investments-and-acquisitions.com/oil-and-gas-drilling-advantages-in-us-tax-code.

Chapter 11

1 Clare Foran, "How Many Jobs Does Fracking Really Create?," *National Journal,* April 14, 2014, http://www.nationaljournal.com/new-energy-paradigm/how-many-jobs-does-fracking-really-create-20140414.

Chapter 12

1 Matthew Rocco, "Shale Boom Spurs Rapid Job Growth," *Fox Business,* August 8, 2013, http://www.foxbusiness.com/industries/2013/08/08/shale-boom-spurs-rapid-job-growth/.

2 Nancy Hodur and Dean Bangsund, "Population Estimates for the City of Williston," Agribusiness and Applied Economics Report no. 707-S, Williston Economic Development, January 2013, http://www.willistondevelopment.com/usrimages/PopulationEstimatesWillistonJanuary2013.pdf.

3 Carly Crane, "North Dakota's Attitude Towards Women is All About . . . Oil?" *Policy.Mic,* April 3, 2013, http://mic.com/articles/32085/north-dakota-s-attitude-towards-women-is-all-about-oil.

4 John Eligon, "An Oil Town Where Men Are Many, and Women Are Hounded," *The New York Times,* January 15, 2013, http://www.nytimes.com/2013/01/16/us/16women.html.

5 Juan Miguel Pedraza, "UND Researchers Probe North Dakota Oil Patch Man Camps," *University Letter: University of North Dakota Faculty/Staff Newsletter,* August 27, 2012, http://webapp.und.edu/dept/our/uletter/?p=31747.

6 Gregg Zart, "Wal-Mart Campers EVICTED! (Live) in Williston ND.wmv," YouTube video, April 1, 2012, http://www.youtube.com/watch?v=_VaAiacfPTA.

7   "North Dakota Sees Increases in Real GDP Per Capita Following Bakken Production,"
    U.S. Energy Information Administration, July 12, 2013, http://www.eia.gov
    /todayinenergy/detail.cfm?id=12071.

8   Blaire Briody, "11 Shocking Facts about the North Dakota Oil Boom,"
    The Fiscal Times, June 6, 2013, http://www.thefiscaltimes.com/
    Articles/2013/06/06/11-Shocking-Facts-about-the-North-Dakota-Oil-Boom.

9   Blake Ellis, "Oil Boom Leads to Surging ER Visits, Wait Times, STDs," *CNN Money*,
    November 7, 2011, http://money.cnn.com/2011/11/07/pf/America_boomtown
    _healthcare/index.htm.

10 Kane Farabaugh, "Oil Boom Crowding North Dakota Schools," *Voice of America*,
    June 9, 2014, http://www.voanews.com/content/oil-boom-crowding-north-dakota
    -schools/1933134.html.

11 Jennifer Oldham, "North Dakota Fracking Boom Leaves Oil Hub a Bust: Muni
    Credit," February 26, 2013, *Bloomberg Business*, http://bloomberg.com/news
    /articles/2013-02-27/north-dakota-fracking-boom-leaves-oil-hub-a-bust-muni-credit.

12 Faith Braverman, "In North Dakota, Walmart Employees Start at $17.40
    /hr," *The Libertarian Republic*, June 11, 2014, http://thelibertarianrepublic.com
    /north-dakota-walmart-employees-start-17-40hr/.

13 Katie Little, "Boom Helps Fast-Food Workers Bring Home the Bakken," *CNBC*,
    June 20, 2014, http://www.cnbc.com/2014/06/19/boom-helps-fast-food-workers
    -bring-home-the-bakken.html.

14 "McDonald's Signing Bonuses: North Dakota Outlet Offering $300 To Potential
    Hires," *Huffington Post*, January 21, 2012, http://www.huffingtonpost.com/2012
    /01/21/mcdonalds-signing-bonuses_n_1220088.html.

15 "America's New Energy Future: The Unconventional Oil and Gas Revolution and
    the US Economy; Volume 3: A Manufacturing Renaissance - Main Report" IHS,
    September 2013, http://www.energyxxi.org/sites/default/files/pdf/Americas_New
    _Energy_Future_Phase3.pdf.

16 Jon Entine, "Will Washington Politics Kill the US Energy Revival and Shale Gas
    Revolution?," *Forbes*, August 22, 2013, http://www.forbes.com/sites/jonentine/2013
    /08/22 will-washington-politics-kill-the-us-energy-revival-and-shale-gas-revolution.

17 Dan Alfaro, "Shale and HF: A 50 State Jobs Plan," Energy in Depth, December 26,
    2012, http://energyindepth.org/national/shale-and-hf-a-50-state-jobs-plan/.

18 Rob Grunewald and Dulguun Batbold, "Bakken Activity: How Wide Is the Ripple
    Effect?" *FedGazette*, Federal Reserve Bank of Minneapolis, May 7, 2013, https://
    www.minneapolisfed.org/publications/fedgazette/bakken-activity-how-wide-is-the
    -ripple-effect.

19 Ibid.

20 Ibid.

21 "Nimby Town to Provide Water for Fracking at Pittsburgh Airport,"
    Marcellus Drilling News, August 30, 2013, http://marcellusdrilling.com/2013/08
    /nimby-town-to-provide-water-for-fracking-at-pittsburgh-airport/.

22 "America's New Energy Future: The Unconventional Oil and Gas Revolution and the US Economy; Volume 3: A Manufacturing Renaissance - Main Report" IHS, September 2013, http://www.energyxxi.org/sites/default/files/pdf/Americas_New _Energy_Future_Phase3.pdf.

23 Dan Alfaro, "Shale and HF: A 50 State Jobs Plan," *Energy in Depth*, December 26, 2012, http://energyindepth.org/national/shale-and-hf-a-50-state-jobs-plan/.

24 "America's New Energy Future: The Unconventional Oil and Gas Revolution and the US Economy; Volume 3: A Manufacturing Renaissance - Main Report" IHS, September 2013, http://www.energyxxi.org/sites/default/files/pdf/Americas_New _Energy_Future_Phase3.pdf.

25 Jeffry Bartash, "Bringing U.S. Manufacturing Jobs Back Home," *MarketWatch*, February 14, 2013, http://www.marketwatch.com/story /bringing-us-manufacturing-jobs-back-home-2013-02-14.

26 Jim Landers, "Dallas-Fort Worth Manufacturing Ready to Compete with the World," *The Dallas Morning News*, November 11, 2012, http://www.dallasnews.com/business /headlines/20121111-dallas-fort-worth-manufacturing-ready-to-compete-with-the -world.ece.

27 *Energy Outlook 2035*, BP, February 2015, http://www.bp.com/content/dam/bp/pdf /Energy-economics/energy-outlook-2015/Energy_Outlook_2035_booklet.pdf.

28 Thomas Miller, "Three Reasons Why US Shale Isn't Going Anywhere," Oilprice.com, March 4, 2015, http://oilprice.com/Energy/Crude-Oil/Three-Reasons-Why-US-Shale -Isnt-Going-Anywhere.html.

29 *Energy Outlook 2035*, BP, February 2015, http://www.bp.com/content/dam/bp/pdf /Energy-economics/energy-outlook-2015/Energy_Outlook_2035_booklet.pdf.

Chapter 13

1 Gary Shilling, "Get Ready for $10 Oil," *BloombergView*, February 16, 2015, http://www. bloombergview.com/articles/2015-02-16/oil-prices-likely-to-fall-as-supplies -rise-demand-falls.

2 Barani Krishnan, "U.S. Crude Down 10 Percent Post-Opec, Brent Breaks Below $70," Reuters, November 28, 2014, http://www.reuters.com/article/2014/11/28 /U.S.-markets-oil-idUSKCN0JC1LO20141128.

3 James Williams, "North American Rotary Rig Counts," *WTRG Economics*, n.d., http://www.wtrg.com/rotaryrigs.html.

4 Collin Eaton, "More Than 500 Rigs May Shut Down as Oil Slides, Analysts Say," *Fuel Fix* (blog), *Houston Chronicle*, December 17, 2014, http://fuelfix.com/ blog/2014/12/17/more-than-500-rigs-may-shut-down-as-oil-slides-analysts-say.

5 Dan Weil, "Ex-Wells Fargo CEO Kovacevich: OPEC 'Wants to Punish Fracking' through Price War," *Newsmax*, January 6, 2015, http://www.newsmax.com/Finance /Kovacevich-OPEC-fracking-oil/2015/01/06/id/616763/.

6   Grant Smith, "Why OPEC Is Talking Oil Down, Not Up, After 48% Selloff," *Bloomberg Business*, January 8, 2015, http://www.bloomberg.com/news/articles/2015-01-09/why-opec-is-talking-oil-down-not-up-after-48-selloff.

7   Afshin Molavi, "Declining Oil Prices: OPEC vs. (Future) Shale?," *El Arabiya News*, December 16, 2014, http://english.alarabiya.net/en/views/business/economy/2014/12/16/Declining-oil-prices-OPEC-vs-future-Shale-.html.

8   Timothy Puko and Ese Erheriene, "Oil Rises on Optimism for Higher Demand, Lower Supply," *The Wall Street Journal*, February 9, 2015 http://www.wsj.com/articles/crude-rises-on-opec-forecast-of-increased-demand-1423485545.

9   "97% of Fracking Now Operating at a Loss at Current Oil Prices," *Daily Kos*, January 6, 2015, http://www.dailykos.com/story/2015/01/06/1355814/-97-of-fracking-now-operating-at-a-loss-at-current-oil-prices.

10 Youssef Ibrahim, "Energy Independence for U.S. Adds up to Strategic 'Game Changer,'" *New York Sun*, July 7, 2013, http://www.nysun.com/foreign/america-crosses-into-new-era-of-energy/88342/.

Chapter 14

1   Bruno Gremez, February 16, 2015, commented on "Oil and Gas Industry in 2015: Is an end to the shale oil boom coming? Or has it come and gone?" Quora (website), n.d., http://www.quora.com/Oil-and-Gas-Industry-in-2015/Is-an-end-to-the-Shale-Oil-boom-coming-Or-has-it-come-and-gone.

2   Keir Yorke, "Why Oil Prices Keep Falling – and Throwing the World into Turmoil," *LinkedIn Pulse*, January 8, 2015, https://www.linkedin.com/pulse/why-oil-prices-keep-falling-throwing-world-turmoil-keir-yorke.

3   Russell Gold, "Back to the Future? Oil Replays 1980s Bust," *The Wall Street Journal*, January 13, 2015, http://www.wsj.com/articles/back-to-the-future-oil-replays-1980s-bust-1421196361.

4   Travis Hoium, "Why OPEC is Playing a Dangerous Game With Oil Markets," The Motley Fool, January 5, 2015, http://www.fool.com/investing/general/2015/01/05/why-opec-is-playing-a-dangerous-game-with-oil-mark.aspx.

5   Margaret McQuaile, Stuart Elliott, Adal Mirza, Jacinta Moran, and Herman Wang, "OPEC Is Playing a Dangerous Game with Oil Markets," *The Barrel* (blog), Platts, November 28, 2014, http://blogs.platts.com/2014/11/28/opec-meeting-nov14/.

6   John Kemp, "Bakken Oil Producers need $55 to Keep Production Steady," Reuters, January 9, 2015, http://www.reuters.com/article/2015/01/09/bakken-oil-breakeven-kemp-idUSL6N0UO1Z520150109.

7   Tom Randall, "Citi: Oil Could Plunge to $20, and This Might Be 'the End of OPEC'," *Bloomberg Business*, February 9, 2015, http://www.bloomberg.com/news/articles/2015-02-09/citi-oil-could-plunge-to-20-and-this-might-be-the-end-of-opec-.

8   Jan H. Kalicki and David L. Goldwyn, eds., *Energy & Security: Strategies for a World in Transition* (Washington, DC: Woodrow Wilson Center Press, 2013), 547.

9   Ibid, 547.

10 Ibid, 548.

Chapter 15

1   Robert Blackwill and Meghan O'Sullivan, "America's Energy Edge: The Geopolitical Consequences of the Shale Revolution," *Foreign Affairs,* March/April 2014, http://www.foreignaffairs.com/articles/140750/robert-d-blackwill-and-meghan-l-osullivan/americas-energy-edge.

2   "U.S. Oil Refining Capability," FactCheck.org, May 12, 2008, http://www.factcheck.org/2008/05/us-oil-refining-capability/.

3   D. Sean Shurtleff and H. Sterling Burnett, "Increasing America's Domestic Fuel Supply by Building New Oil Refineries." Brief analysis from the National Center for Policy Analysis, November 15, 2007, http://www.ncpa.org/pub/ba603.

4   Eloise Ogden, "Tribes Hope to Start Building Refinery in Spring," *Minot Daily News,* January 24, 2012, http://www.minotdailynews.com/page/content.detail/id/562388/Tribes-hope-to-start-building-refinery-in-spring.html.

5   Joyce Lobeck, "Refinery Still Moving Forward," *Yuma Sun,* March 11, 2009, http://www.arizonacleanfuels.com/news/2009/031108_YS.htm.

6   Gregg Laskoski, "Amid Keystone Controversy, Another Energy Project Moves Forward," *On Energy* (blog), *U.S. News & World Report,* October 6, 2011, http://www.usnews.com/opinion/blogs/on-energy/2011/10/06/amid-keystone-controversy-another-energy-project-moves-forward.

7   "U.S. Exports of Crude Oil," Petroleum & Other Liquids, U.S. Energy Information Administration, July 31, 2015, http://www.eia.gov/dnav/pet/hist/LeafHandler.ashx?n=PET&s=MCREXUS1&f=M.

8   Robert Grattan, "U.S. Crude Exports Hit Recent High," *Fuel Fix* (blog), *The Houston Chronicle,* August 7, 2014, http://fuelfix.com/blog/2014/08/07/u-s-crude-exports-hit-recent-high/.

9   Nick Snow, "EIA Conference Speakers Warn of US Light Crude Oil's 'Day of Reckoning'," *Oil & Gas Journal,* July 21, 2014, http://www.ogj.com/articles/print/volume-112/issue-7b/general-interest/eia-conference-speakers-warn-of-us-light-crude-oil-s-day-of-reckoning.html.

10 Edward Dodge, "Daniel Yergin: US Oil Output Helping Avert Crisis," *Breaking Energy,* July 18, 2014, http://breakingenergy.com/2014/07/18/daniel-yergin-us-oil-output-helping-avert-crisis/.

11 Henry Vidas, et al, "The Impacts of U.S. Crude Oil Exports on Domestic Crude Production, GDP, Employment, Trade, and Consumer Costs." Report by ICF International and EnSys Energy, March 31, 2014, http://www.api.org/~/media/Files/Policy/LNG-Exports/LNG-primer/API-Crude-Exports-Study-by-ICF-3-31-2014.pdf.

12 Bernard Weinstein, "World's Energy Landscape Has Changed so Much that 40-Year Restrictive Policy Has Outlived its Usefulness," *Houston Chronicle,* October 23, 2014, http://www.chron.com/opinion/outlook/article/Weinstein-Ban-on-oil-exports-has-outlived-its-5843602.php.

13 "US Crude Oil Export Decision: Assessing the Impact of the Export Ban and Free Trade on the US Economy," Crude Oil Export Special Report, IHS, http://www.ihs.com/info/0514/crude-oil.aspx.

14 Henry Vidas, et al, "The Impacts of U.S. Crude Oil Exports on Domestic Crude Production, GDP, Employment, Trade, and Consumer Costs." Report by ICF International and EnSys Energy, March 31, 2014, http://www.api.org/~/media/Files/Policy/LNG-Exports/LNG-primer/API-Crude-Exports-Study-by-ICF-3-31-2014.pdf.

15 "Recent Improvements in Petroleum Trade Balance Mitigate U.S. Trade Deficit," Today in Energy, U.S. Energy Information Administration, July 21, 2014, http://www.eia.gov/todayinenergy/detail.cfm?id=17191.

16 "Total Petroleum and Other Liquids Production – 2014" (infographic), International Energy Data and Analysis, U.S. Energy Information Administration, n.d., http://www.eia.gov/countries/cab.cfm?fips=JA.

17 Lydia DePillis, "A Leaked Document Shows Just How Much the EU Wants a Piece of America's Fracking Boom," *Wonkblog* (blog), The *Washington Post,* July 8, 2014, http://www.washingtonpost.com/blogs/wonkblog/wp/2014/07/08/could-a-trade-deal-lift-the-u-s-longstanding-ban-on-crude-oil-exports-europe-thinks-so.

Chapter 16

1 "About LNG: Basics," Center for Liquefied Natural Gas, n.d., http://www.lngfacts.org/about-lng/basics.

2 Tyler Crowe, "How Much Natural Gas Can America Export?" The Motley Fool, August 11, 2013, http://www.fool.com/investing/general/2013/08/11/how-much-natural-gas-can-america-export.aspx.

3 "Effects of Increased Natural Gas Exports on Domestic Energy Markets." Report by the U.S. Energy Information Administration, January 2012, http://energy.gov/sites/prod/files/2013/04/f0/fe_eia_lng.pdf.

4 "Natural Gas Monthly," U.S. Energy Information Administration, July 31, 2015, http://www.eia.gov/naturalgas/monthly/.

5   Jon Hurdle, "Gas Industry Urges U.S. to Speed Approval of LNG Export Terminals,"
    StateImpact Pennsylvania, April 16, 2015, https://stateimpact.npr.org/pennsylvania/
    2015/04/16/gas-industry-urges-u-s-to-speed-approval-of-lng-export-terminals/.

6   Timothy Cama and Cristina Marcos, "House Passes Bill to Speed up Liquefied Natural
    Gas Exports," *The Hill* (blog), January 28, 2015, http://thehill.com/blogs/floor-action/
    house/230990-house-passes-bill-to-speed-up-liquefied-natural-gas-exports.

Chapter 17

1   "The State of the National Pipeline Infrastructure." Report by the U.S. Department
    of Transportation, n.d., http://opsweb.phmsa.dot.gov/pipelineforum/docs/
    Secretarys%20Infrastructure%20Report_Revised%20per%20PHC_103111.pdf.

2   Steve Banker, "Aging US Gas Pipeline Infrastructure Costs Consumers Billions,"
    Forbes, September 30, 2013, http://www.forbes.com/sites/stevebanker/2013/09/30/
    aging-us-gas-pipeline-infrastructure-costs-consumers-billions/.

3   Jim Murphy, "New Revelations from Arkansas Spill Highlight Need for Stricter Tar
    Sands Pipeline Safety Standards," *National Wildlife Federation Blog* (blog), August 5,
    2013, http://blog.nwf.org/2013/08/new-revelations-from-arkansas-spill-highlight-need-
    for-stricter-tar-sands-pipeline-safety-standards/.

4   United States Department of State, "Final Supplemental Environmental Impact
    Statement for the Keystone XL Project," Executive Summary, (January 2014),
    http://keystonepipeline-xl.state.gov/documents/organization/221186.pdf.

5   Stephen Dinan, "Red-State Democrats Blast Latest Keystone Delay," *The Washington
    Times*, April 20, 2014, http://www.washingtontimes.com/news/2014/apr/20/
    red-state-democrats-blast-latest-keystone-delay.

6   David Ramsay, "Mark Pryor Responds to Keystone Delay (You'll Never Guess What He
    Says," *Arkansas Blog* (blog), *Arkansas Times*, April 18, 2014, http://www.arktimes.com
    /ArkansasBlog/archives/2014/04/18/mark-pryor-responds-to-keystone-delay-youll
    -never-guess-what-he-says.

7   Christopher Helman, "New Keystone XL Delay: A Stunning Act of Political
    Cowardice," *Forbes*, April 21, 2014, http://www.forbes.com/sites/christopherhelman/
    2014/04/21/new-keystone-xl-delay-a-stunning-act-of-political-cowardice/.

8   John M. Broder, Clifford Krauss, and Ian Austen, "Obama Faces Risks in
    Pipeline Decision," *The New York Times*, February 17, 2013, http://www.nytimes.
    com/2013/02/18/business/energy-environment/obamas-keystone-pipeline-decision
    -risks-new-problems-either-way.html.

9   Bruce Drake, "Why Can't We All Get Along? Challenges Ahead for Bipartisan
    Cooperation," Pew Research Center, November 7, 2014, http://www.pewresearch.org
    /fact-tank/2014/11/07/why-cant-we-all-get-along-challenges-ahead-for-bipartisan
    -cooperation/.

10 Diana Furchtgott-Roth, "Pipelines Are Safest for Transportation of Oil and Gas," Manhatten Institute for Policy Research, June 23, 2013, http://www.manhattan -institute.org/html/ib_23.htm.

11 Christina Nunez and John Tomanio "This Map Shows How U.S. Oil Train Accidents Skyrocketed," *National Geographic*, May 1, 2015, http://news.nationalgeographic.com/ energy/2015/05/150506-crude-oil-trainaccidents-over-time.

12 Jennifer Dlouhy, "Pipelines Are Safer than Trains and Trucks, Report Says," *Fuel Fix* (blog) *Houston Chronicle*, October 17, 2013, http://fuelfix.com/blog/2013/10/17/ pipelines-safer-than-trains-and-trucks-report-says/.

13 Ron Meador, "Why So Much Oil from the Fracking Boom Is Moving by High -Risk Rail," *Minneapolis Post*, September 24m 2014, https://www.minnpost.com/ earth-journal/2014/09/why-so-much-oil-fracking-boom-moving-high-risk-rail.

14 "Oil and Gas Transportation: Department of Transportation Is Taking Actions to Address Rail Safety, but Additional Actions Are Needed to Improve Pipeline Safety" Report to Congressional Requestors, U.S. Government Accountability Office, August 2014, http://www.gao.gov/assets/670/665404.pdf.

15 Incident Detail Reports for 2013, Hazmat Intelligence Portal, U.S. Department of Transportation, Pipeline and Hazardous Materials Safety Administration and Office of Hazardous Material Safety, https://hip.phmsa.dot.gov/.

16 Aman Batheja, "Rail Transport of Crude Oil Increases as Pipelines Fall Short," *The New York Times*, April 12, 2014, http://www.nytimes.com/2014/04/13/us/rail -transport-of-crude-oil-increases-as-pipeline-falls-short.html.

17 "Refinery Receipts of Crude Oil by Method of Transportation," Petroleum & Other Liquids, U.S. Energy Information Administration, June 19, 2015, http://www.eia.gov /dnav/pet/pet_pnp_caprec_dcu_nus_a.htm.

18 Brian Westenhaus, "Trucks, Trains, or Pipelines: The Best Way to Transport Petroleum," OilPrice.com, August 13, 2013, http://oilprice.com/Energy/Energy -General/Trucks-Trains-or-Pipelines-The-Best-Way-to-Transport-Petroleum.html.

19 "Moving Crude Oil by Rail," Association of American Railroads, July 2014, http:// energy.gov/sites/prod/files/2014/08/f18/chicago_qermeeting_gray_statement.pdf.

20 John Frittelli et al, "U.S. Rail Transportation of Crude Oil: Background and Issues for Congress," Congressional Research Service, December 4, 2014, https://www.fas.org/ sgp/crs/misc/R43390.pdf.

21 "Energy, Understanding Our Oil Supply Chain," American Petroleum Institute, n.d., http://www.api.org/~/media/Files/Policy/Safety/API-Oil-Supply-Chain.pdf.

22 David Shaffer, "Blast in Quebec Exposes Risk of Shipping Crude Oil By Rail," *Star Tribune*, July 9, 2013, http://www.startribune.com/business/214699171.html.

23 United States Department of State, "Final Supplemental Environmental Impact Statement for the Keystone XL Project," vol. 3, ch. 4.10, (January 2014), http:// keystonepipeline-xl.state.gov/documents/organization/221186.pdf.

24 Ibid.

25 "Canadian Economic Impacts of New and Existing Oil Sands Development in Alberta (2014–2038)," Briefing paper. Canadian Energy Research Institute, November 2014, http://www.ceri.ca/images/stories/CDN_Economic_Impacts_of_New_and_Existing _Oil_Sands_Development_in_Alberta_-_November_2014_-_Final.pdf.

26 Ibid.

27 John M. Broder, Clifford Krauss, and Ian Austen, "Obama Faces Risks in Pipeline Decision," *The New York Times*, February 17, 2013, http://www.nytimes. com/2013/02/18/business/energy-environment/obamas-keystone-pipeline-decision -risks-new-problems-either-way.html.

Chaper 18

1 Tobey Craig Jones, "America, Oil, and War in the Middle East," *The Journal of American History*, 99, no. 1 (2012), http://jah.oxfordjournals.org/content/99/1/208.full.

2 Conglin Xu, "IEA: Global Demand to Average 92 Million B/D in 2014," *Oil and Gas Journal*, September 13, 2013, http://www.ogj.com/articles/2013/09/iea-global-oil -demand-to-average-92-million-b-d-in-2014.html.

3 Charlie Szrom and Thomas Brugato, "Liquid Courage," American Enterprise Institute, February 2008, http://www.american.com/archive/2008/february-02-08 /liquid-courage-2.

4 Ibid.

5 Ibid.

6 Ibid.

7 Ibid.

8 Hans Binnendijk, Christopher Chivvis, and Olga Olike, "Rapprochement with Russia?" *The New York Times*, December 30, 2014, http://www.nytimes. com/2014/12/31/opinion/rapprochement-with-russia.html.

9 John Scales Avery, "Blood For Oil—The Close Relationship Between Petroleum and War," *Human Wrongs Watch*, September 26, 2012, http://human-wrongs-watch. net/2012/09/26/13188/.

10 James Glanz, "The Reach of War: Maritime Defense; 15 Miles Offshore, Safeguarding Iraq's Oil Lifeline," *The New York Times*, July 6, 2004, http://www. nytimes.com/2004/07/06/world/th-reach-war-maritime-defense-15-miles-offshore -safeguarding-iraq-s-oil-lifeline.html.

11 Tim Arango and Clifford Krauss, "China is Reaping the Benefits from the Iraq Oil Boom," *The New York Times*, June 2, 2013, http://www.nytimes.com/2013/06/03/ world/middleeast/china-reaps-biggest-benefits-of-iraq-oil-boom.html.

12 Adam Wilmoth, "Energy Independence: It would impact U.S. military policy, expert says," *News OK*, October 1, 2012, http://newsok.com/article/3714064.

13 "U.S. Military Involvement in Nigeria." Report by the African Security Research Project, September 2009, http://concernedafricascholars.org/african-security-research-project/?p=83reliablesounds like a single personmmerce & Transportation.

14 Jin Liangxiang, "Is China Really a Free Rider in the Middle East?" *China U.S. Focus Digest*, August 22, 2014, http://www.chinausfocus.com/peace-security/is-china-really-a-free-rider-in-the-middle-east/.

15 Adam Wilmoth, "Retired Marine general explains to The Oklahoman the importance of energy independence," *News OK*, May 18, 2012, http://newsok.com/retired-marine-general-explains-to-the-oklahoman-the-importance-of-energy-independence/article/3676383.

16 Don Smith and Rebecca Watson, "The Global Impact of U.S. Oil and Gas Development," The Denver Post, August 24, 2013, http://www.denverpost.com/ci_23921439/global-impact-u-s-oil-and-gas-development.

17 "Remarks By Tom Donilon, the National Security Advisor to the President at the Launch of Columbia University's Center on Global Energy Policy," press release, The White House, Office of the Press Secretary, April 24, 2013, https://www.whitehouse.gov/the-press-office/2013/04/24/remarks-tom-donilon-national-security-advisor-president-launch-columbia-.

18 Daniel Yergin, "US Energy Is Changing the World Again," *Financial Times*, November 16, 2012, http://www.ft.com/intl/cms/s/0/b2202a8a-2e57-11e2-8f7a-00144feabdco.html.

Chapter 19

1 "World Energy Outlook." Executive summary by the International Energy Agency, 2014, https://www.iea.org/publications/freepublications/publication/WEO_2014_ES_English_WEB.pdf.

2 *Energy Outlook 2035*, BP, February 2015, http://www.bp.com/content/dam/bp/pdf/Energy-economics/energy-outlook-2015/Energy_Outlook_2035_booklet.pdf.

3 Peter C. Glover and Michael J. Economides, "OPEC Fracked: The Days When OPEC Could Hold the West to Political Ransom Are Gone," *The Commentator*, n.d., http://www.thecommentator.com/article/3339/opec_fracked.

4 Ann Myers Jaffe and Edward Morse, "OPEC: Can the Cartel Survive Another 50 Years?" in *Energy and Security: Strategies for a World in Transition*, ed. Jan H. Kalicki and David L. Goldwyn (Washington, DC: Woodrow Wilson Center Press, 2013), 129–132.

5 Ambrose Evans-Pritchard, "U.S. Shale Threatens Saudi Funding Crisis and Demise of OPEC," *The Telegraph*, July 29, 2013, http://www.telegraph.co.uk/finance/newsbysector/energy/oilandgas/10209822/.US-shale-threatens-Saudi-funding-crisis-and-demise-of-OPEC.html.

6 Richard Spencer, "Fracking Boom Frees U.S. From Old Oil Alliances," *The Telegraph*, December 13, 2013, http://www.telegraph.co.uk/news/earth/energy/oil/10476647/Fracking-boom-frees-the-U.S.-from-old-oil-alliances.html.

7   Paul Ames, "Could Fracking Make the Persian Gulf Irrelevant?" *Global Post,* May 30, 2013, http://www.globalpost.com/dispatch/news/business/energy/130529/gas-fracking-hydraulic-fracturing-saudi-arabia-europe.

8   Ben Wolfgang, "Fracking's Rise in the U.S. Inspires the World," *The Washington Times,* January 24, 2013, http://www.washingtontimes.com/news/2013/jan/24/frackings-rise-in-us-inspires-the-world/.

9   Fatima Hansia, "Sinopec Fracking in China Turns Deadly," *CorpWatch Blog* (blog), April 24, 2014, http://www.corpwatch.org/article.php?id=15945.

10 Ruth Morris, "The Next Fracking Frontier: China?" *PRI,* August 15, 2012, http://www.pri.org/stories/2012-08-15/next-fracking-frontier-china.

11 "Update 1—Exxon Mobile Says Hits More Shale Oil, Gas in Argentine Region," Reuters, December 18, 2014, http://www.reuters.com/article/2014/12/18/argentina-exploration-idUSL1N0U21IP20141218.

12 Jan H. Kalicki and David L. Goldwyn, eds., *Energy & Security: Strategies for a World in Transition* (Washington, DC: Woodrow Wilson Center Press, 2013).

13 James Attwood, Matthew Craze, and Pablo Rosendo Gonzalez, "Shale Veteran Takes On Argentina's $6 Billion Shortfall," *Bloomberg Business,* December 15, 2014, http://www.bloomberg.com/news/articles/2014-12-16/shale-veteran-takes-on-argentina-s-6-billion-shortfall-energy.

14 "Shale Gas Exploration Will Be a Game Changer, Says Zuma," South African Government News Agency, February 13, 2014, http://www.sanews.gov.za/south-africa/shale-gas-exploration-will-be-game-changer-says-zuma.

15 Paul Burkhardt, "Blackouts Present Biggest Risk to South Africa's Economy," *Bloomberg Business,* September 14, 2014, http://www.bloomberg.com/news/articles/2014-09-24/blackouts-present-biggest-risk-to-south-africa-s-economy.

16 "Fracking Here, Fracking There," *The Economist,* November 26, 2011, http://www.economist.com/node/21540256.

17 "Shale Gas Explained," Shale Gas Europe, 2014, http://shalegas-europe.eu/shale-gas-explained/shale-gas-and-europe/poland/.

18 Anthony A. Davis, "Taking Flight: Poland Tries to Revive its Shale Gas Hopes as Russia Tightens its Grip," *Alberta Oil Magazine,* November 3, 2014, http://www.albertaoilmagazine.com/2014/11/poland-shale-gas-canada/.

19 Marek Strzelecki and Isis Almeida, "Fracking Setback in Poland Dims Hope for Less Russian Gas," *Bloomberg Business,* October 9, 2014, http://www.bloomberg.com/news/2014-10-09/fracking-setback-in-poland-dim-hopes-for-less-russian-gas.html.

20 John Kemp, "The Big One: Russia's Bazhenov Shale: Kemp," Reuters, July 16, 2014, http://uk.reuters.com/article/2014/07/16/russia-shale-kemp-idUKL6N0PR1OP20140716.

21 Russell Gold, "Halliburton Strategist Ponders: Which Country Will Frack Next?" *Corporate Intelligence* (blog), *The Wall Street Journal,* March 4, 2014, http://blogs.wsj.com/corporate-intelligence/2014/03/04/halliburton-strategist-ponders-which-country-will-frack-next/.

ABOUT THE AUTHOR

Dan K. Eberhart's knowledge of geopolitical energy issues and oil prices have made him a guest on Fox News, CNN, and CNBC International. His editorials and interviews on those topics have appeared in publications such as *The Hill* and *The Economist*. In addition, Eberhart has served as an industry consultant in North America, Asia, and Africa—a role that earned him a place in Hart Energy's influential "30 Under 40" list and inclusion in several U.S. trade missions to sub-Saharan Africa headed by the U.S. Secretary of Commerce and U.S. Secretary of Transportation.

Eberhart is also the CEO of Canary, LLC, which began with the purchase of a small oilfield services company in North Dakota. Under Eberhart's leadership, the company has grown to become one of the largest private wellhead companies in the United States. Prior to serving as Canary's CEO, Eberhart was vice president of acquisitions at two energy companies. He received a Juris Doctorate from Tulane Law School and has dual degrees in economics and political science from Vanderbilt University.

Eberhart is a Georgia native who grew up in a close family with one sister and three brothers. Today, he resides in Houston, Texas, with his wife Farah and daughter Kylee. He enjoys restoring old cars, collecting books, and traveling with his family.

To learn more about Dan Eberhart, please visit www.dankeberhart.com.